A GUIDE TO
JAZZ IN JAPAN

A Guide to Jazz in Japan

By Michael Pronko

Copyright © 2025 Michael Pronko
Formatting by BEAUTeBOOK
Cover Design © 2025 Andy Bridge

Raked Gravel Press

All rights reserved worldwide. This book may not be reproduced in any form, in whole or in part, without written permission from the author.

Follow Michael on Twitter:
@pronkomichael

Michael's Facebook page:
www.facebook.com/pronkoauthor

A GUIDE TO JAZZ IN JAPAN

by Michael Pronko

Raked Gravel Press 2025

CONTENTS

Introduction 7

Where to Go—Jazz Clubs 15

    Straight Ahead 21

    Cozy and close 35

    Neighborhood 43

    Down-to-earth 53

    Corporate-International 65

    Yokohama 73

    Eclectic and blues 81

Who to Hear —The musicians 89

    Drummers 93

    Pianists 99

    Bass Players 111

    Trumpeters 119

    Saxophonists 125

    Trombonists 135

    Guitarists 139

    Unusual instruments 145

    Singers 151

    Big Bands 157

    Hammond B3 Organ Players 163

    Blues, Salsa, Brazilian, and other music 167

- Where to Jam, Hang, and Shop 171
  - Jam sessions 173
  - Jazz Kissaten 183
  - Record Stores 199
- When and Why —History and Culture 209
  - A brief history of jazz in Japan 211
  - How jazz fits Japanese culture 219
  - The Process of Cultural Integration 227
  - Why Jazz Resonates so Far from Home 241
  - Quiet About It Jazz in Japan 261
- Outro 277
  - In Memorium 279
  - My other writing 281
  - Special Thanks 285

Introduction

Dedication

This book is dedicated to the musicians who've made my evenings a serious pleasure. Yes, I have my day job, friends, and family, but more than anything, it's been jazz that made me feel at home in Japan. *Kokoro kara, arigatou gozaimasu.*

About this guide

This guide will introduce you to the small clubs, backstreet kissaten, vinyl stores, jam sessions, and big band contests that make up the vibrant jazz scene in the greater Tokyo metropolitan area. With nearly forty million people within train distance of the heart of the city, that means a lot of different clubs, innumerable musicians, and an incredible amount of great live music every night.

However, the sheer scale of Tokyo and Yokohama can also make it hard to find the best music. This guide points you towards the best places and best musicians. It is intended for people who live here as well as for visitors. It's designed for anyone who likes jazz, is curious about it, or is just interested in a great night out in Tokyo.

The people and places in the Japanese jazz world are generally humble, but intensely devoted to the music. It's not that the jazz world is closed off exactly, but rather those in the know are quiet about it, partly because the jazz scene is so huge, and partly because playing jazz is such an ambitious undertaking.

I've been covering the jazz scene in Japan since 1999 for a series of publications and for my website, Jazz in Japan (www.jazzinjapan.com). Some of the material in this guide overlaps with the website, but a book is a handy reference just the same. In putting this guide together, I feel like a band leader trying to decide which songs to play—there are too many choices.

The guide is not just about great music. It's about culture too. The clubs, groups, and musicians have their own way of doing things, and like so many other "ways" in Japanese culture, jazz has its "way." That an African-American subcultural art form could fill the basement clubs of a city far away is a fascinating phenomenon. It's a story of cultural exchange, globalization, musical passion, and artistic exploration, and the story is far from finished. If anything, the jazz scene in Japan is livelier than ever.

I've divided the book into several sections. In the first part, there's a guide to the jazz clubs. I haven't covered every club in Tokyo and Yokohama, much less Japan, but I've picked a solid selection of the best. I have reviewed those (some are like a home away from home) to give you an idea of the kind of music, the performers, and the atmosphere at over forty clubs. I've organized those by atmosphere and style, but don't take that as a hard and fast rule. On any given night, the music can be unpredictable. But this section will get you where you want to go (and maybe where you need to be).

Second, I've chosen the musicians I've seen and treasured over the years. I've organized them by instrument. That might not be ideal since musicians often play different styles and instruments. But musicians consider their instruments central to their musical identity, so I'll take that as a cue for arranging. Check out the bands that musicians lead or play in, and the descriptions I've added too, for what kind of jazz they usually play. You can also check the Jazz in Japan website for past reviews. Links to their websites, usually with music samples or videos, will give you even more ways to find who you'd like to hear.

Next, I've added some pointers for jam sessions where musicians can meet and jam with other musicians. If you're a musician at any level, bring your instrument and find a time and place to join.

I've chosen a few of the better-known jazz *kissaten* coffee shops, but be advised that there are many more out there, as with clubs and musicians. Jazz fans are enamored of vinyl records, and Japan has many stores where records are sold. Vinyl in Japan is always well cared for and priced accordingly. Jazz kissaten are a unique experience. They are discrete islands of jazz culture and libraries of musical history. This section gives you pointers toward those other aspects of jazz.

In the last part, I've included longer articles about jazz in Japan. Three of my academic works are reprinted from books and journals, and two new essays discuss the history and cultural factors surrounding jazz. They examine why jazz in Japan is so interesting, how it got to Japan, and why it's continued to flourish. There's plenty to think about there.

Take this guidebook as your *genkan*—that little area in every Japanese home just inside the door where you take off your shoes and step inside.

And then go on in.

Irrashaimase!

About the focus

"Writing about music is like dancing about architecture" is a quote attributed to many different musicians, writers, and critics. Reluctantly, I half agree.

In contrast, the essayist and critic Walter Pater said, "All art constantly aspires to the condition of music." I pretty much agree with that.

This guidebook lies somewhere between those two. I feel it's helpful to have writing that provides information and background. Writing can enhance the music by helping listeners go deeper into the work. Listening to jazz is not just an aural pleasure—it's a creative experience. Music is all subjective at one level, maybe at the best levels, but having a guide can help in numerous ways.

This book is primarily a list of people and places I recommend because I've heard them, usually repeatedly, on CD, live, or both, and have found them compelling and meaningful. The clubs are places I've been to repeatedly over many years. One or two are almost like home. I sit in the same seat.

In this age of AI, it's easy to vacuum up information and pass it off as experience. The information here is handcrafted, individually shaped, and personally obtained. I think that fits the nature of jazz itself. It's about individual tone and self-expression. Part of the reason this guidebook is limited is because it's filtered through one person. But I like the human touch with whatever I read, watch, listen to, or consume. I hope you do too.

Because the jazz world in Japan is so huge, I've necessarily had to leave out quite a few places and people. No guidebook can be, nor should it try to be, exhaustive. I have my likes and dislikes too, though overall, I like all kinds of jazz and all types of music—Latin, African, rock, blues, flamenco, Chinese opera, you name it. A broadly appreciative view of all different genres, approaches, and styles forms the framework here.

But if some important musician or club didn't get a mention, that's my bad. I'm not a large travel publication corporation. I'm just a jazz writer.

Likewise, I included "Japan" in the title, but almost all the clubs and musicians are based in Tokyo and Yokohama because that's where I live. Not all are Japanese, either. Many foreign musicians have made Japan their home.

This guidebook is for anyone interested in jazz or in Japan. Sometime fans, short-term visitors, die-hard jazz lovers, long-time residents of Japan, and people just passing through will find recommendations and new possibilities.

Even people who can't visit Japan will find much to consider here, with many links to follow up. The descriptions of the clubs and musicians are more than just a travel guide's to-do list. Combined with the essays about history and culture, they offer insight into another world.

All the clubs and people in this guide are also on the Jazz in Japan site, www.jazzinjapan.com. Over the last twenty-some years, the site has grown into a trove of information about musicians, bands, CDs, backgrounds, ideas, and the jazz scene in Japan. Check the calendar for more on upcoming shows.

With this guidebook in hand, you have forty-some clubs and over two hundred musicians. That should be enough to help you navigate the vibrant musical scene, delve deeper into the music, and enjoy many evenings of great jazz. I hope it opens up a fascinating world of musical experience.

As Nietzche said, "Without music, life would be a mistake." I couldn't agree more with that.

About me

This guidebook is the product of nearly thirty years of listening and reporting on Japanese jazz. I started going to clubs in the 1980s, when it wasn't easy to find jazz spots. Back then, it was word of mouth or sheer chance. I stumbled across spots while walking around the city or caught sight of "jazz" written on a sign from the train window. Friends and acquaintances told me about their favorite places and musicians, sometimes reluctantly, as some were well-kept secrets.

I picked up flyers, announcements, and handouts dangling from a string or clip for other clubs and shows at each club. Those led me into a vast world of live music. The network was there, but was hard to uncover. At that time, the online world was yet to take off, and though there were a few publications in Japanese, there was not much in English.

My first jazz writing gig was at the English-language online mag Tokyo Q, which didn't mean much to musicians or club owners. Still, those musicians and club owners were welcoming, allowing me to take photos, chatting with me between sets, and, maybe most of all, remembering me. That wasn't hard, as there were few other foreigners *to* remember. Their kindness led me to continue.

In 2001, *The Japan Times* invited me to cover the jazz scene. With that *meishi* name card in hand, doors opened more easily. I could ask a staff photographer, who always loved to go and certainly took better photos than my film camera and scanner could produce. The reach of the newspaper was greater, and the name respected. I had a regular column called "Jazznicity." I still like that name.

Working there, I interviewed jazz greats from abroad, such as Herbie Hancock, Michael Brecker, McCoy Tyner, John McLaughlin, and Monty Alexander. I continued going out to hear the best Japanese jazz musicians, all listed in this guide, and writing about them. It was an honor to write about jazz. I was out several nights a week to hear jazz, even while working at my university job. In those days, the band often announced it was time for the last train, in case people wanted to get home, before they jumped into more music.

Way leads on to way, though, so I teamed up with Marco Mancini, who had started a bilingual print magazine called *Jazznin*, which translates roughly as "jazz people." It was a beautiful magazine with great photos and good printing. However, at that time, getting an ISBN was highly restricted in Japan, and distribution was tightly controlled. We got out two years of issues before folding, but the articles I wrote there are now on the website.

Meanwhile, I'd started writing a "Tokyo Eye" column for Newsweek Japan, mostly about my bemused puzzlement about Tokyo life. Other gigs rolled in writing about art, architecture, and culture. I contributed editorials to The Japan Times too. As for jazz, I wrote for a Japanese online streaming service, an Italian jazz magazine, a car magazine, and a few other sites. It was all good.

Writing-wise, I've collected my nonfiction writing on Tokyo into four collections, the Tokyo Moments series. I also write a detective series, the Detective Hiroshi series, set in Tokyo. I've been honored to receive multiple awards and great professional reviews for both series. More on those writings can be found at

www.michaelpronko.com.

Day job-wise, I taught American Literature and Culture at Meiji Gakuin University, publishing academic articles, giving papers, and launching a conference, Liberlit, on teaching literature. My students were serious about English, though, and I learned more every day. One homework assignment for an American Culture class was to review a live show. Many students had never been to hear live music before. I still teach courses on novels, film, art, and music—nothing like a lecture on Bessie Smith to put everyone in a good mood.

Around 2007, I put together the website Jazz in Japan, www.jazzinjapan.com, which is still running. A good friend did the technical work, and I rolled through Joomla, Wordpress, and Squarespace. Ugh. But it was worth it to keep writing a steady stream of live reviews, CD reviews, essays, and a calendar.

Somewhere along the line, a jazz researcher from the UK contacted me and dragged me into jazz studies. That's pushed me to reframe my jazz reporting into an academic framework. I contributed a chapter on Japanese jazz to the *Routledge Companion to Jazz Studies*, among others. A selection of those writings is in this book.

Nowadays, information is not hard to come by—in fact, it's hard to avoid. Every jazz musician has a dedicated homepage, Facebook page, and posts on X (Twitter) or Instagram. There are also lots of videos on YouTube. I encourage you to check them out. I am amazed.

With all that available, you could learn much about Japanese jazz from anywhere in the world—and you should! But much of what I know about jazz in Japan came from the pre-internet days of piecing things together, flyer by flyer, recommendation by recommendation, night by night. That experience runs through these pages, but to be honest, I like having easy access to information nowadays.

No matter how info is acquired, the excitement of heading down the stairs into a dark club on a backstreet of Tokyo for an intense, enjoyable evening of great live jazz hasn't changed.

I wrote this guide because I was excited, fascinated, and pleased. I hope it resonates deeply.

Happy listening! The world is always larger than we think.

* * *

You are welcome to follow me at:
X: @pronkomichael
Instagram: @michaelpronko
Facebook: www.facebook.com/pronkoauthor
LinkedIn: https://www.linkedin.com/in/michaelpronko/
Personal website: https://www.michaelpronko.com/

Where to Go—Jazz Clubs

About the clubs

The larger Tokyo area is one of the largest urban areas in the world. Within train distance, over one hundred clubs (yes, not a math error), offer jazz nightly. From those hundred-some clubs, I've chosen the best I've been to over the past twenty-plus years.

Each listing has links, addresses, and reviews. For more on each club, visit the Jazz in Japan website: www.jazzinjapan.com. Enter the club's name, and you can find reviews of live shows that took place there.

I organized the clubs into the types of music usually played there. But the emphasis is on "usually." Any club could have a different kind of music on any given night. If in doubt, copy and paste the name of the group leader performing that night and check out one of their videos. Some clubs predictably offer one style every night, while others range along the continuum. I've noted that in the reviews.

The review includes a short set of directions, but Tokyo and, to a lesser extent, Yokohama can be difficult to navigate. By all means, save the address in your GPS app! Passersby will usually not know how to direct you, and signs are sometimes small and hard to see.

If you get stuck, look at the list of tenants in the building, look for a rolling sign on the sidewalk, or look up or down for the tiny sign in the basement or higher stories. Tokyo is challenging to navigate, both horizontally and vertically.

Unlike much of Japanese society, there are no strict rules in the jazz world. Nightlife is the time and place to throw off convention and custom and become looser, more human, and more natural.

That said, Japanese fans will strike most foreigners as a bit staid. Jazz clubs are different from izakaya or bars, where people go to drink, eat, shout, and argue. At most jazz clubs, it's quiet except for the music and conversation before, after, and between sets.

Of course, jazz fans applaud, clap along, and even whoop with joy at points, but expressing emotion is generally not what's done in public. Look instead for their feelings expressed in buying a CD and asking for an autograph. Watch how they concentrate and consider what they're hearing. Or consider that they're not spending their money in the thousands of other venues, restaurants, and activities nearby! They vote with their feet. For most Japanese, that's expression enough.

Since Japanese jazz clubs are slightly different, here are a few pointers.

Japanese live shows often start early, at 7:30 or 8, and they start on time. However, starting times can differ on holidays and special occasions, so check closely. Before the Coronavirus pandemic, clubs often started and ran late, but this is no longer the case.

Except at the large corporate-owned clubs, you can stay for both sets, with some exceptions for well-known bands.

Also, some clubs are relatively small, so it's awkward to get in once the music starts. In a couple of the smallest clubs, the pianist or bassist has to stand up and step out of the way for the door to open. In others, the door is kept tightly shut to contain the sound. In others, it's hard to get past others to the empty seats. You get the idea.

Showing up early means getting two full sets and a better seat. If you're a bit late, though, go on in. If the place is full, you might have to stand or wait for the next set. Making a reservation is advised; be sure to tell them when you'll arrive. A reservation assures you of a better seat.

Reserving by email is probably best. Names are hard to catch across languages, but it's OK by phone too. Recently, most clubs have someone who speaks enough English to take your name, phone number, and time of arrival. But not always. Be patient.

Some clubs have an online reservation form, though it's often in Japanese. Music has no language barrier, and that's the main point. But a reservation is practically helpful and a sign of good intentions and interest.

Japanese is a complicated language, and in Tokyo and Yokohama, there are pockets of English friendliness and others that remain steadfastly Japanese. Jazz clubs lie somewhere in the middle. So, for this guidebook, I've also included the Japanese for addresses, names, and other terms. Nowadays, though, most clubs can handle at least a minimal amount of English.

In any event, it's best to double-check details like starting times and entrance fees for each evening. Shows might start at 7:30 one night and 8:00 the next. Also, be sure the show isn't in the afternoon, as a few clubs run afternoon sessions.

Entrance fees vary depending on the size of the band and their fame. Check carefully. The price is usually stated clearly. If you're visiting, the exchange rate can make a big difference in price, but I have listed the usual range of entrance fees for each club. Well-known musicians and larger bands charge more.

Most sets finish by 10:30 or 11:30 at the latest, so people won't miss their last train home. Trains in Tokyo and Yokohama often finish before 1 a.m. If you miss the last train, it means an expensive taxi ride home, a cheap hotel, or an all-night coffee shop. There are plenty of all of those everywhere.

Jazz clubs are not for the claustrophobic. "Rub elbows" is not a metaphor in Tokyo. It's the reality. A few places have ample legroom, but the Japanese are used to being packed into tight spaces. If you're expecting Western-size roominess, be ready to adapt as best you can.

Reservations are advised and highly recommended at bigger clubs or for well-known bands, but it's not always easy without speaking Japanese. Talking with musicians at some clubs in between or after the sets is common. Some musicians love that, and others do not. Many Japanese musicians speak English, but not all. That could be an embarrassment for them, as it is for almost every Japanese person.

During break times, most musicians are happy to chat if they can, but they also want to talk to long-time fans, old friends, students, or bandmates they haven't seen in a while. So please respect the musicians' time during breaks. They are at work, after all.

Jazz clubs differ considerably in terms of food and drink. Do you have to buy a drink or food order? Each club has its own rules, but it's just polite—in that inimitable Japanese way—to follow the club's rule.

Some places serve the bare minimum of nuts or bags of chips. Others might have a microwaved pizza or cheese plate, but others offer a full range of restaurant-quality food. It's good to check ahead. I usually eat before I go in. The focus is on the music, not on Michelin stars.

Whiskey or coffee are the old-school beverages of choice, but wine and craft beer are increasingly common, as are cocktails and non-alcoholic drinks. A few clubs request a one-drink or one-order minimum, but most take it for granted that customers will order. If you're on a budget or don't want anything, at least ordering bottled water or coffee ensures the clubs make a little something.

Look for the lone guy or couple with an entire bottle of whiskey in front of them. Bottle "keeps" used to be common practice. The idea was that you bought the bottle, stored it there with your name on it, and purchased ice and mixers each time. That "bottle keep" system is almost a thing of the past.

The clubs run on tight margins, and none of the owners I've ever talked to is in it for the money. They're in it for the music. Rents can be exorbitant in Japan, and owners and musicians operate at the edges of everyday accounting, so every little bit helps. Of course, there's no tipping anywhere in Japan.

Most clubs are located in lively parts of town with plenty of food and drink options in the surrounding area. If there is nothing to eat near the club, the surrounding streets or the closest station will almost surely have places to eat before and after the show.

Smoking used to be a blight on jazz clubs, but it's much better than it used to be. Smoking is banned in most of them, but there's a soft approach to smokers at some clubs or in the hallway. If you are allergic to smoke or hate it, ask the wait staff to be seated away from smokers. Japanese are almost always polite and accommodating, even Japanese smokers.

Entrance fees can seem quite expensive compared to other countries, but be aware that rents in most Japanese cities are incredibly high. You may have a high price for one evening, but that helps keep the space open for up-and-coming and lesser-known musicians to play on other evenings.

In addition, entrance fees help clubs offer their space for jam sessions and recordings. Some have a night with no music charge and offer discounts to students. Full price supports the music in multiple ways. Having seen the evening's pay divided among the band members after many shows, I can tell you it isn't ever enough.

Musicians almost always sell their CDs at the club. Each musician also leads another group, so their CDs will likely be on sale too. So, if you like the music, pick up a copy. There's usually a table stacked with CDs in the back or by the door. Musicians get a bit more if you buy from them directly, and it can be challenging to track down CDs through music stores or online. And if you get a CD, musicians will happily sign it for you! It's such a common thing to ask that they'll probably have a sign pen ready.

Also, check out the flyers and posters on a stand or hung on the wall. Over the years, I've picked up the best tips about jazz there.

A few of my favorite clubs have closed: Una Mas, Halftone, Hot House, Jazz Spot "J," GH9, and STB139. Sayonara to them. However, many new clubs have opened. Some of them will be included in the next edition of this guidebook and are on my site.

Straight Ahead

Introduction

Straight-ahead and Serious.

Old-school clubs with the cream of the jazz world

The clubs in this section focus on straight-ahead jazz and have a serious atmosphere—they are as much a music hall as a club. Chairs often face the stage, and talking is discouraged during the performance. That doesn't mean you can't talk; it's just that everyone is there to focus on the music, not on socializing.

These clubs are the best-known in Tokyo. They showcase the best musicians in the city and offer a variety. Some are better known for one style of jazz than another, but all of them give their stage to musicians you can count on to deliver great music. You might not like their particular style on any one night, but you can rest assured that the musicians are playing that style at the top of their game.

These clubs also have a history that extends back to the 1960s, when jazz was one of the city's most popular music styles. During the Japanese economic bubble, all these clubs were booming. Still, they survived the lean years when corporate expense accounts shrank, and clubs started to attract more jazz lovers than salarymen entertaining clients.

Some of these clubs have a fifty-year history and an impressive list of Japanese and international artists who have played there. They are also dedicated to presenting the very best in jazz.

Alfie

六本木アルフィー

Top-level jazz in a cool space

Hama Roppongi Biru 5F, Roppongi 6-2-35, Minato-ku, Tokyo

(03)3479-2037

〒106-0032 東京都港区六本木6-2-35 ハマ六本木ビル5F

Roppongi Station (Tokyo Metro Hibiya Line, Toei Oedo Line)

Roppongi Station has many exits. But from the big Roppongi crossing, walk down Roppongi Dori towards Shibuya and Roppongi Hills. You will see the Azabu Police Station, and after 200 meters (long before Roppongi Hills), you can find the club. Look for a small sign on the left and a small entryway to the elevator.

4,950 to 6,600 yen. On weekdays and Saturdays, there are two sets from 19:15 to 20:45. The time and charge depend on the show. Jazz every night. (With some days off irregularly).

http://alfie.tokyo/index.html

https://www.jazzinjapan.com/clubs-and-venues/alfie

https://www.facebook.com/jazz.alfie

https://www.instagram.com/jazz_house_alfie/

https://x.com/jazzhouse_alfie

@jazzhouse_alfie

Alfie is Roppongi's best jazz and most elegant club, and one of the longest-lasting in a nightlife area that is constantly changing. A great space with great music and great food and drinks (did I mention it was great?), it is also a favorite with musicians, and for good reason. Owner Yoko Hino knows how to run a club, and while she hires great managers, she is there overseeing things almost every night. The atmosphere is laid-back, cool, and hip, which is what you want in a club, especially in Roppongi.

The musicians might all be termed elegant in some sense too, but accomplished and professional also apply. The audience is always there for the music, not just a night out —maybe a jazz night out. The musicians play both to themselves and the audience—again, in just the right measure. At Alfie, everything always seems to work just right.

The club features established musicians, often for their CD release parties. But Alfie also offers up-and-coming groups a special chance to get a solid gig (with some pay). The music is usually straight-ahead, but it also includes Latin, funk, fusion, or someone with amazing technique or a special charisma.

Every couple of months, a performer from overseas takes the stage, and sometimes, unique combinations of musicians dedicate themselves to a musician or kind of music for an anniversary or retrospective evening. Every night of the week, though, Alfie offers top-level jazz in an elegant environment.

They have a solid, top-shelf selection of drinks, with delicious wine and food good enough to entice customers from the hundreds of other restaurants in the area. It's one of the premier jazz clubs in Tokyo.

B Flat

ビー・フラット

A big, glorious jazz space

Akasaka-Sakae Bldg., B1, Akasaka 6-6-4, Minato-ku, Tokyo

(03)5563-2563

〒107-0052東京都港区赤坂6-6-4 赤坂栄ビルB1

Akasaka Station (Tokyo Metro Chiyoda Line) and Tameike Sanno Station (Tokyo Metro Ginza Line and Nanboku Line)

From Akasaka Station, it's an easy 4-minute walk. With your back to the large ACT Theatre and TBS buildings, you go uphill, winding a little, and on the right-hand side, you will see a bright red door and sign. Alternately, from Tameike Sanno station, exit 12B onto Roppongi Dori. Turn right uphill on the narrow winding street that goes up and over and down to Akasaka.

3,800 - 7,700 yen, 2,000 -3,100 for students (sometimes more depending). About twice a month, they have no-charge night! The cover charge will rise for overseas acts, but you get two full sets. Sets are from 19:00 and 21:15.

https://bflat.yamano-music.co.jp/

https://www.jazzinjapan.com/clubs-and-venues/bflat?rq=b%20flat

https://www.facebook.com/bflatyamano/

https://x.com/JazzDiningBflat

https://www.instagram.com/jazzdiningb_flat/

B Flat is one of the premier jazz clubs in the city, showcasing the very best in Tokyo jazz every night. After moving from its previous spot in Harajuku (where it went by the name "Keynote"), and with the passing of Sugiya-san, a great human being and an excellent manager always in a bow tie, the club's future seemed in doubt. However, the next owner/manager, Suzuki-san, took on the challenge and ran the club for many years, maintaining a high quality of music, service, food, drink, and sound. When he passed away, the club was bought by Yamano Music. The previous owners will be missed. They were both wonderful people. But at least the club can continue.

History aside, the club's focus is music. Though Yamano is a corporation, it is a music corporation that appreciates the value and importance of music. It runs a student big band contest, offers music lessons, and still sells CDs, music scores, and instruments all over Tokyo, so it's not unusual to run a jazz club too.

B Flat loads the dais with orchestras or big bands several nights a week. That makes for a huge sound, and the sound system handles it with crisp perfection. On other nights, everything from quartets to octets delivers straight-ahead jamming and tight, solid swing of every description. Musicians always like playing there. You can tell by the way they up their level a little. The names of famous performers written in pen on the brick wall attest to the outstanding musicians that have performed there over the years.

You can see well from most seats, but it pays to make a reservation and choose your table ahead of time if you can. B Flat is exceptionally good about reservations, but it is always wise to call or email ahead, even an hour or two. But if you can't, there are standing tables too, for latecomers. Large pillars block a few seats, but hey, that's life. Sitting on the far sides of the stage is fine, though, and the sound is good from everywhere.

Yamano has made an effort to up the level of food and drink too. Drinks are reasonably priced (for Tokyo), but you can also splurge for pricey bottles of wine. The daily special plates are tasty if you don't have time to check out the many eateries in the area. With shows starting at 19:00 most nights, eating there is often easier and worth it.

Body and Soul

ボディ＆ソウル

A soulful hideaway with great music every night

Shibuya Homes B-15, Udagawa-cho 2-1, Shibuya-ku, Tokyo

(03)6455-0088

〒150-0042 渋谷区宇田川町2-1 渋谷ホームズB-15

Omotesando station (Tokyo Metro Chiyoda Line, Ginza Line, Hanzomon Line)

The club is about halfway between Shibuya Station and Harajuku Station on the large-ish Koen Dori Street. It's accessible from either station by walking.

4,500 yen to 8,000 yen. Two sets from 19:30 and 21:00 on Monday-Saturday, 18:30 and 20:00, or a daytime show on Sunday and public holidays.

www.bodyandsoul.co.jp

https://www.jazzinjapan.com/clubs-and-venues/bodyandsoul

https://www.facebook.com/bodyandsoul.co.jp

https://www.instagram.com/bodyandsoul_jp/

One of Tokyo's older and more respected clubs, Body and Soul, has been in the jazz business for fifty years and is run by the same woman. It's an essential part of Tokyo's jazz culture. After moving from its old location on the backstreets of Omotesando, the new location is calming, spacious, and welcoming. Body and Soul expresses true jazz spirit. The club acts as a jazz shrine, but with warmth rather than stuffy religiosity.

    Because of its history, the club has the respect of musicians and listeners alike. The club's and the performers' straight-ahead approach ensures you will have a great night of jazz every night of the week. Most of the very top tier of Japan's jazz musicians play here, some of them regularly. The musicians know they'll have an appreciative audience there and tend to polish things up just a bit more. You can feel the devotion to the music as soon as you enter the door.

The food and drink are of high quality, much better than those of most clubs in the city. If the show starts early, eating there is a good choice. The service is always excellent. The sound system is extremely good, whether it's a trio or a big band. It's easy to hear well from anywhere in the club, which is good because some of the best musicians in Japan gravitate to the club to present their most polished groups and best performances.

It's best to make a reservation on the website ahead of time. You'll get a slightly better seat, but because the new space is much better designed and more spacious than the old one, there is almost always a good seat, even if you come at the last minute without a reservation. Body and Soul perfectly balances its namesake. Exciting and intimate, imbibing and listening, physical and corporal, all the opposites merge.

Keystone Club

キーストンクラブ東京

Stylish newcomer with a lot to offer

2F, JASMINE Bldg., 7-4-12 Roppongi, Minato-ku, Tokyo

(03)6721-1723

〒106-0032 東京都港区六本木7-4-12 ジャスミンビル2F

Roppongi Station (Tokyo Metro Hibiya Line, Toei Oedo Line)

Two minutes walk from Exit 8, Roppongi Station, Tokyo Oedo Line.

The cover charge is from 3,500 yen to 6,000 yen, plus a food and drink order. Shows from 19:00 or 19:30 every night. Times can change. Occasional afternoon shows.

https://keystoneclubtokyo.com/

https://www.jazzinjapan.com/clubs-and-venues/keystone

https://www.facebook.com/keystoneclubtokyo

https://www.youtube.com/channel/UCB7V8MLk5ZcwQjtgN8xCowA

@keystoneclubtokyo6484

https://www.instagram.com/keystoneclubtokyo/

A few blocks from the center of Roppongi, on a quieter street, Keystone Club is just the right-sized club. There are raised seats by the bar and tables close to the stage (shared when it gets crowded). Circular group seating to the side is a good choice to reserve if you go in a larger group. The club's well designed, and it's not cramped like some places are. It's in Roppongi too, so everyone's in their own bubble.

The food is Indian, which is unusual for a jazz club, and extremely good, in my Indian food-loving opinion. It could be a restaurant on its own without the jazz. Oddly enough, curry and jazz go together perfectly, as it turns out! If you don't like Indian, though, there are several other choices equally good.

Drinks are well up to Roppongi standards, a fraction on the pricey side, but then again, so are rents in the area. There is a solid selection of high-end cocktails, whisky, wine, and beer. The service is prompt and attentive, so you don't have to divide your attention from the music to get served.

And for those who love acoustics, the sound system is excellent. They feature jazz every night, but there are some closed evenings and Saturday afternoon shows, so check carefully.

When the club opened, I couldn't get a fix on what music they were aiming at, but after a few years, it's clear—top quality. This is one of the newer clubs in Tokyo, but they have worked hard to make an outstanding venue showcasing some of the best jazz in the city and to make an exceptional club. Jazz is generally straight-ahead, but there's a range inside that category that Keystone covers well.

Naru

ナル　お茶の水店

Elegant space for straight-ahead jazz

Kanda Surugadai 2-1, Chiyoda-ku, Tokyo

(03)3291-2321

〒101-0062　東京都千代田区神田駿河台2-1

Ochanomizu Station (Chuo Line, Sobu Line, Tokyo Metro Marunouchi Line)

From the west exit of JR Ochanomizu Station, go diagonally across the huge, crisscrossed intersection. You can see the club sign from the west exit—just a one-minute walk.

3,500 yen or more. Two sets at 19:00 and 20:30, depending on the night.

http://ocha-naru.com/

https://www.jazzinjapan.com/clubs-and-venues/naru

https://www.facebook.com/ochanomizu.naru

https://www.instagram.com/naru_jazz/

https://x.com/jazzNARU

@jazzNARU

(Naru has a second club in Yoyogi, almost exclusively dedicated to vocalists. Please don't get them confused. If you like vocalists and want to hear established and up-and-coming singers, go to: www.yoyogi-naru.com)

Compact, tidy, and intimate, with no dust on its neat shelves of bottle keeps, Naru is a very comfortable place catering to students on expensive dates, salarymen chilling out, and jazz maniacs of all stripes. Many clubs try hard for "nice," but Naru does it naturally. Food and drinks are several notches above any club in the city and are affordable. Why more clubs do not offer good wine, as Naru does, is a sad mystery to this jazz writer. Perhaps it's the experience that comes from two generations running the same club in the city's center. Maybe it's respect for the sophistication of the music. Whatever the thought and care behind it, it's good.

Their selection of jazz players is excellent, chosen with obvious care and attention. The performers play with great intensity, reflecting their focused and professional sense. The music is typically straight-ahead, but without the feeling of being strangled into traditional patterns. The musicians here always have the artistry to dip into free jazz, clave rhythms, complex harmonies, or "out" soloing, but bring it back to a satisfying resolution. They push the edges here, but fold them back up too. Some nights, singers take the stage, and a slightly less edgy and more soulful feel takes over.

I always feel a respectful hush come over me when I head down the stairs past the musician photos heading into Naru's basement space. Somehow, the intimate setting of upholstered booths, smooth black lacquer, polished brass rails, and curved counter meandering around the piano feels calming and dreamy. Naru's sound is superb, and the drums and sax do not even need to be miked. Always a complete and satisfying night out, Naru offers excellent music in a cool club.

Pit Inn

新宿ピットイン

Premiere jazz listening room for serious jazz

Accord Shinjuku Building B1, Shinjuku 2-12-4, Shinjuku-ku, Tokyo

(03)3354-2024

〒160-0022 東京都新宿区新宿2-12-4アコード新宿 B1

Shinjuku 3-Chome Station (Tokyo Metro Marunouchi Line), Shinjuku Station (JR Yamanote Line, Chuo Line, Sobu Line, Saikyo Line, Shonan Shinjuku Line, Tokyo Metro Marunouchi Line, Oedo Line, Toei Shinjuku Line, Odakyu Line, Keio Line, Narita Express, and more lines)

3,000 yen up to 7,000 yen for special shows. Two sets starting from 19:30. Afternoons from 14:00 to 16:30 pm, 1,300 yen.

http://pit-inn.com/e/

https://www.jazzinjapan.com/clubs-and-venues/pitinn
https://x.com/pit_inn_

@pit_inn_

https://www.instagram.com/pitinn_shinjuku/

https://www.facebook.com/pages/PIT%20INN/158332544182091

More of an intimate listening room than a club, the Shinjuku Pit Inn has had decades of great jazz inside its Zen temple-like space. It's become an institution. Afternoons are given over to promising bands working toward the evening slots or new configurations working out material. Stopping in for an afternoon of jazz by virtually unknown young players shows the depth of jazz talent in Tokyo. Playing the evening there means you have made it as a musician. Their anniversary concert line-ups are an annual who's who of jazz in Japan.

Inside, all the seats attentively face the stage, with plenty of room to stand at the back. Listeners are serious and focused, reading books and jazz magazines during sets and lining up after the show to get autographs on their just-purchased CDs. The Pit Inn is a large place that lets you settle into the music for a concentrated evening of musical meditation. Although it is primarily a beer and whiskey place, many customers stick with coffee too. The audience is there for the music.

The sound system here is always exacting. The right mix of instruments makes an incredible difference to the musical experience, and the Pit Inn offers excellent sound. For some shows, tickets are sold in numbered order, but you can usually line up early for the seat you like. There are no bad seats, though. There is no "scene" either. You can head in, sit down, space out, get lost in the music, and wander home.

Once a month or more, the Pit Inn brings in artists from abroad. Many of these musicians have not burst into big-label contracts, but many hardly care. The vibe is more about getting across the feelings, ideas, and forms of their creative expression than fulfilling contractual obligations. At the Pit Inn, musicians are creating culture, not making money, and the distinction makes for much better music than one might at first imagine.

Often, the foreign musicians team up with Japanese players, and the mix makes for a real intercultural exchange, except that the underlying culture is, after all, jazz. Fortunately, this year, the Pit Inn set up a recording studio across the hall to capture the magic that goes on and give musicians a place to record what they create. Perhaps the most important club for creative jazz in Tokyo, the Pit Inn is a treat.

Someday

サムデイ

Big basement room for great jazz nightly

1-34-8 Schroth Asakusa B1 Kotobuki Taitou-Ku Tokyo Japan 〒111-0042

〒111-0042 東京都台東区寿3-19-2 シュロス浅草　B1

someday@someday.net

070-6986-0822

03-3359-6777

Tawaramachi Station (Ginza Line), Kuramae Station (Oedo Line), Kuramae Station (Asakusa Line)

The easiest way is to check the club map, which is in both English and Japanese. You could also walk from Asakusa Station on the Ginza Line. Once you get close, the sign is easy to find on the main street. It's less than a five-minute walk from each of the above stations.

2,800 yen up to 4,500 for big bands plus one drink and one food order. Two sets at 19:45 and 21:10. There's a slight discount on most shows for foreign tourists with a passport. Don't forget to ask.

http://someday.net/

http://someday.net/english/english-index.html

https://www.jazzinjapan.com/clubs-and-venues/someday

@someday_jazz

https://www.instagram.com/jazz_someday_tokyo/

https://www.facebook.com/profile.php?id=100063893594261

Someday has moved several times in the past decade, from Shin-Okubo to Kagurazaka to Shinbashi to Shinjuku and this year (2025) to Asakusa. The place has hardly changed, though. The owner, sound engineer, cook, manager and "master" Mori-san has finally found a good home. Certainly, this newest space is a bit more intimate, but it's a good, relaxed space with even better sound. It is an easy walk from the nightlife in Asakusa, down a large street in a quieter area a block or two away from the hubbub and near many hotels.

 Since Mori-san was once a sound engineer, the speakers sound superb. He has them set up well, and the acoustics of this newest club are just as good as before. I always try to sit in the middle of the club, just a bit back from the stage, for the ultimate sweet spot in the sound, but closer seats are more fun to watch the band.

 Someday's stage can easily hold a twenty-piece band, whether modern, Latin, or straight-ahead jazz. That stage size alone makes it a unique place, and even more so for the annual big band festival held at Someday over two weeks every spring. Master Mori-san has always had a special fondness for big bands, but the festival is a chance to hear them on successive nights. Most weeks have at least one big band, though, and several of the bands reform themselves from other groups just to play at Someday.

Mori-san also likes to book blues, steel-pan, and hard bop bands as well. He's picky, so the bands are good, with some of the best players in Tokyo coming through regularly. It can be quiet on weeknights, but for the best bands, the club is packed, and the music swings hard. Most of the groups who perform there have a straight-ahead feel, but on other nights, the bands experiment with different configurations, styles, and approaches—hard bop one night, free jazz the next, and guitar trios, Latin. Whoever's playing, it's never a scene, and you can get into the music without the over-cool club vibe some places strive for. It's all about the music. The musicians jam through lengthy, solid sets. The space seems to invite them to stretch out.

You can hear and see well from any seat in the place. Food is basic, hearty, and satisfying- pizza, fried potatoes, salads, fried rice, and the usual nibbles. However, the Asakusa area has innumerable dining choices too. Drinks are reasonably priced, though don't hesitate to wave your hand when you get thirsty to drag over one of the wait staff. The master has a fair bit of English on his website too. The vibe is directed towards the music, and players and listeners take their music seriously here.

Sometime

サムタイム

Everyone likes Sometime, and for good reason

1-11-31-B1, Kichijoji Honcho, Musashino-shi, Tokyo

(0422)21-6336

〒180-0004東京都武蔵野市吉祥寺本町1-11-31 B1F

Kichijoji Station (JR Chuo Line, Sobu Line, Keio Inokashira Line)

From the north exit of Kichijoji station. From Kichijoji Station (Chuo Line), exit in the central north direction (not the Inokashira Park exit). Out of the station, you will see a covered shopping street called Sun Road. Go up there, and NOT to the left down Cherry Road. After a hundred meters or so, turn left on the small side street called Penny Lane. About 20 meters on the right-hand side is a sign for Sometime and stairs heading down.

2,500 yen, a bit more for overseas groups. Two sets at 19:00 and 20:30. Times may vary for three-set evenings. Lunchtime live shows are two sets from 13:00 and 14:30 on weekends and public holidays.

www.sometime.co.jp/sometime

https://www.jazzinjapan.com/clubs-and-venues/sometime

https://x.com/sometime_jazz

@sometimejazzclub

Sometime is one of the premier jazz clubs in Tokyo. Nestled in the dense warren of shops, eateries, and boutiques of Kichijoji, Sometime pulls in a crowd every night of the week. They book the best of Tokyo jazz and have established an atmosphere where the groups play their best. It's an institution in Tokyo jazz. Playing there means you have made it. Nearly every great player in Tokyo has been through here at some point in their career, and often all through their career, as the audience is always filled with the curious, informed, and jazz-hungry. Most performers have a regular monthly gig set up and often appear in interesting re-groupings, swapping the role of leader on different nights.

Interestingly, though, the vibe is very laid back. With a nightly cover charge cheaper than almost any spot in Tokyo, you can wander in without taking out a loan. You can also wander in mid-set and not feel like you are interrupting. There is a constant in-flow and out-flow that is lively, without being a hassle. The wait staff are also excellent, sensing when you want another drink, but otherwise leaving you alone to enjoy the music. Drinks are reasonable and the food quite good.

The stage is smack in the middle of the club so that from almost anywhere, you can hear well. However, the view is obstructed from the back tables on the lower floor (it's split a bit) and one or two tables on the balcony floor. Get there early, call ahead, or beg for a better seat during the break. You can always squeeze in and switch your seat if the first one isn't perfect. The sound is good throughout the club, and you can hear the drum without any miking or amping, as it's smack in the middle.

Seats that arc around the back of the players' heads are terrific because you can see the musicians working up close. One could quibble with the kitschy interior and the acoustics, but after settling in for a few numbers, Sometime starts to look and sound like one of the best spots in the city to hear music. There is now also a live Sunday afternoon show, which is usually quite busy and an interesting way to spend a non-work day.

More than anything, the players relax as much as the patrons, thanks to the mystery vibe that makes all the difference. It's one of the older clubs in the city, and some fans have gone there from college to retirement age. Musicians generally do not depart too far into open, free jazz, but neither do they play predictable standards. Musicians always play their best here and showcase recent compositions and new arrangements. The musicians are also very close to the audience, so they have the human interaction that drives them to play hard and dig deep.

Cozy and close

Introduction

Japan's small spaces are a comfortable intimacy

Space is at a premium in Japan's large cities. Every bit of space is accounted for. However, Japanese urban culture is good at turning limitations into virtues, so these smaller clubs provide an intimate space where you can see and hear the musicians creating music up close. The music feels different when it's near.

The downside is you can't stretch your legs out. But life is full of trade-offs, and the customers that come to these clubs like music made in front of their eyes, not at a distance on a high stage. Musicians who command larger crowds like to play here for the closeness to listeners and fans. They want to see the audience, to respond to them, and to play in duos or trios.

Because these interiors are a bit confined, it's always good to call ahead or email to reserve a seat. When they are full, there is no space even to stand in the back. Food is available, as are drinks of all kinds, but check the review for what's on offer.

Sets generally start on time. Having bumped into drummers and pianists, tripped over other customers' feet in the middle of a solo, and whispered apologies after arriving late on more than one occasion, getting there reasonably on time is highly advised.

Of course, if you are late, go anyway, whatever time. The music you'll catch in these clubs always has a delicacy and energy you won't find elsewhere.

Ginza Swing

スウィング銀座

Long-running and real jazz spot in the middle of Ginza

2F, Ginza Inz2, 2-2, Ginza-Nishi, Chuo-ku, Tokyo

(03)3563-3757

〒104-0061東京都中央区銀座西2丁目2番地 銀座インズ2-2F

Yurakucho Station (JR Yamanote Line, Keihin Tohoku Line). Ginza Station (Tokyo Metro Marunouchi Line, Hibiya Line), and Ginza Itchome Station (Tokyo Metro Yurakucho Line)

A three-minute walk from Yurakucho Station. Also from Ginza Station and Ginza Itchome Station.

5,500 to 7,500 yen. 3,000 for students. (You can become a member for 600 yen, which reduces future entry fees). 2 sets from 19:00 and 20:30. (some nights different).

http://ginzaswing.jp/

https://www.jazzinjapan.com/clubs-and-venues/ginzaswing

https://www.facebook.com/swingsince1976

https://x.com/ginza_swing

https://www.instagram.com/jazzclubginzaswing/

This classic old-school jazz club has featured the best musicians from Japan since 1976. Though it's housed in a shopping mall-like area, once you get inside, you get inside the heart of jazz in Japan. And a shopping mall in Ginza is still Ginza. Inside the club, the outside world falls away, and you can get into the music.

    The musicians range over many styles, but vocalists and straight-ahead jazz take the stage most evenings. The stage also welcomes evenings with talks from musicians about jazz, brought alive with the best examples played by musicians right then and there. The talks are in Japanese, but it is a real treat for those with enough Japanese to hear the musicians talk about their passion. I've listened to talks on a range of musicians, styles, and history. It's interesting to hear them talk and then play the songs right away.

    Even when they're there to play, it somehow feels closer, more understandable, and personal. The musicians are pulled from the top tier of Japanese musicians.

    Ginza Swing is a marvelous space with room to relax. Seats sweep around the stage in a horseshoe shape, so the sound and visuals are great from any seat. The venue has a very intimate vibe, which suits the musicians they bring in. Jazz is visual and aural, so it's great to see the magic of the music up close. Simply put, it's a great jazz club.

Strings

Small, stylish club with an ever-impressive line-up

TN Column Building B1, 2-12-13 Kichijoji Honcho, Musashino-shi, Tokyo

(0422)28-5035

〒180-0004東京都武蔵野市吉祥寺本町 2-12-13 (TNコラムビル地階)

Kichijoji Station (JR Chuo Line, Sobu Line, Keio Inokashira Line)

From Kichijoji station, take the north/Sun Road/main exit. Turn left out of the station and walk to the end of the block. Cross over the large street with a stoplight and enter a smaller street with shops and restaurants on both sides. Turn right on the second street (you can only turn right), and the club is about 50 meters up on the left-hand side with several signs out front.

2,800 to 3,500 yen. 2 sets from 19:30 and 20:45. (Saturday, Sunday and public holidays, two sets from 18:30 and 19:45). Sometimes there are three sets.

http://www.jazz-strings.com/

https://www.jazzinjapan.com/clubs-and-venues/strings

https://www.facebook.com/strings.live.bar/

Strings is a lovely little gem of a club nestled into the lively, hip spaces of Kichijoji's backstreets. It's a small club, but it never feels anything less than warm and friendly. A counter curves around the piano, high tables fill the back, and another counter lines the other wall, and that's about it. You have just enough room for a plate of pasta, a glass of wine, and an *oshibori*. But that's all the space you need, because it is easy to get lost in the music.

Most nights, the musicians play without mics and amps, or not much, anyway. So, the sonic pleasure of hearing the instruments so fresh and direct is part of the charm. With the instruments so close and personal, the musicians play with heightened intimacy and immediacy. There's nothing to separate the audience and musicians anyway, so you feel the whole room being live and alive. Musicians who could command a much larger crowd clearly like to play here for the closeness to listeners and fans. Between sets, there's no place for them to sit, or even stand, so chatting is part of the fun.

The food at Strings is nicely done, and the interior is well-designed. It's a hip, tiny space with delicious food and drinks. It has to be to compete with the many great restaurants, bars, and eateries cramming side streets and backways of Kichijoji. You almost always need a reservation, as it can get crowded quickly, and often, all seats are reserved ahead of time by ardent fans of musicians. If there's room, though, the owner will let people stand at the back until the door is pushed back open.

The musicians who play here consider Strings a regular stop for CD release tours, special groups, and important tours. Many come through every month if they can. The music is not always jazz, but it mixes in bossa nova, Latin, singer-songwriters, and other close cousins of jazz. The common thread is quality and a close appeal. The music always feels acoustic and unplugged in just the right ways. Strings offers handcrafted evenings, making it a great place to go, no matter who is playing. The owner is usually there, making sure everything runs right and that customers enjoy it all.

Absolute Blue

アブソルート ブルー

Close to the station for jazz and more

Toshima-kaikan B2, 1 Chome-15-6 Nishi-Ikebukuro, Toshima-ku, Tokyo

(03)5904-8576

〒171-0021 東京都豊島区西池袋1-15-6豊島会館B2F

Ikebukuro Station (JR Yamamote Line, Saikyo Line, Shonan Shinjuku Line, Tohokuhonsen Tokkyu-Line, Tokyo Metro Fukutoshin Line, Tokyo Metro Marunouchi Line, Tokyo Metro Yurakucho Line, Seibu Ikebukuro Line, Tobu Tojo Line)

3,000 to 5,500 yen. Depending on the night, there are two sets at 19:00 and 20:30. Music is played nightly, though sometimes the club is reserved for jam sessions or private parties.

http://absol.blue/

https://www.jazzinjapan.com/clubs-and-venues/absoluteblue

https://www.facebook.com/absol.blue

https://x.com/AbsoluteBlue00

https://www.instagram.com/absolute_blue_/

Absolute Blue is a lovely club close to Ikebukuro Station, about one minute from the west exit. That location makes it easy to drop by for a set or two, but you'll want to stay longer. The cozy atmosphere of the club wraps around you, and the very comfy seats let you drift into the music. Like many serious-about-the-music venues in Tokyo, the seats face the stage.

The music is the main thing, though the drinks, especially the cocktails, are great, and the food is basic, but good. The stage is designed not thinking of the club owner's needs so much as the musicians' and sound tech guys' preferences. That means even the small-ish space has excellent sound for musicians and the audience. Actually, the quality is impeccable, but not in a way that calls attention to itself. For music lovers who pay attention to sound, that makes a massive difference in the total experience, but for everyone else, the sound is easy on the ears.

While most evenings at Absolute Blue feature jazz, the music often includes funk, blues, rock, and jam bands. Bands usually attract long-time fans, so the atmosphere is always lively. This great club feels like home, where you can turn up the music loud and perfect and let it sink into your bones.

Apollo
アポロ

Funky basement room with loose, fresh jazz

EIKO Bldg B1, 2-9-22 Kitazawa, Setagaya-ku, Tokyo

〒155-0031 東京都世田谷区北沢２-９-２２ EIKO下北沢ビル地下１階

Shimokitazawa Station (Keio Inokashira Line, Odakyu Line)

2,000 to 3,000 yen, plus bar charge 800 yen and drink order. Sets from 19:30. No food. Just drinks and great music.

https://ameblo.jp/430416apollo/

https://jazzshiryokan.net/jazzDB/livehouse_detail.php?recordID=H329

https://www.facebook.com/XiaBeiZeBarApolloaporoShimokitazawaApollo

https://www.instagram.com/explore/locations/280536939/xia-bei-ze-apolloaporo-shimokitazawa-apollo/

Apollo is not much bigger than the Apollo that carried men to the Moon, but it sure is cozier. The vibe is laid-back and relaxed, and there's not only no miking but hardly any place to put a mike! Located on a neat little back street of one of Tokyo's hippest, most music-loving areas—Shimokitazawa—Apollo is more of a newcomer to the jazz scene, but it's made a name for itself.

This four-meter square space on the basement floor is packed with black and white photos of musicians and real instruments hung on the old yellow walls. Lighting is by bare bulb.

The "stage" is the space nearest one corner. There's no need for amplification. A grand piano would be nice, but where would you put it? Instruments hang from the walls like at many neighborhood clubs where musicians of all stripes used to go to jam.

The music is cutting-edge, experimental, free, and sometimes straight-ahead. Musicians clearly love playing there, as the space's underground feel always kicks them into high gear. It's a cool atmosphere for an intimate music experience.

Get there early to get a decent seat. Drinks are good, and they'd probably rustle up some food for you, but it's better to eat at any of the hundreds of eateries in the nearby areas.

Salt Peanuts

そるとぴーなつ

Intense basement room for hard-driving groups

Gracy Mansion 43-B1F, 4-3, Sakae-cho, Nerima-ku, Tokyo.

(03)3993-3400

〒176-0006 東京都練馬区栄町4-3 グレーシーマンション43-B1F

Ekoda Station (Seibu Ikebukuro Line), Shinekoda Station (Toei Oedo Line), Shinsakuradai Station (Seibu Yurakucho Line)

It is a 3-minute walk from Ekoda Station (Seibu Ikebukuro Line) or a 9-minute walk from Shinekoda Station (Oedo Line). From Ekoda, take the south exit, cut right up to the main road, and look for the tiny sign. Then, head downstairs.

There is a 1,500 yen music charge and a 500 yen table charge. There are two sets from 19:30, earlier on Sundays and public holidays.

https://saltpeanuts.jp/

https://www.jazzinjapan.com/clubs-and-venues/saltpeanuts

https://x.com/SALT3400/

https://www.facebook.com/profile.php?id=100051458841243&ref=settings%2F

https://www.instagram.com/saltmaster3400/

A short train ride from Ikebukuro takes you to the lively, small station of Ekoda, which is quickly becoming a hub for music, food, and good times far from the rush and over-building of Ikebukuro. Salt Peanuts is one of the best additions to Ekoda's vibe. Presenting the best of up-and-coming jazz musicians, the club focuses on music first, everything else second.

 Drink choices have a wider range than most clubs, and the free snacks, including the club's namesake, on every table are a welcome freebie. The club keeps prices reasonable, so customers never feel overcharged, and they feel free to keep coming back to hear groups they may not be sure about yet. Salt Peanuts is a joyous bargain in a city where quality is usually priced accordingly.

 The club's atmosphere is characterized by a sense of experimentation. It promotes younger players who have yet to break into the ranks of established players, but it also features the most established musicians.

 The club is a club, instead of a performance hall, a place where musicians still have the freedom to try things out, push their limits, and gauge the reaction of the audience. The atmosphere is generally younger, friendlier, and more switched on to straight-ahead music.

Salt Peanuts, of course, is the perfect name for the club. It comes from the fast-paced, amusing song Dizzy Gillespie and Charlie Parker made famous. That sense of intense devotion to jazz infuses the club. It's a comfortable place, a bit bigger than most clubs, where you can go for the music and linger to unwind, but you can be assured of getting a great evening of jazz.

Neighborhood

Introduction

Neighborhood clubs.

Places to drop by, whether you're a regular or not yet a regular

Neighborhood clubs are among the authentic delights of the Tokyo and Yokohama jazz scene. Small, unpretentious, messy, and welcoming, you can unwind and sink into the music in these small clubs. Musicians like to be able to look their audience in the eye, and when they do, they always seem to play more warmly and richly. That might just be how my feelings run when I'm there, but music, especially jazz, is all about feelings at some level.

These small clubs are usually run by jazz fanatics, so they give top priority to the music, but also to providing an intimate human experience with the music. No club owner is in it for the money, but these neighborhood clubs are hives of friendship, interaction, and devotion to music. They are clubs in the sense of being a collection of like-minded individuals, as much as a space to hear music.

One of the nice parts of these clubs are the regulars. Musicians put these places on their regular circuit of the city because they know many people work late, yet can still make it to a place on the way home for music, even if it's only for the last set. Clubs are often a short walk from the station, and you can feel the calm the farther you get from the busy streets around the station.

Many places double as coffee shops or lunch places during the day, and they are great to visit then too. You're assured of a good playlist of vinyl jazz. Others open for drinks at cocktail hour.

As a result, the vibe is calmer and more unassuming, and the music often comes out that way. Musicians are more reflective and tend to play their personal favorites, new material, and favorites from past CDs, not so much what they "should" play. It's a welcome change from the intensity of other venues and a very different side of the city. Be ready to rub elbows and have conversations. It's a neighborhood, after all.

Harbor Light

ジャズ&バー　ハーバーライト

A harbor in western Tokyo for jazz and drinks

Y's Vision Bldg 4F, Higashi 1-6-2, Kunitachi-shi, Tokyo

(042)577-5510

〒186-0002 東京都国立市東1-6-2 Y's VISION ビル4F

Kunitachi Station (JR Chuo Line)

The club is a three-minute walk from the south exit of Kunitachi Station on the Chuo Line. From the north exit, head left around the rotary and take the angled-left street. The club is on the right-hand side. The map on the club's site (even in Japanese) is clear.

2,500 yen or more. 20% off for students. Two sets from 19:30 and 21:00, depending on the show. There's not jazz every night, but most. Check carefully.

https://harborlight-kunitachi.com/

https://www.jazzinjapan.com/clubs-and-venues/harborlight

https://x.com/Harborlightjazz

https://www.facebook.com/profile.php?id=61556018414167

@Harborlightjazz

Though many jazz lovers head into the middle of Tokyo or Yokohama for their jazz fix, the jazz clubs outside the center are often a great delight. Harbor Light is that and then some. Located close by Kunitachi Station on the Chuo Line, Harbor Light's name is well chosen. It's an intimate, well-designed space that offers safe harbor after a few minutes' walk.

    It also offers great music. The owner, Omura-san, spent years working in the States, and when he retired, he knew what he wanted to do: listen to jazz every night. He's achieved his dream and offered it to others by creating a marvelous space that is equal parts living room, whiskey bar, and club.

    The stage is close to the front tables without feeling crowded. At the long, wide, comfy bar that stretches along the back of the club, the bar stools are raised, making it easy to see and hear the music. The club also has an impressively large selection of whiskeys—single malt, Japanese, foreign, and bourbon—as well as great cocktails. The food menu is simple and of high quality, a wise choice if you don't have time to pop in one of the many eateries close by.

The sound is crisp and clear since the club is acoustically designed to not need too much in the way of amps and mikes, soundboard, or wires. The music surrounds you with clarity and intensity. Harbor Light is a delightful spot that anyone near or far will find to be a great oasis for jazz and a soothing place to kick back.

He doesn't have live jazz every night, but when he does, some of the best musicians in Tokyo, usually ones who live nearby, fill the evening with duos or trios. Other nights, he opens up the space for students to perform or for amateur groups. That's what neighborhood means after all.

Giee

ライブ・カフェ・ギー

A basement hideaway for jazz and more

Sanko Building, Basement floor 1, Honcho 2-3-9, Kokubunji-shi, Tokyo

(042)326-0770

〒185-0012東京都国分寺市本町2-3-9 三幸ビルB1

Kokubunji Station (JR Chuo Line, Seibu Kokubunji Line, Seibu Tamako Line, Narita Express)

Head out the north exit of Kokubunji station. Turn right after the construction, and follow the street filled with restaurants, bars, and noodle shops parallel to the train tracks. When you see the end of that street, called "Daigaku Dori" or University Street, there is an angled street to the left, a bit before the street runs out. Turn left, and Giee will be on the right-hand side. Look for the cool metal sign.

1,500 to 4,500 yen. Two sets from 19:30 most nights, though Tuesdays and Wednesdays are often off. Check the site for details and exact starting times.

http://giee.jp

https://www.jazzinjapan.com/clubs-and-venues/giee

https://x.com/livecafe_giee

Giee is a cozy room—literally a room—that happens to showcase great music from across the spectrum of genres every night. The atmosphere is as friendly as a living room, and it's impossible to keep from chatting with everyone around you. Well-worn seats and a basic drink menu, with food whipped up by the mama-san, is all you need to settle in and hear music close, live, and intimate.

Band announcements for Giee and other gigs line the stairway, demonstrating how much musicians love playing there and how much it serves as a hub for jazz along the Chuo Line.

Nights, the groups tend to be small—duos, trios, or quartets at most, and it's always a pleasure to hear the music so close. Starting times can vary, so check the site before you go. Most shows begin at 7:30, but check the schedule carefully.

Fridays and weekends, there is usually an afternoon session, a jam sessions with everything from chanson to pops to gypsy swing, to blues, and of course, jazz. Giee is a community, in other words, devoted to music and an oasis of musical satisfaction in western Tokyo.

KLAVIER

クラヴィーア

Asagaya Minami 3-37-13-3F, Suginami-ku, Tokyo

(03)3393-0418

〒166-0004 東京都杉並区阿佐ヶ谷南3-37-13-3F

Asagaya Station (JR Chuo and Sobu Line)

Asagaya Station on the Chuo and Sobu Line. From the JR station south exit, step out into the open area with a police box and look up at the third floor of the first building on the right-hand side. It is maybe a one-minute walk if your feet are tired, 30 seconds if you're OK. It is easy to see from the station.

2,500 yen to 3,400 yen, but more for bigger groups and specials. There are two sets at 19:30 and 21:00 on weekdays and 18:00 and 19:30 on

Sundays and Public Holidays. Check carefully as the time depends on the show.

http://www2.tbb.t-com.ne.jp/klavier/www/

https://www.jazzinjapan.com/clubs-and-venues/klavier

https://www.jazzinjapan.com/clubs-and-venues/klavier

The wood-lined walls of Jazz Club Klavier form the perfect resonating board for the small-group jazz and intimate atmosphere showcased there. The wood creates a superb acoustic setting, making the "live" seem much more alive. The horns and reeds do not need any miking, nor do the other instruments, though some sound balance helps coordinate each musician's level and let the music fly.

Even those audiophiles who have spent a lot of time and money creating a great sound setting in their homes will appreciate the beauty of the sound at Klavier. The club's title, after all, comes from the German word for piano, a marvelous instrument at the center of so much jazz and classical music.

The club is small enough to see and hear from anywhere. But it never feels crowded. Service is impeccable without being imposing. Customers can sit and drift off into the music all alone or strike up a conversation, either one easily. The food is good, and there is an excellent selection of drinks, with as many bottles lining the back of the bar as any cocktail specialty spot in Tokyo.

Musicians go there to play in an intimate, relaxed, and individual way. The musicians slip into their finest virtuoso mode too. Some of the best jazz musicians in the city team up with one or two others, often in an acoustic setting, to showcase the interaction and deliberate improvising at the heart of jazz. Musicians there are never trying to prove anything edgy or provocative, but play with the awareness that the audience is there to hear their music closely, calmly, and rather diligently. Klavier is a real jazz place.

Jesse James
ジェシー・ジェイムス立川店

Whiskey, steaks, and small group jazz in a roadhouse interior

Tachikawa Regent Bldg. B1, 2-11-7 Akebono-cho, Tachikawa-shi

(042)525-7188

〒190-0012東京都立川市曙町2-11-7立川リージェントビルB1F

Tachikawa Station (JR Chuo Line)

From the north exit of Tachikawa station, walk north, with Isetan on the left and Bic Camera on the right. Turn right at the first big street, and you'll see the funky Americana sign.

1,200 to 4,000 yen. Two sets from 19:00 on weekdays. Daytime shows from 14:00.

http://jessejames-tachikawa.music.coocan.jp/

https://www.jazzinjapan.com/clubs-and-venues/jessejames

Jesse James specializes in bourbon, steak, and jazz—the holy triumvirate of bodily pleasure. The steaks are fresh, the bourbon unblended or special reserve, and the music red-blooded. The club is lined with wooden mementos, steer horns, black walls, cowboy hats, thick wood tables, and the mouth-watering smell of frying steak and sour mash bourbon. It's easy to willingly enter into that movie-like suspension of your disbelief once inside.

If you're not into Americana, don't worry, they have plenty of other drinks and food. You'll find something. The music makes even the surroundings unimportant.

The band picks up on an American frontier saloon's slightly theme-park feel and plays to the surroundings. You are not likely to hear any arty, airy jazz here, though the groups tend to be duos and trios. It's mostly muscular, straight-up jazz, down-to-earth. The performers here are primarily up-and-comers, but many established players enjoy having the freedom to work through a trio set. All the bands here are good, every night of the week, and weekends especially showcase solid performers.

Jesse James is a fair-sized place, befitting its location in the constantly renewing Tachikawa. The acoustics are good, with decent amps and good sound mixing. You can hear and see well from anywhere in the place. The giant wood seats and thick, solid tables are a relaxing retreat from the cramped, elbow-bumping spots in downtown Tokyo. The openness makes it a different listening experience from other clubs—a nice pleasure in the western side of Tokyo.

Lady Jane
レディ・ジェーン

Booze and jazz and weekend live music

5-31-14, Daizawa, Setagaya-ku, Tokyo

(03) 3412-3947

〒155-0032東京都世田谷区代沢5-31-14

Shimokitazawa Station (Keio Inokashira Line, Odakyu Odawara Line)

The music charge is 3,500 or more, depending on the band. Two sets from 18:30. Live shows are usually on the weekends and public holidays. Closed on Mondays. Check the time carefully as it shifts a bit.

http://bigtory.jp/

https://www.facebook.com/LadyJane.bigtory

Genuine sophistication is a hard quality to achieve, but Lady Jane does that and has been doing it since 1975. It's a cozy, lovely spot that would fit inside any of the other sections equally well. As their website points out, it's flaneur, rhum, and pop culture (I guess meaning pop culture of the 1950s—jazz—and drinks from the Prohibition Era). Nestled into the hip environs of Shimokitazawa for so many years, it feels like the seed from which the rest of the area grew.

The live music they showcase is now mainly on the weekend, but the musicians are always influential, progressive, and eclectic. Don't expect four-beat quartets here; it's more like a sax-drums-koto trio, an electric violinist singer duo (both singing and violining), or cello-alto sax duos. Throw in some ukuleles and accordions, and you get the idea of their wide-ranging sense of jazz.

On non-live music nights, it's a fantastic jazz bar. Their cocktails are some of the best in the city, with ironic names and unique mixes. With a sleek, dark interior, the place feels like a speakeasy during prohibition. There's always a feeling of doing something a little naughty when you enter. And that makes it all the more of a delight.

The club has been a mainstay in the jazz scene, with an amazing history of musicians who've played there or dropped by. It has kept its importance by focusing on an atmosphere where people, music, and pleasure blend effortlessly.

Art x Jazz M's

(アート×ジャズ　エムズ)

Warm and welcoming spot for jazz and jamming

B1 Myojo Bldg., 2-7-5, Honcho, Kokubunji-shi, Tokyo

(042)325-7767

〒185-0012 東京都国分寺市本町 2-7-5 明星ビルB1

Kokubunji Station (JR Chuo Line, Seibu Kokubunji Line, Seibu Tamako Line, Narita Express)

Head north out of Kokubunji Station and take the first street to the right. On the second street to the left, take a left and a left (yes, it's still Tokyo's winding streets). On an angled street, you will see a long row of windows to the half-basement room.

The charge is 2,000 to 3,000 yen. The shows start around 19:30 or 20:00, and Sundays and Mondays are jam sessions.

http://artjazz-ms.com/

https://www.jazzinjapan.com/clubs-and-venues/art-x-jazz-ms

https://www.facebook.com/artjazzms/

https://www.instagram.com/artjazzms/

https://x.com/artjazzms

This great club presents jazz nightly without pretense, but with plenty of impact. It's a small place that hardly needs a mic so that you can hear the instruments closely and clearly. It's a real jazz lover's place but laidback enough that anyone would feel comfortable. Getting there early is best, as the best seats are limited. If you do wander in later, though, someone will find you a chair. Reservations are always good to have, but not always necessary.

The groups are usually straight-ahead jazz, but on some nights, the groups stretch out to play more freely and wildly. Typically, it's duo or trios, but quartets and even quintets play. There's a dedication to jazz in the place that really comes through. The up-and-comers from the jam sessions often attend. Monday nights and Saturday afternoons are usually jam sessions. They are welcoming to serious musicians.

Sunday afternoons run into Sunday evenings with the "Sunday Jazz Happening," when new music is played and a relaxed vibe flows. On other nights, jazz lectures and explanations take over. It's cool to hear pros talk about their work and what they love. The club is a genuine incubator of jazz, playing and listening. You can hear up-and-coming players and old stalwarts too. It's off the beaten path but really on its own path.

Manhattan

(マンハッタン)

A trackside engine of jazz

3F Kiraku Bldg., 2-2-7, Asagaya-kita, Suginami-ku, Tokyo.

(03)3336-7961

〒166-0001 東京都杉並区阿佐ヶ谷北2-2-7喜楽ビル3F

Asagaya Station (JR Chuo and Sobu Line)

Head out the north exit of Asagaya Station and turn left. The club's about two buildings down on the other side of the street that runs along the Chuo Line train tracks.

The cover charge is 2,500 yen with a two-drink minimum. 2 sets from 19:30 and 20:45. There is a jam session on Thursday nights and Sunday afternoons. Closed on Mondays, Tuesdays, and Sunday nights.

http://www.ateliermw.com/manhattan/

Manhattan is an unassuming little place, unlike its namesake. Like its namesake, it has excellent music. The interior is a bit rundown and messy, but there is an air of indifference to any concerns except jazz. Fair enough.

The club's blog, "Jazz Never Sleeps," describes its mission well. Although I say "club," it's also a jazz school, a rental space with rental instruments, and, until the pandemic, a spot for all-night jam sessions.

It's a small space, and depending on the set-up, the bass player has to move over to let in late-arriving guests. It's not so easy to keep the beat when you're leaning out of the way of the door, but most bassists manage pretty well.

Food and drinks are basic, but that's all that's needed. On the same street, or on the other side of the train tracks too, are numerous small eating places of every description.

This place has helped many musicians advance from their beginnings to the level of pros. The club still has weekly jam sessions and lessons, but plenty of musicians who have "made it" return for the vibe and the good company. The club rents out its space (and space isn't cheap in Tokyo) for practice sessions, recordings, and tryouts. It's a hardworking place.

With all that going on, the evening gigs seem like a chance to unwind, listen, or play after a hard day's work. And hard night's work, too, as the Thursday jam session starts at ten p.m. If you want to see how jazz "works" in Japan, this is a great spot to see just that.

Down-to-earth

Introduction

You sometimes want to avoid the hip atmosphere, polite service, or out-on-the-town drama. You want to sit in a chair and soak up the music, not read a complicated menu or act pleasant to the wait staff. Those are the days you go to these clubs.

Japan is famed for having neat, clean spaces with everything all in order. But that's only one side of Japan. The other side of Japan is an ignore-the-world carelessness that might feel a bit sloppier, but also much more human. These places rest on a nonchalance that's inviting. They are super casual and very funky.

You won't see musicians in suit coats or neat outfits in these joints. They come from their practice sessions that afternoon directly to the club warmed up and ready. Musicians come as they are, ready to play. The audience comes ready to listen. That's it.

These clubs typically offer limited food and drink choices, but are still ready for customers. They're all located near nightlife, standing bars, ramen shops, or yakitori joints, so you can always eat beforehand.

In some ways, these are the most Japanese types of clubs, where everyone is more themselves. While musicians play from the heart in any venue in Japan, the music at these places is less filtered, more direct, and unadorned, like a conversation with a good friend at your favorite bar.

Koen Dori Classics

公園通りクラシックス

Neat hideaway tucked inside a parking garage

B1 Tokyo Yamate Church, 19-5, Udagawa-cho, Shibuya-ku, Tokyo

(03)6310-8871

〒150-0042 東京都渋谷区宇田川町19-5 東京山手教会B1F

Shibuya Station (JR Yamanote Line, Saikyo Line, Shonan Shinjuku Line, Tokyu Toyoko Line, Tokyu Denentoshi Line, Keio Inokashira Line, Tokyo Metro Ginza Line, Tokyo Metro Fukutoshin Line, Tokyo Metro Hanzomon Line). From the Hachiko exit of Shibuya station, pass Hachiko exit and head to the right of the Starbucks. The next large street, curving up to the left, is Koen Dori. It's a big street, and the club is about 100 meters up on the left side. It's under a church, though it doesn't look like a traditional church. There is an unimposing cross a couple of stories up on the wall, but it's hard to see. Instead, look for a basement entrance with a small sign to the left and head down into the parking lot.

The cover charge is 3,000 yen or more, depending on the group. There are two sets from 19:30. On weekends, shows can be in the afternoon. There are shows most nights, but not every night.

http://koendoriclassics.com/

https://www.jazzinjapan.com/clubs-and-venues/koen-dori-classics

https://www.facebook.com/KoendoriClassics

Koen Dori Classics is an unusual place to hear jazz—not just near a parking lot, but actually inside a parking lot. The venue is just the right size, though, and the managers are picky about who plays there. Only the most intriguing and unique artists are invited, so it's always cutting-edge and unique.

 Musicians from overseas are prominently featured, often playing with Japanese musicians, so there's a real sense of exchange. And a real sense of creating improvised music in unique combinations.

 The venue does not have music every night, but when it does, it's always stellar. From intense free improv to gentle Brazilian guitar to collaborations of all kinds, the club showcases an eclectic line-up of engaging musicians playing sometimes challenging, but always satisfying music.

 Seats are limited and ring around the stage, depending on how the performers set it up. But you can hear and see well from wherever you sit. The sound system is excellent and always mixed carefully.

 Seats are often limited, so it's essential to book ahead. Most performers have mailing lists, so it can sell out even before it's listed.

There are standard drinks at the small counter but not much food. That's fine, though, since it's in the middle of Shibuya, where it's easy to find whatever food your stomach desires.

Don't be put off by walking through an underground parking garage. Just follow the signs and wave away the carbon monoxide, and the club will appear at the bottom of the slope to the right. The entryway is odd, but once inside, it's a great venue to hear a fascinating selection of improvised music.

Organ Jazz Club

オルガンジャズクラブ

Hammond B3 Organ Heaven

Numabukuro 1-34-4 B1F, Nakano-ku, Tokyo-to

(03)3388-2040

〒165-0025東京都中野区沼袋1-34-4 B1F

Numabukuro Station (Seibu Shinjuku Line)

From Numabukuro station's north exit, veer to the right, though not the sharp right. About 100 meters down on the right-hand side, you will see a sign and a closed circuit TV broadcasting from inside (unless it's raining). Alternatively, Numabukuro is only a short taxi ride from Nakano station. Hop in a taxi and take it to Numabukuro station, only about one tick.

The cover charge is 3,000 to 4,000 yen. Two sets from 19:30 to 20:00, sometimes starting earlier.

https://ojcabecafe.jimdofree.com/

https://www.jazzinjapan.com/clubs-and-venues/organjazzclub

https://www.instagram.com/explore/tags/organjazzclub/

https://www.facebook.com/profile.php?id=100042370039697

@沼袋Organ Jazz Club

The passion for the Hammond B3 organ sound has seized many Japanese jazz fans. The famed organ company, whose transforming of the Hammond from respectable church accompaniment to the funkiest jazz instrument around, is maybe the best example of popular music's revenge. It has found a home in Japan! Get your dose of vitamin B3 right here!

Organ Jazz Club opened in 2006, and the owner did everything right. The club is smallish but comfortable, with a fantastic sound system, superb acoustics, and a huge mirror set up behind the organ so you can watch the organ players' hands work the two layers of keyboards and fiddle with the stops. Not every night at OJC features organists, but most do. Build it, and they will come!

Surprisingly, many fans dig the B3 in Japan, and the steady stream of full-time B3 players has increased. Knowing that, Organ Jazz Club has a vintage B3 installed (try carrying one down the stairs!) with Leslie rotating speakers to get that perfect sound. All the other amps and equipment are also done just right, and musicians respond by treating the gear and the music with respect.

On non-organ nights, other jazz musicians perform. A grand piano fills the other half of the stage. But even when it's a guitar-based group, the B3 vibe informs the music. It's a place for really laid-back, soulful music.

And if you need more soul, they serve some of the best tacos in Tokyo! The drinks and other food are solid and filling, but the tacos fit the B3 well.

This club is heaven for fans of the Hammond B3-based style of funky soul jazz. For those who like great, fun music, it's close to heaven!

Apple Jump

アップル・ジャンプ

A compact basement room to listen closely

Tobu West Ikebukuro Sunlight Mansion B1, Nishi-Ikebukuro 3-33-17, Toshima-ku, Tokyo

(03)5950-0689

〒171-0021東京都豊島区西池袋3-33-17東武西池袋サンライトマンションB1

Ikebukuro Station (JR Yamamote Line, Saikyo Line, Shonan Shinjuku Line, Tohokuhonsen Tokkyu-Line, Tokyo Metro Fukutoshin Line, Tokyo

Metro Marunouchi Line, Tokyo Metro Yurakucho Line, Seibu Ikebukuro Line, Tobu Tojo Line)

A few minutes walk from exit C3, down an underground walkway from the station, west side of Ikebukuro Station. Straight out the exit, head down Rikkyo Dori, and veer left, and you can see the club to the right of a good-sized park. Map and photos on site.

The cover charge is 3,000 yen to 3,800 yen. There are two sets from 19:30 and sometimes daytime shows on weekends or public holidays. There are also occasional days off.

http://applejump.net

https://www.jazzinjapan.com/clubs-and-venues/applejump

https://www.facebook.com/AppleJump/

@applejump2009

https://x.com/applejump2009

Apple Jump is a relative newcomer to Tokyo's jazz scene, but it has gained a reputation for opening its space to the best new musicians in the city. Most musicians play as support for other bands, but once they start to have several CDs in their names, they often play Apple Jump as their first regular leader live shows. Some of the best keep coming back year after year.

And understandably, since Apple Jump is an easy place to like. Unpretentious in design, its simple, focused, box-like interior is all that is needed. There's nothing extra. It's a compact, cool-looking box of a basement room. The musicians and audience sit close, on the same rough concrete floor as the "stage," so everyone joins together as one.

There is no feeling of being a customer here, just another human being needing music. The musicians also love playing here since they do not need to separate themselves. The space looks like a practice room, but feels like you have lucked upon a special conclave of esteemed musicians.

Drinks and food are simple, but done right. Pizza toast is about as advanced as the food gets, but the range of drinks is extensive. It is an easy place to ease into a right-at-home feeling. Chairs are simple but comfortable, and you can move them around without bashing into the person beside you.

The building is in a lively area not far from Ikebukuro station, with plenty of other cafes, bars, and restaurants that like to be off the well-beaten paths of the bigger roads. The owner clearly loves music. His calming presence keeps things running smoothly without all the pressures of most clubs.

The club also has excellent sound dynamics, without any need for miking and amping. The room is "live" but in a way that sounds natural. Hearing instruments directly makes the music that much more special. The laidback vibe is infectious to musicians, fans, and all who pull back the heavy front door and sit down.

Ko-Ko

渋谷ココ

An intense dynamo of a club

Himawari Building 2F, 2-26-5 Dogenzaka, Shibuya-ku, Tokyo 150-0043

(03)3463-8226

〒150-0043 東京都渋谷区道玄坂2-26-5　ひまわりビル2階

Shibuya Station (JR Yamanote Line, Saikyo Line, Shonan Shinjuku Line, Tokyu Toyoko Line, Tokyu Denentoshi Line, Keio Inokashira Line, Tokyo Metro Ginza Line, Tokyo Metro Fukutoshin Line, Tokyo Metro Hanzomon Line)

Shibuya station. From Hachiko Square, go across the intersection towards the Shibuya 109 building. Veer to the left up the large street, going uphill to the second street on the right. Go under the overhead sign with a huge yellow ramen shop on the corner. Ahead, you'll see a Lawson convenience store. Walk to the Lawson and turn right. You can see the orange-yellow Ko-Ko sign on a building about 50 meters ahead. The club is on the second floor. Ko-Ko is smack in the middle of the love hotel section of Shibuya, if that helps you locate it more easily.

The cover charge ranges from 2,500 to 3,300 yen. Two sets from 20:00 to 22:30 every night except Monday. Sundays and Tuesdays are jam sessions starting at 19:00 or 19:30 and 3,100 jam session charge.

https://jazz-koko.com

https://www.jazzinjapan.com/clubs-and-venues/koko

An intense dynamo of a club, Ko-Ko has expanded from its long-ago spot, Sonoka, in Meguro and the smaller-sized first space, upgrading, enlarging, and nice-ning things up bit by bit to the just-right form it is in today. That makes Ko-Ko an easy place to hang out and hear good, solid music. The name, of course, has multiple meanings, coming from a Charlie Parker song title. But of course, "koko" is also the Japanese word for "Here!" The club draws a bit from each of those allusions, but Parker's intensity is the influence.

Most of the groups playing at Ko-Ko dig into quick-tempo-ed, long-soloing jazz. They come here to let fly. The space is just right for being close enough to feel part of the proceedings, but still being large enough to relax. Many nights offer vocals, and not every band jams long and loud, but the exciting bebop vibe, no doubt also influenced by the love hotels and cheap bars in the area, is the predominant one.

Part of the appeal of Ko-Ko is that the musicians like to interact and drive each other to better, faster, or more interesting playing. Musicians like to try out old songs, dig into standards with a new attitude, and interact on the bandstand in a truly improvised fashion. That makes for earthy, serious music with the right degree of spontaneity. The sense is not so much of having to worry what the audience would think, but neither do the musicians lag into jam session mode, either. Except when it is a jam session, and then the evening is great fun of another sort, with musicians jumping in for in-the-moment arrangements and lots of supportive interaction.

If Shibuya did not have a club like Ko-Ko amid all its other offerings, it would have to be invented. Food and drink are right to the point here, but certainly with no fancy frills of any kind. There are fill-me-up, cheese-based dishes, pasta, and the usual finger food, all good. That's good enough in the middle of Shibuya, where you can find whatever you like to eat or drink before or after the show.

Ko-Ko is always a short walk up the hill and in the middle of a lively area. Its location seems fitting since jazz was a music born in the pleasure quarters of New Orleans. Ko-Ko's jazz fits perfectly into the lively evening hills of Shibuya.

Aketa no Mise
アケタの店

Funky basement room for wild jazz

Yoshino Biru B101, Nishi Ogi Kita 3-21-13, Suginami-ku, Tokyo

(03)3395-9507

〒167-0042 東京都杉並区西荻北3-21-13 吉野ビルB101

Nishi-Ogikubo Station (Chuo Line, Sobu Line, Tokyo Metro Tozai Line)

Nishi-Ogikubo Station (Chuo Line). From Nishi-Ogikubo Station, go out the north exit and cross over the small-ish bus and taxi area to a winding street lined with noodle shops, yakitori places, and various restaurants. Walk down this street until you get to the first large cross street. Turn right, and it is a couple of buildings on the right-hand side.

The cover charge is usually 3,000 yen (which includes one drink). Live shows from 20:00. Saturday midnight show from 24:00-01:30 is 1,400 yen. Sundays and holidays often start in the afternoon. Closed on most Mondays. So check their schedule before you go.

http://www.aketa.org/mise.html

https://www.jazzinjapan.com/clubs-and-venues/aketanomise

Aketa no Mise is more of a converted college dorm room than a club. The furniture was rescued from big trash day, light bulbs dangle by thinning wires, the carpet is frayed, and plastic beer crates hold up the speakers. The back wall is covered in a primitivist mural painted by an artist who does not follow all the substance control laws in the country.

The first time I went, I was a little surprised as the place was packed, but then, around starting time, everyone in the audience got up and went onstage! They were the musicians. Left behind were the band's girlfriends and me. Sadly, the owner Shoji Aketagawa passed away in 2024, but he'd be pleased to know his club is running on like it has for decades. He was an ocarinist, pianist, CD producer, radio DJ, big band leader, and friend to musicians and fans who like unusual approaches to jazz. He's missed.

The musicians at Aketa are playing to satisfy themselves. Because they are pushing boundaries, that approach never seems to result in self-indulgence, but rather intriguing, beguiling music. Don't let the funkiness fool you. Aketa showcases some of the most cutting-edge music in Japan. The intensity of performances here stays up at levels in inverse proportion to the casualness of the interior. This is a serious jazz studio—with plenty of edges. Aketa no Mise is a space for avant-garde, offbeat, unpredictable jazz, and straight-ahead, no-nonsense jamming.

Musicians come here because they know they can play in their own way and have an interested audience that knows what they are trying to do. Experimental approaches and full-on jams are the mainstays here, but on many nights, solid musical weight is the main course. Aketa's is home to what might be called "Chuo Line Jazz" if the musicians could in any way be grouped. But resisting categorization is how they play instead, and if any place in Tokyo could exemplify creativity and sincerity in music, it's Aketa.

The surrounding area, Nishi-Ogikubo, is a very cool area too. On the way to the club, check out the hundreds of eateries on the north side (and again on the south). There's not much in the way of food at Aketa, just standard drinks and some snacks, but you don't go to Aketa's for the clean crystal. Get something beforehand or after. The area stays open late. Shows hit at 20:00. Aketa also puts out its own CD label, many recorded live, and samples line the small shelves along the walls. Aketa is one of my favorite places in Tokyo.

Live in Buddy

ライブハウス バディ

Shape-shifting club with great variety

Futaba Kaikan B2F, 1-77-8, Asahigaoka, Nerima-ku, Tokyo.

(03)3953-1152

〒176-0005 東京都練馬区旭丘1-77-8 双葉会館B2F

Ekoda Station (Seibu Ikebukuro Line)

The cover charge is 3,000 yen to 4,000 yen, but it is higher for some live shows.

The shows usually start at 19:30 unless otherwise noted on the schedule. Live shows are not available every day since many days are reserved for private party reservations.

https://www.buddy-tokyo.com/

https://www.facebook.com/ekoda.buddy

https://x.com/BUDDY_TOKYO

https://www.instagram.com/ekodabuddy/

Eclectic in the extreme, Live in Buddy (yes, an odd name) is a venue that is large, unpredictable, and interesting. The spot can be rented out for special groups, and it often is, but most nights it showcases one or another variety of jazz, everything from big band to free jazz to klezmer, and all points in between. You never know what type of music will be there.

It's a chameleon-like place that takes on the color of the band and fans on that evening. Most people go there just for the band, notified through mailing lists and band websites. Other nights, they rent it out to university or amateur big bands.

It's a rather big space with big tables, chairs, and a solid sound system. It never feels cramped. There is standard bar food, though eating at one of the small spots nearby is also a good option. The drink menu is extensive.

Live in Buddy is not a place to go just for the atmosphere or for a random jazz night out. Before you go, be sure of who's playing. Once there, it's a very laid-back place. Ekoda is a nice little area with its own atmosphere. It is also home to the Salt Peanuts club.

Knuttel House

Knuttel House

なってるハウス

Can't get freer than here

4-1-8 Matsugaya, Taito-ku Tokyo

(03)3847-2113

〒111-0036 東京都台東区松が谷4-1-8 1F

Iriya Station (Tokyo Metro Hibiya Line), Asakusa Station (Tsukuba express, Tobu Isesaki Line, Toei Asakusa Line, Tokyo Metro Ginza Line, Tobu Skytree Line, Tobu Nikko Line, Tobu Kinugawa Line), Uguisudani Station (JR Yamanote Line, Keihin Tohoku Line), Taharacho Station (Tokyo Metro Ginza Line)

The cover charge is 2,500 yen to 2,800 yen. Live shows start at 19:30, and on most (but not all) Saturdays and Sundays, afternoon shows start at 14:00.

http://www.knuttelhouse.com/

https://www.facebook.com/profile.php?id=100072032922858

https://www.instagram.com/knuttelhouse1/

https://x.com/Knuttelhouse1

Knuttel House is the leading club in Japan for free jazz. Though free jazz, free improv, and experimental music of all kinds can be heard in many different venues, Knuttel House offers it every night. Progressive free jazz, improvisation workshops, a biwa trumpet duo, electronica, or a butoh dancer and sax improv, the musicians get together there to let loose.

    And by loose, it's very loose, inventive, unpredictable, and wild. Whatever the combination of performers (even confining it to "musicians" feels restrictive), the club's atmosphere and reputation push everyone into a freer approach to music that is always inspiring, even if you're not a free jazz fan.

    While the club is dedicated to improvisation and free jazz, many groups who play here are less concerned with pushing the edges or fitting into a wild genre. They take boundary-breaking seriously and the sense of searching for a unique brand of music. It's not that they ignore the audience. It's more that they want to create music free from any limitations, based on their musical vision. In that sense, this club is devoted to artistic freedom.

    Drinks are basic fare, but there's no food here. The club's located in *shitamachi*, the old part of Tokyo, and there are plenty of traditional eateries nearby. Recently, a few Western-style restaurants have sprung up too.

Corporate-International

Introduction

The clubs in this section have nothing particularly Japanese about them. You can reserve, order, and pay in English. Their websites are translated perfectly into English. If you were blindfolded and dropped into one of them, you wouldn't know what country you were in.

That sounds critical, but because of their large scale and corporate stature, they bring in world-class music and present it in near-perfect conditions. You can see most of their monthly lineup at any other similar club in any city around the world. And yet, it still feels Japanese. These are important places that showcase jazz in elegant settings.

Also, these places regularly feature Japanese groups in and around the international stars. When the line-up doesn't have a big-name American or European artist, local groups fill the bill. It's a great place to see those musicians, and in fact, any musicians. But you definitely pay for the privilege.

If you're looking for a Japanese experience, you won't find it here, though service is impeccable in the way the Japanese do so well. If you're looking for great music and don't mind paying for it, these clubs have tremendous offerings every night of the year. The seats are comfortable, the drinks exceptional, and the food deserves all the stars it receives.

JZ Brat

ジェイジーブラット

Swank service and great sound

Celurian Tower Tokyu Hotel 2F, 26-1 Sakuragaokacho, Shibuya-ku, Tokyo

(03)5728-0168

〒150-0031 東京都渋谷区桜丘町26-1 セルリアンタワー東急ホテル2階

Shibuya Station (JR Yamanote Line, Saikyo Line, Shonan Shinjuku Line, Tokyu Toyoko Line, Tokyu Denentoshi Line, Keio Inokashira Line, Tokyo Metro Ginza Line, Tokyo Metro Fukutoshin Line, Tokyo Metro Hanzomon Line)

From the Tokyu Plaza west exit of Shibuya station, head south towards the overhead highway, route 246. Walk uphill along the highway (away from Aoyama towards Sangenjaya) about 100 meters. On the left, you will see the multi-story Tokyu Hotel in a skyscraper called the "Cerulean Tower." On the second floor, wander around to the "back" following the guide map of the hotel complex.

Cover charge ranges from 5,000 to 9,900 yen. Usually, there are two sets from 19:00 or 19:30, but sometimes each set is charged separately.

www.jzbrat.com

https://www.jazzinjapan.com/clubs-and-venues/jzbrat

Everything except the name JZ Brat speaks of elegance at this Shibuya club with nightly music. From the elegantly dressed, attractive staff in constant microphone contact to the under-floor lighting and retro-60s designs, JZ Brat tries hard. And almost always, they succeed. The club does not jam you in cheek and jowl, and the service is excellent, if a bit hotel-like. However, it should be noted that hotels have long served as venues for some of the most essential jazz clubs.

    Fortunately, JZ Brat offers an excellent selection of players. The atmosphere is international, with many hotel guests stopping in. They feature groups from abroad, but most musicians are local to Tokyo. They up their game a bit, it might be said, when playing to a swank venue like this one.

    Whoever chooses the bands knows his/her stuff. The musicians span a variety of genres and styles, (there are plenty of non-jazz nights on the calendar), but are consistently top-notch and well-established in Tokyo's jazz scene, or abroad. The sound system is excellent, making the club one of the best places to hear a singer's voice. Other nights, JZB (sounds better than Brat) offers quality bebop, modern, and hard-swinging jazz, as well as the occasional pop-oriented rhythm and blues act. Musicians like to play here. You can see it in their top-notch performances.

Once a month or so, jazz groups from abroad play. On those nights, the cover charge increases, which is understandable, and the club also reverts to the "Blue Note" system of getting one set only. Even if you pay for the second set, the songs are often the same as the first. Ask ahead, or check it out during the break to be sure of that night's system.

The sound system is solid and clear, with large blue cushioning pads along the back wall to boost the interior acoustics. The mixing board is always right. Be careful not to get stuck behind the couple of huge central pillars. Get there early for the best seats.

The food is exceptionally good, with a range of neo-European dishes and daily specials. The drinks too, are top-notch. Once inside, though, it is easy to sink into the fancy atmosphere, and the surroundings don't matter once the music starts to carry you away.

Blue Note Tokyo

ブルーノート東京

A large concert hall that's run like a club

6-3-16 Minami Aoyama, Minato-ku

(03)5485-0088

〒107-0062 東京都港区南青山 6-3-16

Omotesando station (Tokyo Metro Chiyoda Line, Ginza Line, Hanzomon Line)

From Omotesando station, exit B3, turn left down Aoyama Dori toward Shibuya. At the large T intersection, turn left. Walk down Kotto Dori Street until you can look left at another. Turn left and look for a large banner 100 meters down on the right.

The cover charge is 6,000 to 25,000 yen for one set, depending on the day and group. There are separate sets at 18:00 and 20:30. The times differ on holidays and Sundays, so check closely.

www.bluenote.co.jp

https://www.jazzinjapan.com/clubs-and-venues/bluenotetokyo

https://www.facebook.com/BLUE.NOTE.TOKYO.official/

https://x.com/BlueNoteTokyo

The Blue Note Corporation is one of the world's largest companies dealing with jazz. Initially, a recording label, Blue Note Records, is still thriving. Their name is synonymous with the classic jazz recordings of the hard bop and post bop masters in the '50s and '60s. Those records, many remastered with added tracks, still stand the test of time and sound fresh even now. Even their record covers have become exemplars of a particular visual style.

With all that history, the clubs of the same name started only in the early 1980s in New York. From there, they spread to China, Brazil, Italy, and more, along with many unaffiliated clubs using the name in slightly altered forms. The Tokyo club continues that high level of international excellence.

And yet, the club always feels like an MBA designed it. That means efficiency and sound business strategies, but music does not always fit those confines as easily as one might hope. As with many large-ish corporations, there are plenty of quibbles. Ticket prices are too high and sets too short. Food and drinks are worthy of review on their own, but pricey. There is a seat-you-and-see-you-out pushiness to everything from ordering (on mini-computers) to paying the bill (with neat little plastic tags). You have to wait in the lovely wood décor of the lobby perusing info on upcoming gigs before you're let in. It rankles a bit to see great music packaged as a consumer product, but then again, it's packaged so well!

But that's the deal at Blue Note, and if the slickness can be set aside, the incredible artists they bring in remain amazing. In Tokyo, only Blue Note can afford to bring in jazz giants and current masters to an expensive city like Tokyo without trying to sell out a large hall or stadium. The quality of music is never in doubt. Whatever night you go, you can rest assured that the music will be top class in its genre.

The entrance fee, typically 8,000 to 10,000 yen, gets you one set, often just 80 minutes long, about the length of a CD. The Blue Note feels like a concert hall dressed up as a club, and that's just fine for most people. It's not a weekly outing, but a special occasion.

You can eat, drink, relax, receive excellent bilingual service, and, most of all, hear superb, top-class music. The sound system is excellent, and you can see well from any seat. The second sets are better after the musicians are warmed up, and going on the second or third day in their run lets them overcome the inevitable jet lag. Like many things in life, it's priced just higher than you'd like, but go anyway.

Cotton Club
コットンクラブ

Top-end food, service, and music near Tokyo Station

Tokia 2F, Tokyo Bldg., 2-7-3 Marunouchi, Chiyoda-ku, Tokyo

(03)3215-1555

〒100-6402 東京都千代田区丸の内2-7-3 東京ビルTOKIA 2F

Tokyo Station (JR Yamanote Line, Chuo Line, Joban line, Keihin Tohoku Line, Keiyo Line, Takasaki Line, Tokaido Line, Utsunomiya Line, Yokosuka Line, many Shinkansen lines, Narita Express, and more lines)

From the main Tokyo Station, take the Marunouchi South Exit. That will deliver you to a big open area with taxis. Walk south (left if you come out directly) towards Yurakacho station, following the tracks. Go past the Tokyo Central Post Office, and the next building is the Tokia Building. It's easy to see with a big-windowed restaurant on the first floor and well-lit signs. Take the escalator up to the second floor and follow the signs. From Tokyo Station, it is just a couple minutes' walk. Instructions and maps on the website in English are clear too.

The cover charge is 6,500 yen to 10,000 yen for one set. Occasionally, it jumps to 22,000 yen for special events. There are two sets, from 18:00 to 20:30. Saturday and Sunday sets start earlier, at 16:30 and 19:30.

http://www.cottonclubjapan.co.jp/

https://www.jazzinjapan.com/clubs-and-venues/cottonclub

https://www.facebook.com/cottonclubjapan/

https://x.com/cottonclubjapan

https://www.instagram.com/cottonclubjapan/

https://www.youtube.com/user/CottonClubJapanTV

The Cotton Club is fancy, sleek, chic, posh, and overall, an impressive place. It's so lovely they have filmed scenes for films and TV dramas there. Like with the Cotton Club's close relative, Blue Note, a show-event-spectacle experience is more the norm here than a hot jazz jam session. Enjoying the food, drink, and atmosphere, together with music, is a large part of the appeal. The sophisticated atmosphere, gourmet food, and attentive service are top-notch.

Of course, someone has to pay for all of that, which means the entrance fee is never cheap. Yet, when you are going out without worrying about money, it's a good place to go. It's just money, after all, right? (Right?)

Usually, groups play several days in a row, making it much easier to find a night to go. Rarely, though, do the groups (or "acts") play other dates in the Tokyo area. They tend to play the club as an exclusive engagement. That means it's hard to catch them at a cheaper venue afterward. All the music is professional and impressively performed. The sound system and production values are excellent.

Musical types at the Cotton Club range widely. For serious jazz fans, the Cotton Club has plenty of consistently straight-ahead performers, along with great jazz from Europe. Other nights feature stars of soul, funk, smooth jazz, vocals, or other pop music, often from the past. Mixed in between the jazz and pop are other styles: off-beat singer-songwriters, local jazz, and sort-of-jazz groups with a solid following. That means the audience is always enthusiastic, which increases the excitement level. The club is quite large, but retains enough intimacy for bands to respond.

The Cotton Club is a pricey place, but it's value for money when everything's right. As with the Blue Note, you cannot see some of these great musicians anywhere else.

(Don't confuse this club with the smaller Cafe Cotton Club in Takadanobaba, which features jam sessions.)

Billboard

ビルボードライブ東京

Famed international-minded club in Roppongi

4F Tokyo Midtown Garden Terrace, 9-7-4 Akasaka, Minato-ku, Tokyo

(03)3405-1133

〒107-0052 東京都港区赤坂9丁目7番4号 東京ミッドタウン ガーデンテラス4F

Roppongi Station (Tokyo Metro Hibiya Line, Toei Oedo Line)

From Roppongi Station, follow the signs to Tokyo Midtown. There's an exit from one of the underground passages directly into the vast shopping, dining, and entertainment complex. Or go in from the street. Either way, follow the signs toward the Garden Terrace section. It's on the 4th floor. Getting lost in the wide shopping arcade and long escalators is easy, but you'll get there if you follow the signs.

The cover charge for one set ranges from 6,500 yen to 12,000 yen (occasionally up to 30,000 yen). Weekday sets are from 18:00 and 21:00, and on weekends, there are two sets from 16:00 to 19:00. Times can change, so check carefully. Occasionally, there's only one set.

https://www.billboard-live.com/tokyo/details

https://www.facebook.com/BillboardLiveTOKYO/

https://x.com/billboardlive_t

https://www.instagram.com/billboardlive_tokyo/

Billboard is not strictly speaking a jazz place, but it inevitably has a lot of jazz, and all of it is very good. The sister clubs in Osaka and Yokohama are similar in setup: They have a stage that's really a stage, shared tables, predictably good service, and very decent food and drinks delivered with attention to service.

Music ranges from jazz to southern rock bands, retro soul bands, '60s stars with one member remaining, Swedish jazz fusion band, singer-songwriters, and plenty of other combinations. It's a place you go when you know who the band is and want to see them. International jazz stars take up maybe a third of the line-up, but that's enough to get most jazz fans there occasionally.

With Billboard, as with the other large corporate venues, there's nothing to dislike exactly, and there's the music to like a lot. The food is very tasty and the drinks are better than at most places. Be sure to reserve early to ask for your desired seat. And don't forget your credit card.

But when everything fits together and the band is cooking, it is a place to hear fantastic music.

Yokohama

Introduction

Yokohama can rightly claim its status as jazz's original home in Japan. Kobe and Osaka might challenge that, but the port city of Yokohama was lively in the early twentieth century when jazz started arriving with American and Filipino musicians playing on ocean liners. They hopped ship and started frequenting, and often staying in Yokohama, after Japan ended its seclusion in the 1850s.

Yokohama became a foreign trading port, with a large Chinatown, an English-language newspaper, foreign-style restaurants, and one of the first railway stations. By the 1920s, jazz bands played there frequently. That atmosphere has never really changed in Yokohama, a city that is traditional and progressive in equal measure.

After World War II, American troops stationed there during the Occupation helped re-invigorate the scene. Clubs catering to service personnel featured jazz. The longest-running jazz kissaten, Chigusa, opened in 1933, is located there, as are numerous other jazz clubs, large and small, featuring live and recorded jazz.

Yokohama also holds the annual Yokohama Jazz Promenade, a weekend of jazz in mid-October that is a great chance to hear all the best musicians in Japan at one go, and quite a few who've been invited from abroad, too.

The clubs in Yokohama that hold onto the jazz tradition are excellent. The fans, too, are dedicated regulars. I selected several favorites and long-running spots and included a complete list. Yokohama is much closer to Tokyo than it once was, with more train connections than ever before. Tokyo sometimes threatens to overshadow the slightly smaller and calmer city, but Yokohama maintains its own vibe and atmosphere. History feels even closer there than in the swirl of Tokyo.

Airegin

横濱エアジン

One of the longest-running jazz clubs in Yokohama.

5-60 Sumiyoshi-cho, Naka-ku, Yokohama-shi, Kanagawa-ken

(045)641-9191

〒231-0013神奈川県横浜市中区住吉町5-60

Bashamichi Station (Minatomirai Line), or Sakuragicho Station (JR Negishi Line, Yokohama Subway Blue Line)

From Kannai Station, head towards the smell of Yokohama Bay. It's only a few short cross streets, and Yokohama is laid out fairly much in a grid. From Sakuragicho, head over the river and it's about the same distance. From Bashamichi, head away from the bay, over the large, busy street, and into the small lanes. It's in a busy area. The signs are easy to see.

The cover charge is 3,000 yen to 4,500 yen. Two sets from 19:00. Sundays and public holidays from 15:30 or 18:30. Closed Mondays and Tuesdays, and Wednesdays too (usually).

http://www.airegin.yokohama/

https://umemotomusica.jugem.jp/

https://www.facebook.com/aireginda

https://x.com/UmeMotto

Airegin is named after the song by Sonny Rollins (spelling Nigeria in reverse), and the club keeps the intensity of that song in its atmosphere and in the music it offers. It's been in business since 1969 in one of the liveliest areas of Yokohama, so clearly, they know what they're doing. As far as I can tell, the sign out front hasn't changed or been washed since it was first hung out.

    This is a no-frills place with chairs and tables that work and brick and plaster walls that keep the music up-close and loud. Drinks are sufficient, and they probably have something to nibble on, but you don't come here to dine, you go to listen. There are plenty of places to eat on the surrounding streets.

The listening here is always intense. You're seated not far from the band, and the bass might use an amp, but no one else in the band does much.

A veritable who's who of jazz has played there, certainly every well-known Japanese jazz musician, and some of the greats from America and Europe too. With all that history, playing there is hard without cranking up the energy level several notches.

The bands push the boundaries of straight-ahead jazz and usually delve into freer territory and stretched-out modes. It depends on the band, though. Temperatures run high, and creativity runs wild. It's a very cool place.

Dolphy

ドルフィー

Focused, intense space for the very best musicians

2F Daiichi Nishimura bldg., 2-17-4, Miyagawa-cho, Naka-ku, Yokohama-shi, Kanagawa-ken

(045)261-4542

〒231-0065 横浜市中区宮川町2-17-4 第一西村ビル2F

Hinode-cho Station (Keikyu Line), Sakuragicho Station (JR Negishi Line, Yokohama Subway Blue Line)

A short walk from Hinode-cho Station or Sakuragicho Station. From Sakuragicho, head away from the bay. From Hinedocho, head towards the bay. It's easy to find, and the green sign will guide you.

The cover charge is 3,800 to 5,000 yen, sometimes more for more famed acts. Two sets from 19:30 nightly. From 19:00 on Sundays and public holidays. Sundays often have afternoon sessions, too, from 13:30.

https://dolphy-jazzspot.com/

https://www.jazzinjapan.com/clubs-and-venues/dolphy

https://www.facebook.com/jazzspotdolphy/

https://www.youtube.com/@jazzspotdolphy3280

https://www.instagram.com/jazzspotdolphy/

Dolphy has been dishing out music from the best jazz musicians in Japan for forty-some years. A couple of jazz musicians joked with me once that they moved to Yokohama to play there more often. It was a joke, but also true. Dolphy has the best musicians in Japan playing there every single night. It's hard to think of a single great jazz player who has never been on stage there.

Because of that history and the expectations surrounding it, the jazz at Dolphy is always played with great care and attention. Musicians bring their best band members and best new compositions with them. Check out the links to musicians on the website. It reads like an encyclopedia of Japanese jazz musicians.

It's a small, unpretentious place that never feels overcrowded—except on some nights when customers keep flowing in, and chairs keep getting set up for them. Making a reservation is always best, but a last-minute arrival will surely get you at least a foot in the door.

The food is good and solid. It's nothing special, but it's definitely nice to nibble on small dishes at an affordable price. The drink list is extensive, so you have everything you need. Service is warm and easygoing. A jam session is reserved for the fourth Monday of every month.

Together with Airegin, Dolphy is the heart of Yokohama jazz. It's a comfortable club with great music, pure and simple, or rather, complex and exciting.

BarBarBar

バー バー バー

Relaxed venue for good food and great jazz

1F, 2F, Wakaba Unyu Bldg., 1-25, Aioi-cho, Naka-ku, Yokohama

(045)662-0493

〒231-0012　神奈川県横浜市中区相生町1-25若葉運輸ビル1F・2F

Kannai Station (Yokohama Subway Blue Line, JR Negishi Line), Nihon Odori Station (Minato Mirai Line).

The club is halfway between Kannai Station and Yokohama Stadium.

The cover charge ranges from 2,750 to 4,950 yen. Two sets from 19:00, but sometimes earlier. Be sure to tell them when you'll get there when you reserve. Closed on Sundays and Monday holidays.

https://www.barbarbar.jp/english.html

https://www.facebook.com/barbarbar.jazz

https://x.com/Bar3_mt

https://www.instagram.com/barbarbar_jazz/

BarBarBar feels like the kind of jazz place that would have been packed in the post-war years. There's a surprisingly long bar counter on the first floor and a spacious room for jazz on the second. It's packed most nights. The location is perfect, in a lively area of Yokohama, and the club is spacious compared to most.

 The vibrant atmosphere of the club comes not just from the wait staff or the musicians, who have a place to play to an audience that's into jazz, but also from the audience, who can get a delicious meal and a decent bottle of wine along with their music. It's a well-run place that matches the well-played music.

 Most of the musicians are based in the Yokohama area, and though that may not be as many as in Tokyo, it still means a lot of musicians. There are often vocals, and while a few musicians may not play their most cutting-edge style here, they play with heart and a sense of how music makes an evening special.

 Many of the best musicians in Japan stop by here to play for long-time fans, and while those nights are special, so are all the rest. It's a very relaxing and comfortable spot to kick back for a night of jazz.

Kanmachi 63

上町(かんまち) 63

Neat basement hideaway devoted to jazz

B1F Trust One Bldg., 5-95 Aioi-cho, Naka-ku, Yokohama

(045) 662-7322

〒231-0012 神奈川県横浜市中区相生町5-95 トラストワンビルB1F

Bashamichi Station (Minato Mirai Line), Sakuragicho Station (JR Negishi Line, Yokohama Subway Blue Line), Kannai Station (JR Negishi Line, Yokohama Subway Blue Line).

It's about equidistant from all three stations, so if you can mentally triangulate from the map, you'll find it on a lively street with many other restaurants and bars.

The cover charge is 3,300 yen plus one drink. (A bit more for the rare quartet). (Student discount 2,750 yen). Two sets from 19:30 and 21:00. On Saturdays and Sundays from 15:00 and 16:30. Mondays usually closed.

http://jmsu.web.fc2.com/63/

https://www.facebook.com/Kanmachi63/

https://x.com/kanmachi63live

https://www.instagram.com/kanmachi63/

Kanmachi 63 is a simple space with a bar, a handful of tables, a piano, and just enough room for a small drum set, bass, and a horn player. There's an upright piano. That's about it. But really, that's all you need. It's a teensy sliver of a club tucked into a basement room not far from Sakuragicho and Kannai Stations, but the *master* brings in some of the best musicians in the city. He's a real jazz fan. You can tell from the stacks of CDs and who he invites to play.

    A bit newer than the other long-running clubs in the area, the sleek room is neat, tidy, and easy to enjoy. The stage is one corner of the room. Drinks are simple but quite good. Get a bite to eat nearby before you go. There are plenty of dining options in the surrounding streets.

    And then, sit back and enjoy. There's no miking or mixing to fiddle with. You're close enough to hear the squeak of a bass string and the flap of a sax key.

    Groups are typically trios, which is about all that fits in the corner. But that's enough when the musicians are so close and present. It's as close to earphones as a club could get!

    The music zings through the room with a fresh, live energy. The musicians interact with the audience—they have to—because they listen so closely, physically and mentally. That gives this club a special atmosphere.

Other Yokohama clubs

Far Out

ファーラウト

TS bldg. 2C 2nd floor, 51-2, Nishidori, Fukudomi-cho, Naka-ku, Yokohama-shi, Kanagawa-ken

(045)261-5635

神奈川県横浜市中区福富町西通51-2 TSビル2F

Kannai Station (Yokohama Subway Blue Line, JR Negishi Line), Hinodecho Station (Keikyu Main Line)

Charge is 2,000yen to 3,000yen. Mostly jam sessions. Usually the show starts from 19:00.

https://www.facebook.com/jazz.farout/

A lovely space with windows, a rarity in the jazz world. Jazz almost every night, with jam sessions on Saturdays and Sundays. Lessons all through the week. It's a busy place.

Minton House

ミントンハウス

1F, Hamada Bldg., 276 Yamashita-cho, Nakaku, Yokohama-shi, Kanagawa-ken

(03)5370-4050

神奈川県横浜市中区山下町276 浜田ビル1F

Ishikawacho Station (Minato Mirai Line)

https://bar-navi.suntory.co.jp/shop/0456622586/

More of jazz kissaten than a place with regular live shows, it's still one of the coolest spots around. If you don't salivate seeing the rows and rows of vinyl records, you will after you start listening to them.

Speak Low

スピークロウ

2F, 2-11, Tokiwa-cho, Naka-ku, Yokohama-shi, Kanagawa-ken

(045)263-6777

〒231-0014 神奈川県横浜市中区常盤町2-11 常盤行ビル 2F

Kannai Station (Blue Line, Negishi Line)

Charge is 5,000 yen for men and 4,000 yen for women. The show is from 19:30. Closed on Sunday and Public Holiday.

https://speaklow.shopinfo.jp/

Dedicated to vocalists, usually with piano or guitar accompaniment. It's a lovely little spot that has found its niche.

Yokohama Jazz First

Hinodecho Station, Keikyu Main Line, three-minute walk

京急日ノ出町駅下車徒歩3分、神奈川銀行本店前

Dai-ni Yoshida Building 1F, Chojamachi 9-140 Yokohama-shi, Kanagawa-ken

〒231-0033　横浜市中区長者町9-140 第二吉田ビル 1F

The cover charge ranges from 2,000 to 3,500 yen plus two-drink minimum.

Evening after 18:00. 045-251-2943

Daytime from 19:00. 045-252-8414

https://jazz-first.com/

https://www.instagram.com/yokohama.jazz.first

https://www.instagram.com/yokohama.jazz.first

This long-running club has recently started getting more popular with fans and musicians alike. With live jazz almost every night, the manager has started to pull in top-tier musicians. It's a real jazz lover's spot.

Eclectic and blues

Intro to eclectic and blues

Many clubs in Tokyo cater to a range of musical types. I've included them in the guidebook to jazz because they often have jazz, and when they don't, the music is still improvised. Blues jams, bluegrass runs, and Indian ragas all draw from the same universal musical well as jazz does. It's similar to jazz for in-the-moment spontaneity and fresh creativity, even when it's another genre altogether.

These clubs also have a similar atmosphere as all the jazz clubs, whatever music is on. Jazz maintains a certain social appeal and a cachet that not all clubs want to maintain seven days a week. Having a laid-back atmosphere and music that appeals to diverse customers is also important for many places, both practically and aesthetically.

These clubs regularly feature jazz, but because they also offer other musical genres, you may not get jazz every night, or at all, strictly speaking. So, be flexible if you go and check ahead. I'm sure that even the most die-hard jazz lovers listen to other music from time to time.

What you can be sure of is engaging, intriguing music and a great atmosphere. Many of them change their line-up and style nightly, so when you head there without planning, you're often in for a surprise, but a delightful one.

Otoya Kintoki Live House

音や金時

Earthy vibe with acoustic world music

Kishi Coop B1, 2-2-14 Nishi-Ogi-Kita, Suginami-ku, Tokyo.

(03)5382-2020

〒167-0042東京都杉並区西荻北2-2-14 喜志コーポB1

Nishi-Ogikubo Station (Chuo Line, Sobu Line, Tokyo Metro Tozai Line)

Nishi-Ogikubo Station (Chuo Line). From the north exit, look to the right at the crossing and turn right there. Follow the side street (running parallel to the tracks). You veer to the left and back to the right at a 7-11 convenience store. The live house is about 100 meters from there on the right-hand side, down one floor. There's only a tiny sign, but the total time from the station is just a few minutes, depending on how busy the big street is.

2,300 to 3,500 yen. Two sets from 19:00, usually.

http://www2.u-netsurf.ne.jp/~otokin/

https://www.jazzinjapan.com/clubs-and-venues/otoyakintoki

This lovely club is like stepping back into the 1960s: curry, Asian beer, warm wood tables, Indian cotton cloths hanging on the walls, incense, and an artsy handwritten schedule. It's delightfully retro.

However, the soundstage is up-to-date, with a clarity that lets you hear the instruments, even fingers moving along strings. And strings of all sorts: Spanish guitar, oud, Celtic harp, sitar, or any of hundreds of other ethnic instruments.

The place is a musical world tour, drawing from a diverse range of traditions—jazz, of course, but also Celtic, tango, Persian, Indian, Chinese, bluegrass, and seemingly all combinations thereof! On any two nights in a row, music might come from opposite sides of the globe.

The care and attention to a perfect evening of music and all-around general comfort is very welcome. It's the kind of place where you feel comfortable chatting with the people sharing your table, a bit like spots where travelers eat while backpacking through Asia. It's a community center of sorts—a broad and broad-minded community.

The live schedule is written by hand in Japanese and changes every month. If it's hard for some to decipher, stick with it. Eclecticism requires effort. The same goes for the menu! It's worth puzzling it out.

If you want to hear something a little different from the average live house and listen to it in an intimate, laid-back setting, there is no better place than Otoya Kintoki.

Blues Alley Japan

Blues Alley Japan

ブルース・アレイ・ジャパン

Blues, jazz, and pops in a dinner club setting

Meguro Holic Hotel B1F, 1-3-14 Meguro, Meguro-ku

(03)5496-4381

〒153-0063 東京都目黒区目黒1-3-14目黒ホリックホテルB1F

Meguro Station (JR Yamanote Line, Tokyo Metro Nanboku Line, Toei Mita Line, Tokyu Meguro Line)

It's a few minutes walk downhill from Meguro Station on the Yamanote line. From the west exit of Meguro station, two parallel streets head downhill away from the station. Take the right-hand street (Meguro Dori) and go downhill. The club is about 200 meters down on the right-hand side. Look to the right carefully, or you can walk right past it. If you get to where the two streets join back together, you've gone too far.

The cover charge ranges from 4,000 to 8,000 yen, and sometimes more for name acts. Two sets from 19:00, but times can vary highly.

www.bluesalley.co.jp

https://www.jazzinjapan.com/clubs-and-venues/bluesalley

www.bluesalley.co.jphttps://www.facebook.com/profile.php?id=100060216738252

https://x.com/BLUESALLEY_jp

https://www.instagram.com/bluesalleyjapan/

Blues Alley Japan has a swankiness that relaxes. Out of the way of the big entertainment areas of Tokyo, the club has a snug, unimposing calm. Large, wooden tables fill the large (by Tokyo standards) space. Tables are not packed in too tightly, so you never feel cramped. The space is small enough to maintain real intimacy and atmosphere. You can see and hear from any seat.

 Service is impeccable, but never imposing. They'll hang your coat up for you, and you don't have to beg for a glass of water. None of this comes with fake politeness. Instead, the club has a natural feel for comfort.

Food and drinks are reasonably priced and appetizing. Very decent plates of pasta and French-cum-Californian dishes are served up in solid, satisfying portions. Wine too, is a nice change from the canned beer, bitter coffee, and bottled whiskey of most jazz joints. The sound system here is always set right, even though two central pillars and oddly angled walls threaten to disrupt it. The sound is loud for some shows, but the mix is always right.

Performers here are drawn from a spectrum of blues, jazz, and other genres. The choice of acts is from the upper tier of Tokyo performers. Even if you do not like the style on one particular night, the music is one of the most accomplished in that style. It's a stop on many CD release tours, so the playing quality gets an extra kick.

Keep an eye out for foreign blues musicians featured once every couple of months. Those nights are always special at Blues Alley, as the place is packed with enthusiastic blues fans. Blues has a loyal contingent of fans in Tokyo who know how to get cranked up for the real players, and on those nights, Blues Alley shows its character.

On non-blues nights, the performers range through an intriguing variety. Jazz musicians here are always ones with a well-established group, usually with recent CDs, and always ready to respond to the club's good vibes with more of their own. Other groups ranging from contemporary big band to Latin to soulful pop have their followings, and on those nights, the club can be standing-room only.

Be sure to make reservations in advance and try to arrive on time to get a good seat.

Blues Alley is a very easy place to like.

Rooster

荻窪ルースター

High-energy blues and jazz in a plain, pure blues-loving space

Kyoritsu Dai 51 Bldg. B1, 1-24-21, Kamiogi, Suginami-ku, Tokyo

(03)5347-7369

〒167-0043　東京都杉並区上荻 1-24-21 協立第51ビル B1

Ogikubo Station (JR Chuo Line, Sobu Line, Tokyo Metro Marunouchi Line)

The club is a short walk from the north side of Ogikubo station. Head out the north exit and go left down the large street parallel to the train line. You'll pass seven or eight streets to the left, but the sign is visible from the sidewalk.

The cover charge ranges from 2,500 to 5,000 yen. Two sets from 19:30. Sometimes daytime shows are held on the weekend, but please check the schedule as starting times vary. Some nights are given to university jazz circles or rental parties, so check ahead.

http://www.ogikubo-rooster.com/

https://www.jazzinjapan.com/clubs-and-venues/rooster

https://www.facebook.com/ogikubo.rooster

https://x.com/ogikuborooster

https://www.instagram.com/hiroosatoh/

The rooster is a character in many blues songs, full of sly implications and double meanings, a kind of trickster figure that always delivers delight. That's the right name for the proud, potent, cock-a-doodle-do music that Rooster features. Strictly speaking, Rooster is a blues club, but they have jazz, Latin, and Brazilian between nights of blistering electric blues. All the music, not just the blues, is played loud and low down.

If you want a down-home feel for a live blues joint, you get it at Rooster. They moved from their old spot on the south side of Ogikubo to this new space, which is bigger and better. The sound system is excellent, with the master at the control panel, so you can hear every note and feel every vibration.

Other than that, seats and food are all that you need. Drinks are solid and straight, with no fancy-name cocktails. Food will fill you up. It's a place to listen to music, not splash out on food and drinks.

Rooster has a great atmosphere devoted to music. The crowd is mixed: young people on dates, neighborhood regulars, blues societies, band fans, and people out to shake loose from the uptight hassles of living in the megalopolis. During the break, the master keeps things lively with jokes and magic.

Most performers are rooted in blues tradition and not only have perfected the riffs and rhythms of other eras and other climes, but serve it up by the gutbucket-ful. On some nights, the musicians let loose. Being at Rooster gives them permission. And on other nights, you get to hear music made with just as much respect.

The club is intimate, as if everyone knows everyone else just by being there. It's the kind of place where you chat with strangers, ask them if they liked it, and know the answer you'll get. If Rooster didn't exist, someone would have to open it.

Moon Stomp
ムーンストンプ

Koenji hangout with jazz and other music

B103 Canyon Plaza Osuga, 2-22-6, Koenji-kita, Suginami-ku, Tokyo

(03)3310-6996

〒166-0002 杉並区高円寺北2-22-6キャニオンプラザ大須賀 B103

Koenji Station (JR Chuo Line, Sobu Line)

It's a three-minute walk from the North Exit of Koenji Station on the JR Chuo Line. Walk straight up the larger street running north away from the station dropoff area. When you reach a 'T' in the street, the building is straight ahead and down the stairs.

The cover charge ranges from 2,000 to 4,500 yen, primarily based on how big the band is. There are two sets from around 19:00. Music almost nightly, but Mondays and Tuesdays are often closed.

http://bighitcompany.com/moonstomp/

https://www.jazzinjapan.com/clubs-and-venues/moonstomp

Moon Stomp is a great little club in the hip hustle of Koenji. They offer a range of music, from blues to jazz, bluegrass, gypsy swing, world music, Latin, country, folk and more. The place has a relaxed vibe that fits with the rest of Koenji. Whenever I go there, it feels like a college party.

Even compared to the other great eateries in the area, their food is satisfying and their simple dishes well-prepared. Good drinks are always ready and delivered right away.

This would almost feel like a neighborhood place, but the impressive music lineup makes it feel like a big-city venue without the big-city prices. It's a small place, but hearing and seeing the music up close is great. There's no pretence or pressure here—it's just a place to get into the music.

There's music every night except Mondays, some Tuesdays, and whenever the staff needs a night off. A glance at the schedule, though, teases anyone's musical likes. Dixieland jazz one night, Professor Longhair cover the following, folk after that, each genre falling over the others in delightful succession.

Koenji has now been proclaimed one of Tokyo's hippest areas, and Moon Stomp is the perfect example of why.

Bright Brown

ブライトブラウン

Blues you can use in a stripped-down, easy-going space

2F Yuzawa Daini Bldg., 5-59-9, Nakano, Nakano-ku, Tokyo

(080) 3024-4685

〒164-0001 東京都中野区中野5-59-9 湯澤第二ビル2F

Nakano Station (JR Chuo Line, Sobu Line, Tokyo Metro Tozai Line)

Head out the north exit and look for a sign that says "Nakano Broadway" or "Nakano Sun Mall." That's a covered street lined by shops. Head down that street past three "bigger" streets to the right. On the third, turn right, and the club is just a few steps on the left-hand side.

The cover charge runs from 1,500 yen to 3,500 yen. Two sets from 19:00, 19:30, or 20:00. Check the schedule carefully. Blues jam sessions are held every Thursday. Sundays usually have no music, and Mondays are always closed.

https://brightbrownnakano.wixsite.com/brightbrown

https://www.facebook.com/blues.BrightBrown

https://x.com/NakanoBB

https://www.instagram.com/nakano.brightbrown/

Long a blues mainstay in Tokyo, Bright Brown is an unassuming spot that jumps you right into the music. The stage is the floor space next to the wall, but it comes alive once the music starts. Being there is like hanging with musicians and music-loving friends.

And like hanging out at a diner in the States. Food is homey and filling, with pizza, pasta, gumbo, and hot dogs served up quick and hot. Not many places serve chili-cheese dogs in Tokyo. Few would dare. But having those, along with polish sausage, nachos, chile, and fries as the main menu items, should give you an idea of the vibe there. There's other food too, though, so don't panic. All the food is tasty.

The craft beer selection is solid, and unlike most music venues, the menu includes Japanese sake, a rare treat, and a nice assertion of Japanese culture in the face of American blues, but maybe I'm reading too much into it. A good time is a good time, though.

Blues is the mainstay here, but there's also jump, jive, and jazzed-up blues. Check ahead to be sure to get the kind of blues you like to use. Whatever night you go, though, you'll get a full dose of blues power. There's no live band some nights, so selections from the blues CD and record collection take over. Nakano is also an interesting area packed with shops, restaurants, bars, and other venues.

Who to Hear —The musicians

Introduction

Musicians are undoubtedly the coolest people I deal with in Tokyo. They're spontaneous, creative, hard-working, and humble. They have stepped away from the mainstream currents of Japanese conformity to make a life in music. They live jazz.

Musicians don't always make much money, and what they do make comes in unpredictably. It's hard to say how un-Japanese that is. They practice, study, compose, and often teach. They manage bookings and travel for gigs. They fill in when colleagues can't make a gig. A few write books about jazz theory or put together instruction manuals or practice guides. They record and spend time in the studio. It's a life.

Talking with them between sets and after shows has enlightened me about how jazz works and what values and mindsets keep the music fresh and meaningful. I love it when a musician expresses frustration about teaching students. It's fascinating when musicians ask me if I think jazz is global. I like to hear what they're thinking, how they're working, what they're writing. It's been an education.

Like the clubs, the list selected for this book is not meant to be complete. Far from it. Some of these musicians I've heard play for nearly thirty years, hearing their music develop, evolve, deepen, and expand. Many younger musicians constantly arrive in the community, but sometimes fly below my radar. Others have been there for years without my notice. Others stop playing live for periods or engage in other projects. They get ill and recover. Some go abroad and return. It's hard to keep up.

As one person, I can't cover everyone. The Tokyo metropolitan area is enormous. Add on Yokohama, Saitama, and Chiba, and it's even more immense. "Way more crowded than New York," my friends from the Big Apple always tell me when they visit.

In short, if a musician is in here, they're great, but if they're not in here, they could be great, too.

Apologies to musicians who are not in this initial version of the book. The musicians here are all people I've listened to over many years and recommend confidently. This list is intended to give you a start on finding the marvelous people who have devoted their lives to making jazz, but it's not a complete directory. If I were to hear jazz seven nights a week, I still wouldn't get to all I'd like to. So be it, but this is a good start.

If you are searching for a specific musician you want to hear, follow the link beside their name. More and more musicians use Instagram, Facebook, and X (Twitter) than ever. However, they sometimes use the romanization of their names, sometimes the Japanese kanji. I've included both. You should also be aware that some musicians put a lot of effort into ensuring the info about gigs is easy to find, while other musicians don't worry much about self-promotion.

Another point is that almost all of them play in different groups. If you want to hear them as leaders, with their original compositions, arrangements, and approach, check that their name is first on the list. On club listings, the first name listed is (almost always) the leader. On their website, they will sometimes write, "Leader live."

You won't miss out if you want to hear them with another group, though. Often, the "leader" is whoever arranged the gig, and the musicians are often long-time bandmates who don't care too much who's in charge. Everyone gets a chance to solo.

These days, you can hear many of these musicians on YouTube videos too. But often, the sound is weak or the camera static. The proliferation of videos is impressive, but live music is always better than a video and even better than a CD. Still, previewing their playing before you hear them live adds a dimension. But there's nothing better than hearing jazz live.

Also, what you hear on YouTube may not be how they always play. They might play free jazz with some friends on one night, pristine post-bop on another night, or join the horn line of a Latin jazz group on another. Or debut a new direction for their music. Cross-pollination is, after all, one of the inner strengths of jazz creativity, along with openness and flexibility. That's especially true in Japan, where musicians often play with different groups.

If a musician catches your fancy, check the Jazz in Japan website www.jazzinjapan.com for reviews of their live shows and CDs. I put their names in both languages, but maintained Japanese order for the Japanese, which is family name first and given name second, and Western order for the English, meaning given name first and family name second. If that's confusing, you're right, it is.

Musicians are listed alphabetically by family name according to their primary instrument. The order has no hierarchy or other meaning. Organizing them by instrument instead of their style makes it harder to understand who they are and how they play. But as I said in the introduction, musicians consider their instruments central to their musical identity, so I'll go with that.

There are some fascinating people here. I know you're going to like them and their music. I know I do.

Drummers

Introduction

A band is only as good as its drummer. That saying is as true in Japan as it is in the rest of the jazz world. Tokyo and Yokohama, in particular, have many amazing drummers, and more come in regularly for special shows.

The best drummers are always in demand, but you can always trust the quality of a group based on how in-demand the drummer is. These drummers here are first-call drummers whose schedules are booked months in advance. This list is just scratching the surface as younger drummers keep arriving and making their mark.

Japan has a tradition of drumming, the most famous being taiko, and drums are essential to traditional festivals. But that seems a separate river of percussion from jazz drumming. The rhythms are so different. Most Japanese jazz drummers strive for the classic Blue Note sound or a free approach unmoored from traditional time changes.

Latin polyrhythm is another thread that runs through the music in Japan, but it's almost always contained in specifically labeled Latin, salsa, Caribbean, or South American music. It always strikes me that instruction in percussion is handled at a very high level in Japan. Alternatively, drummers travel to the US or Cuba to learn techniques directly from other traditions and styles.

However it's learned, the drummers propel the music. The more I listen to jazz, the more I listen to drummers first, and then the other instruments.

Drummers

Yoshihito Etoh 江藤良人

https://eto.mockhillrecords.com/

A confident, relaxed drummer with an original sense of contributing to whatever group he's in, especially the ones he leads. He's exploratory and engaging. Always stellar. His CDs are exceptionally well done.

Atsuo Fujimoto 藤本敦夫

https://najanaja.net/atsuo_top.html

Unique and creative, he's a drummer who isn't afraid of a groove or a singer in front. His music is his own, well-crafted, unusual, and highly original.

Dairiki Hara 原大力

http://www.haradairiki.com

One of the most laid-back and yet, most intense drummers. He runs his own band and powers others with intense swing, free rhythms, and incredible energy. He's always a pleasure and revelation to hear.

Tamaya Honda 本田珠也

https://tamayahonda.blogspot.com/

He comes from a musical family—his mother is a singer, and his father is a pianist—and has absorbed much of both. He plays with the best cutting-edge groups in Tokyo. Any group with him on drums will always shine with fresh, original music. Check out Zek 3, Dojo, or any group he's in.

Yoshinobu Inagaki 稲垣貴庸

https://sites.google.com/arounds-band.com/inagakiyoshinobu/

An exceptionally pristine and subtle drummer who leads his own big band, forms the engine of others, and plays with straight-up great groups. Spot on, hard-swinging, and energetic.

Tappy Iwase 岩瀬立飛

https://x.com/tappiiwase

Whether playing Latin clave or straight-ahead 1950s jazz, he's a solid and enjoyable drummer. Deeply involved in education, he's a masterful drummer. But check out his Latin jazz and salsa groups.

Gene Jackson

https://www.genejacksonmusic.com/

First-call drummer and a delight to hear. He makes complex music look easy and ups the level and energy of every group he plays with. If he's in the group, it'll be authentic jazz.

Yoichi Kobayashi 小林陽一

https://monkykoba.wixsite.com/jjmproject

The leader of the Japanese Jazz Messengers, a group in various incarnations that's run for 40 years. He's a drummer and a leader who has the Blue Note canon down with band members young and old. He also works through musician's oeuvre in dedicated shows.

Nobuyuki Komatsu 小松伸之

http://nobuyukikoma2.web.fc2.com/

Loose is good. Tight is good. He's got them both and adds some tasteful additions to every group he performs with. He's been a hard-working drummer who plays most nights.

Blacky Kuroda 黒田慎一郎

http://odd-bowz.com/kuroda.html

A confident and energetic drummer with an amazing circle of bands. Playing with foreign musicians and local friends, he finds the rhythms that fit and adds textures, feelings, and propulsive energy to every group.

Takeo Moriyama 森山威男

https://bowz.main.jp/take-0/news/index.html

A power drummer whose groups deliver high-energy jazz. He's been a top-level player on the jazz scene in Japan for more than 50 years, and more fiery with each passing year. It always seems like he's two drummers.

Kenichiro Murata 村田憲一郎

https://murakenjazz.exblog.jp/

A sleek, nimble drummer who plays with many groups around Tokyo. His style is about keeping the swing for the forward flow and keeping the energy level high. He's played and recorded with Yuji Ono, Lisa Ono, and a range of Japan's top-tier jazz musicians.

Shingo Okudaira 奥平真吾

http://pit-inn.com/okudaira/

A prodigy of sorts whose home base of the Pit Inn welcomes him regularly. His band, The New Force, is aptly named. Solid, straight jazz rarely comes out so pleasingly complex.

Masahiko Osaka 大坂昌彦

https://osaka-masahiko.com/

First-call drummer with a deep sense of jazz, both from the past and the present. Whatever group he plays with is worth hearing. He makes everyone look good while tucking in impressively nimble and original rhythms.

Hidenobu "Kalta" Otsuki 大槻カルタ英宣

http://www.kaltek-musik-engine.com/

Who says the Japanese aren't funky? No one after hearing "Kalta" drumming. Be ready to sweat—he always lays it down with a groove and kick. Always a pleasure.

Mike Reznikoff

https://x.com/mike_reznikoff

Always exciting, dynamic, and inventive. As melodic as rhythmic in his playing, he plays with smaller groups, intent on tight interplay. He works the drums like he wants them to be more than one instrument, and usually succeeds.

Akira Sotoyama 外山明

https://akirasotoyama.wixsite.com/officialwebsite

Backing some of Japan's most inventive and wild bands, his playing is less "back" than out front. When he lifts off his drum seat, expect the group to start flying. He plays some wild rhythms that always work.

Masahiro Tajika 田鹿雅裕

http://masahirotajika.web.fc2.com/

Old-school, taut, precise, and yet still exploratory. He's played with the best jazz musicians in the country and has done it with a deep sense of jazz cool.

Shinnosuke Takahashi タカハシシンノスケ

http://masaaki-imaizumi.music.coocan.jp/index.html

Straight ahead drummer who's anything but just straight ahead. He's accomplished as a classical drummer as well as a jazz drummer, and he blends both of those deeply. His virtuosic devotion to jazz is something to hear. Hear him with the New Japan Philharmonic.

Toru Takahashi 高橋徹

http://torutakahashi.com/

He's played with every big name in Japanese jazz. He adds that unique extra dimension that makes every band he's with stand out.

Kazuaki Yokoyama 横山和明

https://blog.goo.ne.jp/klookmop

Younger drummer (relatively) with a fresh, modern take on jazz and its surroundings. Very modern take on how drums work with the rest of the musicians.

Yasuhiro Yoshigaki 芳垣安洋

https://y-yoshigaki.com/

Encompassing many genres and approaches isn't easy, but making them all your own is even more challenging. He makes every live show interesting, even when he's not leading it—original and inventive music.

Pianists

Introduction

The piano can be played in as many ways as there are keys, and then some. Many, maybe most, pianists in Japan get their start as classical pianists. You can hear it in their technique—precise, tempered, controlled. But others come from a wilder tradition, from rock bands, doodling around at home, or from heavy listening to jazz recordings. Others started in university jazz circles, dragged away from classical music to the improvised delights of jazz.

Once upon a time, the standard route for jazz pianists was getting into Berklee College of Music or other American jazz schools. But nowadays, Japanese music schools employ many great teachers who teach a steady stream of students. Senzoku College of Music, the first college to teach a full range of jazz courses in Japan, along with the traditional classical music conservatories that now offer jazz courses. That has contributed to the development of a whole new generation of jazz keyboardists.

But of course, school is school and the stage is the stage. The pianists here cover a wide variety of styles and approaches. The piano trio remains a standard format that can be heard at hotel bars and cocktail restaurants, which commonly feature piano trios playing standards. That provides suitable employment for pianists working on their jazz technique.

However, free jazz is almost as common as the traditional approach. Some of Japan's pianists are pushing the boundaries of the keyboard in all directions. Some have been doing that since the 1960s. Others run big bands, composing and arranging charts.

Electric piano and synthesized keyboards also have their place in many bands, though they are rarer than acoustic piano. But electric groups with various keyboards driving their sound can be found too.

And don't forget the Hammond B3 organ players, those funky keyboardists. I like them so much that I put them in their own section.

Pianists

Toshiko Akiyoshi 穐吉敏子

One of the most important jazz musicians of the twentieth (and twenty-first) century, she started playing after World War II in American service clubs and has gone on to lead a big band in America, together for many years with husband and collaborator Lew Tabackin. She's traveled and played around the world. Her piano trio and small group recordings are as impressive as her big band works. It's appropriate that she's at the top of this list, and she doesn't need a link. She fills a Wikipedia entry and then some. A quick count of her recordings runs to 70+.

Yuki Arimasa ユキ・アリマサ

http://www.yukiarimasa.com/

A tasteful pianist with exceptional technique and jazz sense. Though he's a teacher and administrator at Senzoku Gakuen College of Music, his career of stellar recordings and moving live performances is impressive.

Toshiyuki Daitoku 大徳俊幸 https://site-1378842-9693-181.mystrikingly.com/

About half the time, when I see an interesting gig, I find he's the pianist. Whether playing in Latin groups, hardcore bop, or backing singers, he seems to do it all and do it well.

Katsunori Fukay 深井克則

https://www.facebook.com/Katsunorindo/

He doesn't only play Latin, but almost always, and when he does, the clave burns. His Latin piano trio is the real deal, and his Latin orchestra is even more real. Hearing Latin music that is vital and natural in Tokyo is always a kick, but the music would be great anywhere.

Shigeo Fukuda 福田重男

https://shigeofukuda.com/

His live shows are as much events as club dates. He plays to keep. His deep interaction with his bandmates, whether on his tunes or theirs, brings out the hidden beauty in every song. His improvisations are complex and thoughtful, heartfelt and potent.

Satoko Fujii 藤井郷子

https://satokofujii.com/jindex.html

She seems indefatigable, perhaps the most prolific recording and touring pianist of Japan's avant-garde jazz. Her approach, whether solo, duo, collective, or her famed big bands, is to create improvised music of intensity, unexpectedness, and originality. She has recorded each of these bands well, and all of her CDs are worth hearing and owning for their improvised energy.

Ichiko Hashimoto 橋本一子

https://www.najanaja.net/profile_ichiko.html

A pianist with a unique sensibility and a club jazz feel. Her voice adds unique layers and textures, somewhere between singing, scatting, and humming.

Masaaki Imaizumi 今泉正明

https://masaaki-imaizumi.music.coocan.jp/

One of my long-time favorite pianists, he has a penchant for bop groups. That fits since he has fire, speed, and an unerring sense of the right notes. Wait for him to play a blindingly fast, thoughtfully intricate Bud Powell song.

Yuichi Inoue 井上祐一

https://x.com/yuichiinoue

Straight-ahead leader who knows how to compose and play, lead and improvise. He's not afraid to play standards and make them his own, with fleet solos and rich harmonies. His compositions are gems, and he often delivers them at blistering tempos.

Akira Ishii 石井彰

http://www.akiraishii.net/

Comping, chording, or playing melody, his calm, assured approach adds textures to his recordings and live shows. He is especially impressive in smaller groups and interactions with just one or two musicians.

Fumio Itabashi 板橋文夫

https://bowz.main.jp/itabashi/index.html

To hear one of his shows is to feel loose within half a song. He has a unique vision of jazz as an open, investigative undertaking that isn't just played—it's lived. His music is raucous and rowdy, but there's a heart of pure jazz inside.

Jonathan Katz

https://www.jkatz.net/

Whether leading the Tokyo Big Band with his compositions and arrangements or in trios or duos, he brings a lot of American jazz to his adopted home of Japan. He is consistently solid as a leader and shows himself to be a startlingly good pianist in every show.

Satomi Kawakami 川上さとみ

http://satomikawakami.com/

With a delightfully musical approach, she mainly plays originals influenced by jazz standards without being stuck in the past. Her tunes are always fresh and new in her velvety hands. Check out her piano trios—gorgeous music.

Kei Akagi 赤城ケイ America

http://www.worldcom.ne.jp/~yamagen/kei/top-info.htm

A tremendously talented pianist who played with Miles Davis and other stalwarts like Art Pepper, Charlie Haden, and Al DiMeola, among many others. He's spent most of his career outside Japan, performing and recording for years and then as a teacher at the University of California

Irvine. His recent piano trio recordings impress just as much as his resume. Live, he's one of my favorites.

Yuichi Kudo 工藤雄一

https://yuichikudo.jimdofree.com/

He writes many of his tunes, often very conceptually, but delivers them with energy, vibrancy, and a keen sense of the piano. His tone is gorgeous without losing drive.

Dennis Lambert

https://www.dennislambertpianist.com/

A relative newcomer to the Tokyo scene, he's made a big splash and garnered many fans. His compositions are intriguing and pleasing, and at live shows, he has a serious approach, but also knows how to have a good time. Keeping the quality high in every group he joins or leads, he's here in Japan to play.

Hakuei Kim ハクエイ・キム

https://www.hakueikim.com/

When he solos, he never seems to need to stop and come up for air; the ideas keep flowing. He is an asset in every group, and his solos and duets open up fully. He is a great pianist with strength and verve.

Ai Kuwabara 桑原あい

http://aikuwabara.com/

She's released a series of thoughtful, focused piano trios that have gained many fans. Dividing her time between Tokyo and LA, she's recorded with Will Lee and Steve Gadd, among others. Whether on her compositions or arrangements of rock tunes or jazz standards, she has a delicacy of touch and a depth of delivery.

Akane Matsumoto 松本茜

http://www.akanejazz.com/akanejazz/

Extremely talented, she plays jazz with an accomplished sense way beyond her years. Whether in a small group or with others, she always draws the biggest applause of the evenings. Lyrical and elegant, but rumblingly rhythmic too.

Keiji Matsumoto 松本圭司

http://keijimatsumoto.com/

An up-and-coming player with his style who plays with many young-minded groups. He ranges from funky to soulful to hard bop and back again. His ease at the keyboard is why he's playing most nights of the week.

Hiroshi Minami 南博

https://airplanelabel.com/minamihiroshi/

A pianist with a distinctive voice and approach working mainly with quartets. He is also a writer, with books on jazz and improvisation. He teaches too. When he sits at the piano, it's a flow of fascinating, inventive ideas.

Jun Miyakawa 宮川純

https://www.jun-miyakawa.com/

He's already well-established as one of the younger players on the scene. He doesn't mind a driving groove and an electric sound, easily switching from acoustic to organ or electric piano. Someone to watch develop. His Hammond B3 style is especially fine.

Hiroshi Murayama 村山浩

https://www.facebook.com/hiroshi.murayama.94/

A pianist with a lush, lyrical, and expansive vision, he makes his home in France. He's also a composer incredibly talented at ballads, lyrical melodies, and full harmonies, even with his piano trio. He's not afraid to swing hard, though, and his trios do just that.

Toru Nakajima 中島徹

https://www.facebook.com/toru.nakajima.7543/

A powerful Latin player who takes the keyboard spot in every Latin ensemble in Tokyo. Having played with the best Latin groups for many years, he's earned the spot. A talented player, he does drop in on bop gigs, but his Latin groups really shine.

Hitomi Nishiyama 西山瞳

https://hitominishiyama.net/

A powerhouse of a pianist with a string of intense and evocative CDs. She's so fluent that it's hard to keep up with her keyboard moves. She has a range of groups she leads, but especially fascinating are the covers of heavy metal songs. Always a pleasure to hear.

Junko Onishi 大西順子

https://junkoonishi.jp/

One of the most accomplished Japanese pianists, she's also one of the most popular, especially with serious jazz fans. After living, playing, and recording in the US, she took a break from music for several years before returning with just as impressive an approach. Trios and quartets give her more time to express her jazz sense fully.

Yuji Ono 大野雄二

https://www.vap.co.jp/ohno/

He's had the good fortune to do the soundtracks for the animated version of the Lupin the Third manga series. That's brought him a broad following, but he's a dedicated jazz pianist with two excellent groups, the Lupintic Six (sometimes other numbers) and his trio.

Makoto Ozone 小曽根真

https://makotoozone.com/

As well known in America as in Japan, he's an outstanding player who returns to Japan regularly to perform, record, and hang with bandmates and jazz friends in Japan. When he does return, he fills up big venues. Big recording contracts aside, he plays with intensity and elegance.

Tom Pierson

https://tompierson.bandcamp.com/

He is a fascinating pianist and composer who has lived in Tokyo for many years. His expansive, eclectic, emotional, and intimate works, which include film scores (for Woody Allen, no less), big band arrangements, and piano trios, are always moving.

Masahiko Sato 佐藤允彦

https://www.mmjp.or.jp/m_satoh/

He's recorded with Eddie Gomez and Steve Gadd, to name a few. After studying at Berklee, he returned to Japan and has continued to release recordings prolifically. A pianist with a modern sensibility and incredible technique, he is also a magnificent composer of jazz music and film scores.

Takeshi Shibuya 渋谷毅

https://www.facebook.com/takeshi.shibuya.39

It's hard to know where to start. With his wild romping orchestra, his delicate arrangements of Ellington for uniquely instrumented quartet and quintet, his piano solos, or his backing of vocalists, he does play it all, and all of it well. A delight on stage every time.

Yutaka Shiina 椎名豊

https://yutakashiina.sakura.ne.jp/

With a sleek, professional approach that harkens back to the classic Blue Note sound in all the best ways. He only plays with the top-notch musicians of Japan. He's also a big promoter of jazz with students and the general public. His piano trios are especially impressive.

Kurumi Shimizu 清水くるみ

https://www.facebook.com/kurumi.shimizu.1/

A powerful pianist with an open view of what jazz can be. Take her Zek3 trio, which only plays Led Zeppelin. Who could think of that? But it's marvelous. Every group she plays with is just as fascinating and unique.

Hiroko Takada 高田ひろ子

http://www.camerata.co.jp/artist/detail.php?id=2003

An old soul with youthful fingers, she knows how to get inside a tune and make it come alive with fresh harmonies, fluid rhythms, and a deep sense of how jazz works and should sound.

Aki Takase 高瀬アキ

http://akitakase.de/

A consistently impressive pianist who resides in Berlin and plays with some of Europe's most cutting-edge, conceptual musicians. Pushing the boundaries is only part of her approach—delivering intense musical energy is the other part. She's released avant-garde, free improv, and genre-bending works since the late 1970s and shows no signs of slowing down.

Daisuke Takeuchi 竹内大輔

https://www.pftakeuchi.com/

Youthful and calm, and not afraid of mixing in an electric sound, he's part of a movement to upgrade classic jazz in one sense. Still, if you listen to Kurofune, where he plays with shamisen, it's something else altogether—something that works well.

Naoko Tanaka 田中菜緒子

https://tanakanaoko.com/

Pulling great musicians into her orbit, she always has the backup to make her compositions and hard-driving approach to jazz a strikingly polished experience. Solid, strong, and deep piano jazz.

Nobumasa Tanaka 田中信正

http://tnobumasa.com/

An intense, two-fisted player who puts energy and ingenuity into his work. He always sounds passionate and potent, making the rest of the band sound that way too.

Masayasu Tzboguchi 坪口昌恭

https://www.tzboguchi.com/

An impressive player who has recorded several CDs with a Weather Report vibe (a real one), he also plays in small ensembles with a classic jazz approach. Consistently inventive and expansive, his style shifts, but he never does. He's always in charge at the keyboard with weighty, rich ideas and an explosive cool.

Hiromi Uehara 上原ひろみ

https://www.hiromiuehara.com/

Now residing in the US, she's made it big with Blue Note contracts and recordings with Chick Corea, Stanley Clarke, and a list of top-tier jazz artists. She's released a dozen-some recordings and is as popular in the US as in Japan and, indeed, around the world. Japanese jazz fans always love artists who make it outside Japan, and she's no exception.

Tadataka Unno 海野雅威

https://www.tadatakaunno.com/

He's made his home in the US, even after a terrible attack in New York City that put him in the hospital. He's recovered and revitalized his spirit and body without losing a note in his playing. He's played with Jimmy Cobb and Roy Hargrove, among others, and continues to write new music and keep a busy performance schedule. His playing is a wonder to hear, either live or recorded.

Chihiro Yamanaka 山中千尋

https://www.chihiroyamanaka.net/

With a flair for upbeat, contemporary melodies and arrangements, she's developed many fans with support from her Universal Blue Note contract. She's appeared with renowned contemporary jazz artists and continues to record and perform. Jazz purists might shy away from the lush arrangements, but listen to her dig into a Bud Powell tune with energy and insight.

Yosuke Yamashita 山下洋輔

https://www.jamrice.co.jp/yosuke/

Perhaps the most important jazz pianist to emerge from the local scene, he's been playing modern jazz since the 1960s, in New York and Japan. He composes for big bands, small ensembles, and Japanese instruments combined with Western ones. He's also a great mentor, bringing many younger musicians onto his stages. In addition, he's a writer, with many books published. In some groups, the collective ages of his bandmates don't add up to his, but no matter, he sounds as young, or as old, as he wants to. With him, every group is a delight every time.

Hideaki Yoshioka 吉岡秀晃

http://hideakiyoshioka.com/

An old-school pianist who's not afraid of any new school playing. With a particularly funky and groovy style at times, he's a student of the jazz piano masters, and his recordings show his devotion and accomplishment. His piano trios are especially appealing live.

Hajime Yoshizawa 吉澤はじめ

https://ameblo.jp/hajime-yoshizawa/

A contemporary jazz exponent, his groups dig into complex music and send it off with a driving force. His solos are exciting and complex, a challenge to follow for their unexpected shifts, but a delight in their resolutions.

Bass Players

Introduction

In some ways, bass players are the shape-shifters of any group. They play to fit and are fit to play with almost any configuration. That doesn't mean they don't have their own style, but rather their style is flexible enough to fit with whatever kind of group they join. I often think of them as the group's anchor, holding them in place and together. But just as often, they provide the buoyancy that lifts the group and helps it sail.

For whatever reason, Japan has a wealth of bass players, and they are often in high demand. A few become leaders of their own groups, where they get to really listen to the best musicians and then invite them into their groups. Maybe bass players play with more types of groups than other musicians, but that's a good thing, escalating their versatility and sensibility.

Getting around Tokyo isn't easy to do with a light bag, so imagine hauling a giant bass onto a crowded Tokyo train, or even a Shinkansen train, and you'll have a lot more sympathy for what bass players go through. In some clubs, between sets, there's hardly any room to set the bass down on the small stages.

The bassists here play with the best groups in Tokyo, and many of them also lead their own groups. Bassist-led groups are some of the most dynamic in Tokyo. They put the bass at the center of the sound, which embraces you, hits you corporally, and sinks into your soul.

Bass players

Shigeo Aramaki 荒巻茂生

https://www.airplanelabel.com/aramaki/
Check out his Aramaki Group for an intense quartet that always delivers. The energy level rises when he's in the group, pushing the high-energy post-bop jazz into new directions. He's a force of nature.

Jeff Curry

https://x.com/theouterrim

An intense player who moves between jazz and hardcore music, he delivers the goods with versatility, verve, and a love of being on stage in the middle of the music. He can also lock into a groove that gets listeners moving.

Mitsuaki Furuno 古野光昭

https://fullnotes.net/

A virtuoso player who plays with the best jazz musicians in Japan. A solid center to any band. He has a long history of being the go-to guy for recordings and important gigs.

Daisuke Fuwa 不破大輔

https://x.com/28poi

The leader, creator, and force behind Shibusa Shirazu, one of the wildest ensembles in jazz, he also plays fascinating trios and other ensembles. Still, Shibusa Shirazu is enough to cement his claim to fame. There's nothing quite like seeing a butoh dancer creep around the side of his bass.

Alan Gleason

https://www.facebook.com/profile.php?id=100011985641959

A solid, hard-playing bassist with a command of bop and post-bop, but who also digs into the blues and gypsy jazz manouche. He leads some of the best unsung groups that play in the many clubs along the Chuo Line.

Pat Glynn

https://www.benthictones.com/

A first-call player who backs many groups in Tokyo. His tasteful playing has adorned many groups' best performances. An unapologetically straight-ahead bassist. Check out his compositions on his CD too.

Takeharu Hayakawa 早川岳晴

https://hayatake319.top/

His intensity has added fire to free jazz, rock and roll, and electric groups. He plays with great ferocity and a sense that there's always more music to come if you just keep playing, experimenting, and searching for more.

Marty Holoubek

https://www.martinholoubek.com/

A transplant from Australia, he's jumped into the cutting-edge jazz scene and formed many partnerships. His creative, sensitive approach flourishes in his groups, and jazz flourishes in them.

Nobuyoshi Ino 井野信義

https://www.facebook.com/nobuyoshi.ino.9

Soulful, tasteful, and a rock-solid core to any band, he has worked with the best musicians in Japan and continues to do so. His presence in any band is a mark of sophistication and jazz sense.

Yosuke Inoue 井上陽介

https://yosukeinouejazz.sakura.ne.jp/

Collaborating with musicians in New York and in Tokyo comes easy for him. He's done both and then some. His albums are wonderful explorations of modern jazz, with his arrangements driving the music. He's a first-call bassist for serious recordings.

Hiroyasu Ito 伊藤寛康

http://itohiroyasu.com/

A laid-back bassist who's a pleasure to hear. He usually plays Latin, Brazilian, and other "exotic" music and plays it magnificently, smoothly combining various rhythms and styles with a jazz sensibility.

Shin Kamimura 上村信

http://kamimurashinbass.g2.xrea.com/

A hard-working, straight-ahead bassist who adds another layer and dimension to the bands he plays with. He's the kind of bassist who reads the lead sheet once and is off and running. He makes you like bass lines.

Kiichiro Komobuchi コモブチキイチロウ

https://comobass.com/

He started as the bassist for Lisa Ono and her Brazilian songbook, but he still joins many Latin groups. Still, he can play Jaco style with intensity, lyricism, and melodic touches that work with every group he joins.

Masatoshi Mizuno 水野正敏

https://www.mizunomethod.com/

He is mainly an electric bass player with an upbeat approach to hard-driving modern jazz. Pleasant and always a promoter of jazz, his groups have a distinctly fusion approach that works side-by-side with the best electric guitar players in Japan.

Hiroaki Mizutani 水谷浩章

http://www.ab.cyberhome.ne.jp/~mizmzic/index.html

Prolific and active, it's no surprise his schedule is packed. He's worked in many top-notch groups over the years, with many more to come, some experimental, some electric, and some classic jazz. Give him an opening, though, and he'll keep things very open.

Yasuhito Mori 森泰人

contrabass, composer

https://morimusic.net/

A bassist and producer based in Sweden, he regularly facilitates a Japan-Sweden connection of jazz musicians, bringing Swedish jazz musicians to Tokyo and taking Japanese musicians to Sweden to perform and record.

Koichi Osamu 納浩一

https://www.osamukoichi.net/

Electric or acoustic, four-string or six-string, he lays down a solid groove that forms the foundation for whatever group he's in. His groups range along many styles. Check out EQ, CODA, and the intriguing Acoustic Weather Report.

Yasuhiko "Hachi" Sato 佐藤"ハチ"恭彦

https://www.facebook.com/yasuhiko.sato.509/

His bass playing sets fire to live shows most nights of the week, but he's also a lyrical and tasteful player with a deep sense of the music. You can tell the other musicians love playing with him.

Takashi Seo 瀬尾高志

https://seotakashi.theblog.me/

A wild and expansive player who doesn't believe in genres, styles, or limitations. He's a spot-on bassist who adds colors, touches, textures, and energy to every group he's with. After you hear him, you never hear bass quite the same again.

Akiyoshi Shimizu 清水昭好

https://akiyoshishimizubassist.weebly.com/

Part of the younger generation of jazz musicians, he plays with many up-and-coming groups. With a sleek and complex approach to bass lines, his compositions and his first CD show great promise. But don't wait, he's worth hearing now.

Takashi Sugawa 須川崇志

https://www.tsgw.net/

With a very modern, versatile sense of music, he plays with many serious groups. He's busy most days of the week, delivering his signature sound in compelling groups—modern jazz bass playing with a keen sense of the instrument's possibilities.

Tomokazu Sugimoto 杉本智和

http://bassist.s7.xrea.com/p/index.htm

An intense bassist with a taut tone and very rhythmic sense. He has played with some of the best groups in Japan, usually in small ensembles. With a full, deep tone, he's also very melodic.

Yoshio "Chin" Suzuki 鈴木良雄

https://chin-suzuki.com/

A master bassist who played with Stan Getz, Art Blakey, and others back in the day, as a regular touring bassist. He returned to Japan and has collaborated with many musicians in the jazz scene here, forming groups such as East Bounce, Bass Talk, The Blend, and Generation Gap. He plays with longtime colleagues but also brings up younger players. He is always a delight to hear play anywhere.

Getao Takahashi 高橋ゲタ夫

https://guetaito.jimdofree.com/

A natural performer who'd be great on any stage doing almost anything. He brings positive energy to every performance, so much so that it's easy to overlook his bass chops. But when he gets turned loose on a Jaco-style solo, you can hear them. He plays Latin, funk, and jazz, but Latin groups are his thing.

Mark Tourian

http://www.marktourian.com/marktourian/webpages/index-mj.html

A transplant from America, he's played with some of the top performers in Japan. He leads his sextet, MT6, and a big band, the Sun and Moon Orchestra. His compositions are featured in those groups alongside his rock-solid bass playing and overall musicianship.

Koji Yasuda 安田幸司

http://jmsu.web.fc2.com/koji/

Straight-ahead bassist with some of the most hard-driving jazz groups. He meshes with whatever song is called in every group, pushing the rhythm and adding harmonies and melodies with style.

Daiki Yasukagawa 安ヵ川大樹

https://daikiyasukagawa.com/

He always adds a fascinating element to the groups he plays with. Having played with most of them, he knows just how. He has consistently been ranked as one of the top bassists in Japan by the famed Swing Journal. You can catch him almost every night because he plays nearly every night.

Yasushi Yoneki 米木康志

https://bigband-jazz.com/cast/yoneki-yasushi/

He's played in many forward-thinking groups, and his solos are consistently jaw-dropping. You wonder where all those ideas and that intensity come from, but definitely from deep inside. In groups like Zek3, he brings pristine jazz, rock energy, and a fluid style together as one.

Trumpeters

Introduction

Though Miles Davis probably has had more influence on Japanese musicians than any other artist, the number of trumpeters in Japan often seems fewer than expected. Of course, big bands can fill out their horn section with phenomenal players, and the musicians who do play trumpet are masterful. But compared to the saxophone, there never seem to be as many as one might hope for.

Most trumpeters start in brass bands at school before moving on to big bands at university jazz circles. However, developing an individual style requires hard work, practice, and understanding, as with any instrument. Perhaps because a long line of trumpeters was so essential in jazz history, some musicians in Japan might have shied away from the instrument. I'm not sure.

But I am sure that when a trumpeter leads the band, they light up the room. The trumpet's sound is robust and commanding, echoing off the walls of small clubs with extra force. Bands led by trumpeters have energy and impact. Many are not constrained by classic jazz style but branch off into freer styles just as much as other instruments do. Most, though, play trumpet that bears the mark of the classic jazz trumpeters, even as they go their own ways.

Trumpeters

Mitsukuni Kohata 木幡光邦

https://x.com/kunizobb

With his distinctive Mohawk haircut, when you hear him, you'd think he'd blow the hair off when he plays—he's a powerful player. In big bands, the musicians in front of him lean to the side. A fixture in every good big band, he also knows what he's doing in small groups.

Tomonao Hara 原朋直

https://tomonaohara.com/

One of the most tasteful players with an astonishing technique, Hara plays in and leads small ensembles devoted to keeping contemporary jazz alive. He's serious about playing, composing, leading, and teaching. His CDs, which include his compositions, are especially good.

Hikari Ichihara 市原ひかり

https://hikariichihara.com/

If there could be a female Chet Baker, it would be her (without Chet's complications). With a calm, sonorous tone and focused manner, she sings as well as she trumpets. The rare female trumpeter in Japan, she has the tone and creative improvising to back up any praise. She also sings wonderfully, with all the nuance and control of her trumpet playing.

Issei Igarashi 五十嵐一生

https://ameblo.jp/ii1965/

The title of his 2017 release, "Ballads of a Sullen Horn Man," might hit too close. Still, he's a fascinating musician whose lush ballads glow with deep emotion and intricate nuance—intimate contemporary jazz trumpet at its best.

Takuya Kuroda 黒田卓也

https://www.takuyakuroda.com/

Consistently inventive and forward-moving, he plays trumpet surprisingly well. Still, it's his way of rearranging the jazz vocabulary, shifting the instrumentation, and generally defying expectations that make his music intriguing. He brings in studio sounds, hip-hop, whatever catches his fancy, but he always makes it work.

Eric Miyashiro エリック宮城

https://www.ericmiyashiro.com/

Born in Honolulu, educated at Berklee, and living in Tokyo, he has played with some of the best musicians worldwide, including Maynard Ferguson, Buddy Rich, and Woody Herman. He leads his own big and small bands. When he hits those high notes, it's thrilling and, as he says, stratosphERIC.

Keisuke Nakamura 中村恵介

https://blackdevil729.wixsite.com/keisuke-nakamura

I'm always impressed by his solos whenever he plays. They draw you in and give you that "how can he do that?" feeling. His releases are sophisticated modern jazz with great lead lines and old-style cool.

Keiji Matsushima 松島啓之

http://matsushimakeiji.com/

What I like about him most is that he always comes to play—and plays hard. He steps on stage and blows, and when the set is over, and you are left astonished at his nimble bebop solos and heartfelt ballads, he's back to being a kid in a baseball cap.

Shunzo Ohno 大野俊三

trumpet

https://www.shunzoohno.com/

A trumpeter who has made his home in the US for many years, he's played with Herbie Hancock, Machito, Art Blakey, Gil Evans, and other heavyweights. His fifteen-plus recordings showcase his pure tone, compositional prowess, and leadership. He also adds electric arrangements, which lets him soar even further.

Yoshiro Okazaki 岡崎好朗

http://www.yoshirojazz.sakura.ne.jp/

Long one of Japan's most highly regarded and busiest trumpeters, he studied in America, lived and played there for several years, and returned home. He is an all-around trumpeter with a keen sense of how music should and could sound. He's always so tasteful.

Shinpei Ruike 類家心平

https://ruikeshinpei.com/

With a sophisticated and expansive view of jazz, he plays outside and inside simultaneously. On record, his electric groups dig deep into electric jazz where Miles Davis left off. You can see the creative impulse at work on his face—always impressive.

Shiro Sasaki 佐々木史郎

http://schedule0522.blog33.fc2.com/

A trumpeter who loves playing and enjoys it for that very reason is rarer than one might think. He always brings pleasure into the mix, whether with his Latin-esque Caoba Big Band or his intensely funky The Boogaloo Band.

Ryuichi Takase 高瀬龍一

https://www.facebook.com/p/%E9%AB%98%E7%80%AC%E9%BE%8D%E4%B8%80-100001944470462/

He plays with the best. A trumpeter who seems to appear on every serious jazz recording made in Japan, he is always amazing to hear in person. He's respected for his tone, extended clean solos, and the seriousness he brings to the stage.

Hino Terumasa 日野皓正

https://terumasahino.com/

One of the leading trumpeters and jazz musicians in Japan. You can hear his virtuosity and experience in every note. His muscular tone sits well with electric backing, but equally well with a hard driving band. His ballads make you lean in to experience the subtlety and depth of feeling. There's not enough space to do him justice, but suffice it to say his debut album was in the late '60s, and he hasn't made anything but great ones since.

Natsuki Tamura 田村夏樹

https://natsukitamura.com/

Ingenious, avant-garde, brilliant, convention-flouting...pile up the adjectives because they all fit. His broad boundaries extend to include pure improv with his wife, Satoko Fujii, and range through the Latin (kind of) Gato Libre, duets with biwa, 5 trumpets (and all the percussive items they can grab), as well as big bands (my favorite is one where the band stops and shouts for tea!). Wildly inventive and startlingly profound.

Toku (flugelhorn)

https://www.tokujazz.com/

More flugelhorn than trumpet, and sometimes vocals, he oozes cool. With an enormous sense of jazz as a music and a culture, his recordings are consistently original. Live, he's captivating. Even setting the cool aside, he creates jazz music that's captivating and pleasing, yet challenging and cutting edge. He fits into the vocal section just as well.

Luis Valle

https://luis-valle.com/

As the pre-eminent Latin player in Tokyo, his trumpeting brings all the energy and excitement of music from his home country, Cuba. His long-running Afro-Qbamigos takes you to Havana and back. He plays in most of Tokyo's big bands, not just for his high notes. He's a substantial addition to any band, jazz, Cuban, and all points in between.

Saxophonists

Introduction

Even though this is the largest group, I've still left out a lot of saxophonists. I've concentrated on the ones that have consistently been satisfying in live performance and on recordings. There are always new sax players coming up to join various groups. I seem to always see a new one.

The allure of the sax means lots of young musicians want to be out front with the complexity of the sax in hand. If there weren't such a thing as electric guitar, sax would be upfront, out loud, and charismatic in front of every musical group.

These sax players cover a huge variety of styles and deliver the goods in ways that any listener can find several players who fit their taste. They are also often the leaders of their own groups, and most are very accomplished composers, too. More women have taken up the sax too, which is a welcome change.

Of course, the sax is always out front, but the best players know that music is all about group interaction. That's especially true in Japan, where humility is a virtue and helps create music that cherishes the ensemble more than the individual.

Sax players, though, like their soloing time, even in a big band. They often drive the improvisation after laying down the lead lines and pushing for more while trading bars with the drummer and other soloists.

Sax purists will note that I didn't divide into alto, tenor, soprano, or even baritone. Sorry about that. But many musicians play several instruments, including the flute. It's hard to divide them into styles, as sax players push for their style. For historical and technical reasons, the sax, perhaps, is the instrument that pushes exploration. If there's a common thread, it's probably that.

Typically, sax players know how to keep their melodic explorations out of the way of other musicians. They are like the chatty participant in a conversation. The best ones layer their sound onto the others and set it inside the forward flow of the music with a special artistic feeling.

Maybe that's why there are so many of them, which is, after all, a very good thing.

Saxophonists

Gustavo Anacleto

https://www.facebook.com/gustavo.anacleto/
Brazil's loss is Tokyo's gain. He keeps the Brazilian and Latin music flame burning bright, but is just as comfortable ripping into a classic 50s jazz number. He always has something interesting to say—and with huge heart and deep reserves of energy.

Andy Bevan

https://www.instagram.com/andybevanmusic/
Sax, flute, didgeridoo, and world rhythms are the core of his approach. Check out his work with Trio Lindo and Tatopani, two intriguing groups, among many others. Didgeridoo fits jazz a lot better than you'd think. A very tasteful player.

Jim Butler

http://www.interjazz.com/jimbutler/
Although he's a relative newcomer to the Japanese scene, he's made his mark quickly. His recordings are exceptionally well done, with intriguing compositions and strong performances. His groups swing hard, but his ballads are just as thoughtful and moving.

Ryosuke Hashizume 橘爪亮督

https://www.facebook.com/hashizume.ryosuke
With a fine string of recordings, he doesn't play live as much as fans might want, but when he does, usually at the Pit Inn, he can knock you

out with a full palette of originality, a deep soundscape, and a unique balance of lush melody and searching drive.

Sachi Hayasaka 早坂沙知

https://sachihayasaka.site/

She is always a pleasure to have onstage. Her playfulness and seriousness are infectious, but what stands out is her serious, longstanding approach to jazz. Her fifteen (and counting) recordings are impressive in number and quality. South American, out, or straight-ahead, she's a great performer who leads with warmth, camaraderie, and a deep sense of jazz.

Eiichi Hayashi 林栄一

https://www.eonet.ne.jp/~n-east/index.html

I can't sit too close when he's in the band. It's too intense. He rips into solos like it's the last one he'll ever play, and the result is pure energy, shaped and molded by experience and an underground sensibility—one of my favorites.

Junji Hirose 広瀬淳二

http://www.japanimprov.com/jhirose/index.html

Dedicated to free improvised jazz in its most fully in-the-moment form, his concerts are potent statements of sonic exploration. Often, with only one other musician, he can create once-in-a-lifetime aural experiences that you won't soon forget. Hardcore improv at its most improvised.

Hiroshi "JuJu" Inoue 井上"JUJU"博之

http://juju.papi4.com/index.html

The house loosens up when he steps on stage, and the fun begins. He has a loose way of playing, which in this case is good, as it helps him wiggle into the deeper parts of songs and bring out the loveliest and most interesting elements. He's one-fourth of the fascinating Saxophobia too.

Atsushi Ikeda 池田篤

https://ameblo.jp/ats-music1963/

A highly accomplished player who's made his mark with some of the top-notch groups in Japan. He combines a lightness of touch with improvisational fluency. When Makoto Ozone needs a sax player, he gets the call.

Tetsuro Kawashima 川嶋哲郎

https://tetsurokawashima.com/

Some sax players are more likable than others, and he's on the likable side and then some. Whether exploring a unique concept or jamming with old friends, his jazz sense always comes through. He is one of the most interesting sax players and wields integrity, originality, and technique.

Naruyoshi Kikuchi 菊地成孔

https://www.kikuchinaruyoshi.net/

His musical genius expresses itself in his compositions, the groups he assembles, and his sax technique. And it's not a sometime genius—he has a constant flow of fascinating ideas, performances, concepts, and explorations. His Dub Sextet is exceptionally fertile and fluid, but every group he puts together has something new to say.

Osamu Koike 小池修

https://www.facebook.com/osamukoikesax/

Whether it's a tribute to Michael Brecker, recording with strings, playing with Yosuke Yamashita, or backing singers, he has a strong sense of the music. Where he also really shines is with his EQ (Earth Quartet) quartet, a muscular, full-toned, hard-driving quartet.

Ayumi Koketsu 纐纈歩美

http://a-koketsu.com/

Women continue to find recognition, and for all the right reasons, in the jazz world in Japan. She's one of the top women saxophonists and one of the top sax players all around. With nine recordings, she's just getting started.

Kazuhiko Kondo 近藤和彦

http://www.kazuhikokondo.com/

He's one of the busiest and most well-established players. He joins a wide variety of groups, shining especially with Junko Moriya. But he's playing more with his groups these days and puts together great groups. A sax player of the old school, with full-bodied tone and well-crafted solos.

Raymond McMorrin

https://www.facebook.com/raymond.mcmorrin/

A tasteful, thoughtful sax player who steals the show with extended solos that you want to keep going. However, Connecticut's loss is Tokyo's gain, and he has a tasteful style that appeals.

Toshio Miki 三木俊雄

http://www.mikitoshio.com/

If he were only known for his Front Page Orchestra, a full-toned, satisfying mid-size band with lovely charts, that would be enough, but he's also a composer and adds his sax to numerous groups. He has an enthusiasm for the music and the technique to back that up.

Kosuke Mine 峰厚介

http://www.worldcom.ne.jp/~yamagen/mine/top-info.htm

Old-school in all the best ways, he's been an integral part of the jazz scene in Japan since 1970. He's picked up every jazz style since then and mastered them all. He plays with all kinds of jazz groups, but always sounds like himself. A gem of the jazz world, he's respected by all other jazz musicians.

Seiichi Nakamura 中村誠一

https://seiichijazz.com/

Energy and passion count a lot, but they count even more when combined with exceptional technique. His full-on tone surrounds the melody, lifts it, and carries it in interesting, unexpected directions. Check out his quartets (which have various amusing names).

David Negrete

https://truenoteinc.wixsite.com/davidnegrete

He is a relatively recent transplant from California who's more than made his mark in Tokyo. He's taken the place by storm. He's a regular on recent CDs, including his own, and live, he summons up a full range of fascinating textures, tones, and takes.

Makoto Oka 岡淳

https://www.oka.net/profile.html

A sax player who covers the flute with equal skill and taste. He helps power the front line of many mid-size groups and always adds great soloing and melodic sense. One of the founding members of Saxophobia, a sax quartet with a wild approach.

http://saxophobia.papi4.com/

Masanori Okazaki 岡崎正典

https://masanoriokazakisax.jimdofree.com/profile-1/

Pristine tone and well-constructed solos count for a lot. When top jazz leaders need just that right tone on their recordings, he gets the call for groups like No Name Horses, the Junko Moriya Orchestra, or the Blue Note All Stars. A regular fixture on the Japanese jazz scene and always great on stage.

Ken Ota 太田剣

http://www.kenota.net/

He's carved out his path by leading interesting groups and recording fascinating CDs. His recordings always have a neat focus, whether it's groove meets swing, heartfelt and upbeat songs, or funky organ trios. He's always a pleasure to hear, and always new.

Hideo Oyama　大山日出男

https://www.oyamahideo.com/

Possibly the purest tone and cleanest lines of any saxophonist in the city. He starts out impressing with technique but ends up blowing you away with solo after solo by the end of the second set. He's an exponent of pure jazz, if there is such a thing, but at least note by note, it exists in his hands.

Steve Sacks

https://www.stevesacks.com/english/

Playing sax and flute with equal skill, he has made a career in Brazilian and Latin music, having played with some of the best, including Paul Simon, Tito Puente, Astrud Gilberto, and David Byrne, among others. His Brazilian Minaswing and the current Mambo Inn have carried the torch of South American rhythms. Oh, and don't forget his jazz!

Akira Sakata 坂田明

http://www.akira-sakata.com/

I always brace myself when he's on stage. Since the late 1960s he's held the banner of intense free jazz of the very best kind. There's no cutting-edge player he hasn't worked with, not just in Japan, but worldwide. Powerful stuff—he's a force of nature and not slowing down a bit.

Tatsuya Sato 佐藤達哉

https://tatsuyasato.com/

Whenever he's on stage, I know the evening will be a satisfying one of fully played, fully felt jazz. Ballads, bop, contemporary, and occasionally out music all seem easy in his hands.

Hisatsugu Suzuki 鈴木央紹

http://www.hisax.net/

He is a very pleasing, yet wholly original sax player. His voice and approach to contemporary jazz are unique. His recordings are both meditative and dynamic. He can play in any group, but it's most fascinating when he roams freely in fluid solos.

Seiji Tada 多田誠司

https://www.tadasei.net/

With a distinctive voice and a long series of excellent recordings, he's always a pleasure to hear live. He has a real sense of the possibilities of small groups and uses them all. He's popular with fans for all the right reasons, and with titans like Yosuke Yamashita and Terumasa Hino, who include him in their groups. He has a long series of impressive CDs.

Tomoki Takahashi 高橋知己

https://www7a.biglobe.ne.jp/~tomokey/

With an uncompromising and raw approach to sax, he knows how to blow freely, but also when to focus his tone on squeezing the notes into the right shape. He has a visceral, almost visual, power to put notes into interesting patterns. He debuted in 1972, and his playing piles on those years of experience into an impressively unique style. He's one of my longtime favorites.

Nao Takeuchi 竹内直

https://takeuchinao.com/index.html

He plays a full-bore tone and moves from one configuration to the next with equal attention and delivery. When he plays solo, you feel like there's a whole band behind him. Innovative and intense at times, he can send a ballad that'll make you cry. Everyone has their favorites, and he's one of mine. He is also fascinated with jazz's ideas and theories that add to his playing.

Erena Terakubo 寺久保エレナ

https://www.jamrice.co.jp/erena/

While her career is mainly in New York, her roots are still in Japan. She's recorded with some legendary musicians. Not everyone can call in Kenny Barron and Jimmy Cobb for a session. Fortunately, she returns to Japan regularly and plays at her world-class level every time.

Kenta Tsugami 津上研太

https://kentatsugami.amebaownd.com/

He's part of some of the most interesting groups, ones who switch around instrumentation, reconfigure chords, and play with a fresh, new approach. Check him out with Saxophobia. His recordings are fascinating works of unique combinations of harmonies, melodies, and instrumentation.

Kazutoki Umezu 梅津和時

https://www.amagaeru.com/u-shi/ume/

Unceasingly original and full of mindboggling new ideas, he's a sax player whose technique matches his conceptual vision. Whether he's with his electric Kiki Band, Komatcha Klezmer, or combos like *enka* on woodwinds, it's simply amazing to hear. He always comes up with fascinating, sui generis music that sounds like no one else—a personal favorite of many people, not just me.

Sadao Watanabe 渡辺貞夫

https://www.sadao.com/en/

It would take a book to cover his entire life and career, maybe several books. He started playing clubs right after World War II and has never slowed down. He was one of the first Japanese jazz musicians to go to America and bring back the secret of jazz to his homeland. Playing with Toshiko Akiyoshi, among others, he released his first recording in 1954. Moving between hard bop and more listenable recordings, he's been a driving force in Japanese jazz since regularly filling large venues around the country.

Andy Wulf

http://www.andywulf.com/profile.html

A Canadian saxophonist who's made his home in Tokyo, he's a busy man with duets, small groups, studio work, and big bands. He has a big sound that fills the room, often without miking. He's been an essential part of the jazz scene in Japan since the early 1990s.

Joh Yamada 山田穣

https://johyamada.com/

Another of my long-time favorites, he leads quartets and quintets that explore his originals and well-chosen standards. Then, he starts disassembling them to understand how they work, putting them back together in unexpected ways while delighting in the whole process. His mastery of the instrument and of improvisation is highly appealing. He is a personal favorite.

Mabumi Yamaguchi 山口真文

https://mabumi.com/

He is an unapologetically straight-ahead sax player who has a knack for lovely melodies, neat arrangements, and following his own direction. He plays without fuss or pretense—he sits down and the melodies stream out. Ten recordings (so far) capture his inventive, melodic approach and confirm him as a serious reed player with a great sense of composition.

Ryuichi Yoshida 吉田隆一

https://www.facebook.com/ryuichi.yoshida.1614/

There are not many baritone sax players in Japan or the world, but he's one of the best. He puts the bari and the tone in baritone. He's a fine improviser with a penchant for free jazz and a rich storehouse of technique that fills out every group he plays with.

Trombonists

Introduction

While the number of trombone players can't compete with sax players, the trombone is relatively common on Tokyo stages. Most trombonists are in demand to fill out big bands. The trombone tone adds a unique dimension to many groups, often as a second bass line counterpoint, but also as a different way of improvising. The trombone was essential to the earliest styles of jazz and later to the classic Blue Note sound and West Coast jazz groups, all of which often grace the stages in Japan.

The trombone lines in many of the big bands are robust and elegant. They always seem to have a particular pride in their instrument, perhaps because it's more unusual than trumpet and saxophone. I'd say it's loved all the more for its rarity.

The preponderance of big bands and high school brass bands undoubtedly contributes to maintaining the trombone population, but that's all to the good. Trombone is also a staple in the Latin and salsa bands of different sizes.

You have to love an instrument that often gets overlooked. After you've heard a trombone filling out the front line, the fullness of tone can seem missing in other groups. Whenever a trombone does appear, it changes the dynamics of the group and the harmonies of the lead lines in interesting ways.

Its hint of Dixieland, the echoes from bebop trombone masters like J.J. Johnson, and that dash of salsa energy make the mix of tones, jazz eras, and improvisational styles fascinating.

Trombonists

Taisei Aoki 青木タイセイ

https://taisei1231.wixsite.com/taiseiaoki

With a lightness of touch and an ability to switch instruments, he's always a live wire in the bands he joins. I always like how he listens to his bandmates and plays what they're missing. If he's on stage, it'll be interesting.

Masaki Domoto 堂本雅樹

http://jmsu.web.fc2.com/domoto/

With a complete technique and a great tone on bass trombone, he's often lead trombone in Tokyo's many big bands (he's in almost all of them), but his small group work is just as compelling. I like him, especially in Four Trombones, a group which is, as it suggests, four trombones playing lush jazz harmonies and riveting lead lines.

Yuzo Kataoka 片岡雄三

https://www.jat-home.jp/profile/kataoka.html

He plays modern jazz in his quartet, belongs to the best big bands, and has a dulcet tone that invites you inside. Whenever any group needs a fuller, rounder sound, he's called in and delivers.

Osamu Matsumoto 松本治

https://x.com/03440588011F

He's a lovely player who doesn't play often enough live, but it's a treat when he does. With a soft, full tone and a way of turning melodies into even lovelier shapes, he leads groups and joins many others.

Shigeharu Mukai 向井滋春

http://www.s-mukai.com/

He's been playing live since the early 1970s and has never let up keeping the trombone flame alive. His Four Trombones group pays tribute to the instrument he's mastered and brought fully into the heart of Japanese jazz. His Super 4 Brass group is just as great, but the names hardly matter—it's his intimate knowledge of the songs he plays, the horn he uses, and the way beauty is created through sound.

Yoichi Murata 村田陽一

https://note.com/yoichi_murata

His big band is funky, high-energy fun, but he's also recorded with Ivan Lins, arranged beautiful charts, and plays a fierce trombone. He's an all-around musician who taught me that Japanese can be as funky as anyone on the planet. Always a pleasure to hear.

Hideaki Nakaji 中路英明

http://blog.livedoor.jp/obatala/

A superb trombonist who plays in as many big bands as his schedule allows, he's also a great composer and arranger with a penchant for Brazilian and Latin rhythms. His deep sense of musical cool comes through, no matter the rhythm.

Koichi Oshida 忍田耕一

https://www.facebook.com/profile.php?id=100085572124229

He leads the Black Elephants, a horn band that digs into Latin, funk, and New Orleans second-line rhythms with equal abandon. He also joins the horn line-ups of some of the best bands in Tokyo.

Haruki Sato 佐藤春樹

https://satohharuki.wixsite.com/home

Another trombonist with exceptional technique, he plays in many big bands, leads quintets, and plays in other small ensembles with verve, experience, and power. He also leads a 5 Trombone Unit that is making waves.

Junko Yamashiro 山城純子

https://www.facebook.com/junko.yamashiro1

She plays in numerous big bands and small ensembles, such as Junko Moriya's sextet and Makoto Ozone's No Name Horses. She also contributes her indelible technique on bass trombone to them all. She often plays in different groups around Tokyo and Yokohama and leads her own.

Guitarists

Introduction

The guitarists in Japan are outstanding. Like the piano, the guitar draws in future musicians at a young age and propels them toward more complicated music than rock and pop. The guitar also sets future jazz guitarists on their path. The number of live houses for rock music would take an entire book (or two), but the guitar is a gateway drug for jazz.

It's rare to commute without seeing one or two guitars being protected in the crowd. When I talk to my students who play in bands, they always respect jazz and aspire to play it, even while enjoying what they're already playing. I usually have to carry earplugs when I go out to hear them play in rock bands in tiny live houses since it's so loud. It's cathartic and energetic, but because jazz is ingrained in Japanese culture, those student musicians always know there are more settings than 10.

If pianists from the classical music world import virtuoso technique into Japan's jazz scene, ex-rock guitarists bring in a high-voltage electric sound. That's not always the case, of course. Jazz guitarists play in a variety of styles at a variety of volumes. No matter what style they develop, the influx of musicians from other genres helps keep jazz fresh and fertile—and loud.

The electric guitar's energy melds well with Japanese jazz groups, especially the more experimental ones. Guitars can be tuned in various ways, adding textures and complex harmonics and easily shifting from rhythm to melody. They also fit well physically—an amp is smaller than a grand piano, which is no small consideration in many jazz interior spaces.

Guitarists who are leaders tend to focus on an electric sound, but the ones on this list don't stop there. They go deep into the styles of jazz forged in America in the late '50s and '60s as guitarists came out front to be headliners themselves and to develop jazz guitar as a substantial jazz idiom of its own. Jazz guitar is alive and well in Japan.

Guitarists

Tomoya Hara 原とも也

https://www.facebook.com/tomoya.haradasd

One of the most tasteful and versatile guitarists, he loves music of all kinds and plays it with a massive sense of how it all works. Jazz might be just one of many genres he's mastered, but it's with jazz that he shines.

Mei Inoue 井上銘

https://mayinoue.com/

He's someone that established musicians like to team up with. His recordings have been consistently impressive, even though he plays with a lightness of touch and delicacy of phrasing. He's a marvelous player who's developed his sound at a young age and plays it exquisitely.

Akihiro Ishiwatari 石渡明廣

https://www.facebook.com/IshinamidaAkimaro/

A wild and uncategorizable guitarist who plays with very intriguing and inventive groups, from Shibusa Shirazu to the Shibuya Takeshi Orchestra to Mull House. When you think he's going in one direction, he goes in several others. Check him out backing butoh dancers. Always original and imaginative, he's one of my favorites.

Takayuki Kato 加藤崇之

https://www.facebook.com/takayuki.kato.58/

His career playing the smallest, funkiest clubs shouldn't overshadow how interesting his fretwork is. He has a distinctive sound and a unique way of playing electric and acoustic, jazz and Brazilian, and all points in between.

Natsuki Kido 鬼怒無月

https://mabokido.web.fc2.com/

A blend of progressive rock and jazz falls magically from his fingers. Whether collaborating with Kazutoki Umezu or leading groups like Bondage Fruit and Warehouse, he knows how to pump up the gain and distortion, throw in a French jazz touch, and let the music fly. He's intense, original, and uncompromising.

Yoshiaki Masuo 増尾好秋

https://www.ymasuo.com/top.htm

Making his home in the U.S., he plays in Japan annually and draws crowds who've listened to him for years. Sadao Watanabe selected him for an early-on band, and he's never looked back. He's played with Sonny Rollins, Elvin Jones, and others and is accomplished as a producer too.

Hiroki Miyano 宮野弘紀

https://www.facebook.com/hiroki.miyano.9/

A staple in the Gypsy jazz manouche community, with a strong style of acoustic jazz that impresses with technique, energy, and accomplishment. He is also a composer with a gentle approach to combining sounds to create lush soundscapes. Acoustic guitar jazz doesn't get any better.

Yoshiaki Miyanoue 宮之上貴昭

https://www.miyanoue.net/

His thumb- and finger-picking style of jazz harkens back to Wes Montgomery. It's startling to hear because it's so impressive. Sleek, stylish, and soulful, he plays jazz guitar classics and his compositions with equal virtuosity. His live shows are always a pleasure to hear.

Sadanori Nakamure 中牟礼貞則

http://www.aoki2.com/zest/zest.html

Still performing and recording in his 90s, wonderfully, with his debut in the early 1950s, is something of a record. He's seen and heard—and created—a lot of music over the years, and that experience informs his playing. He is an audience favorite not just for his staying power but for his keen sense of jazz guitar in all its complexity.

Iwao Ochi 越智巌

http://www.iwaoochi.com/

Funky, fusion-y, and fun, he's the on-call guitarist for Hammond B3 organ trios and groups needing that extra push into high-energy jazz. His groups, like Speaker Sgt., are steeped in funk and urban blues, but stretch into glorious soloing. Check out "Bad Baby City," a favorite of mine.

Ryo Ogihara 荻原亮

https://ryoogihara.jimdofree.com/

The kind of guitarist who gets on stage, plugs in, and plays without fuss. He's a favorite of other musicians. Look at all the CDs he's played on, and you get a sense of how he's received, called on, and long since paid his dues. Now, he's making his own recordings and leading funky groups.

Yoshiaki Okayasu 岡安芳明

https://www.yoshiakiokayasu.com/

A guitarist of the old school of early Jim Hall, Kenny Burrell, and other '50s and '60s masters of that jazz guitar form. He's an old-school stylist and makes the past impressively alive. His CDs are consistently pleasing, virtuosic, and unapologetic about playing with lyricism and nimble soloing.

Yosuke Onuma 小沼ようすけ

http://www.yosukeonuma.com/

An extremely talented guitarist who has played with many of the funkiest groups in Tokyo. He puts a lot of soul into his playing and always sounds fresh and new. He searches for a big soundscape, finds it, and explores. He also branches into flamenco, bossa nova, and other guitar-loving styles.

Yoshihide Otomo 大友良英

https://otomoyoshihide.com/

One of the most intense and freest guitarists, he pushes every boundary he can, and when the guitar isn't enough, he turns to the turntable and electronics to get his ideas and passions across. He's also worked on soundtracks, but I like him best live when he's letting loose.

Ryoichi "President" Saito 斉藤"社長"良一

https://x.com/shachoxno1

He plays with some of the most eclectic groups, ones with an unpredictable spirit and exploratory drive. He adds a unique set of textures and a big sound to every group, always with one ear to the band and one to the call of the wild.

Gene Ess Shimosato ジーン・エス・シモサト

https://gene-ess.com/

Residing in America most of the year, but playing regularly in Japan, he made his name in the US with such stalwarts as Ravi Coltrane, not to mention Archie Shepp, Reggie Workman, and other heavyweights. He's released over ten recordings, which have received well-deserved critical praise (from me too). Live, he stretches out as a marvelous improviser.

Haru Takauchi 高内春彦

https://www.facebook.com/harutakauchi/

One of the most accomplished and experienced guitarists in Japan, he keeps putting out great recordings and forming great groups. That's just what he does. Modern jazz guitar doesn't get better in Japan. He makes the music happen in small or large groups with a complete sense of jazz, a laidback approach, and handfuls of experience.

Shunji Takenaka 竹中俊二

https://www.facebook.com/ShunjiTakenakaMusic/

A tasteful and talented guitarist who works on a surprising number of projects all at the same time—all of them interesting. He plays rock, soul, and, well, anything that fits onto his fretboard. But it's when he takes off with an extended solo in front of a funky, bluesy, jazzy band that he impresses. He's the man about town and always great to hear.

Bob Ward

https://www.facebook.com/bob.ward.1276/

A welcome transplant from America, he's a great guitarist, sound technician, and recording engineer. Catching him live, though, is a special pleasure. He fits into every group and bears down on the solos to make them special.

Koichi Yabori 矢堀孝一

http://www.yabori.pro/index.html

A guitarist with a unique voice and direction, his recordings have just gotten better and better over the years. With a fluid approach and consistently stellar bandmates, his live shows are top-notch modern jazz. He has an electric sound, but not one that's dependent on the "electric" side of it. His solos fly with nimble fretwork and a driving energy.

Unusual instruments

Introduction

Many of the masters of less common instruments originally studied a different musical tradition: Japanese, classical, Latin, or Indian music. Some edged over into jazz because of the strictness of those forms or the lack of venues to play, or maybe they were just interested. All of them, I'd guess, are attracted to jazz's rich tradition of improvisation. It's not that other musical traditions don't improvise—many do—it's just that jazz puts it front and center.

Most of these musicians have that musical drive for the right blend of generic styles and traditional instrumentation that takes the music to a higher level. Most succeed. It's not just the instrumentation that's unique, but also the way of thinking, feeling, and creating music. It's always fascinating to see if such musical differences can be resolved like a neat ii-V7-I chord progression.

It isn't always that easy, but it's still fascinating. I like to see how such instruments transform, strengthen, and lift a jazz group and occasionally make it something other than jazz.

This section includes percussion, vibraphone, biwa, and koto, among many others. Jazz koto? Very definitely, and very wonderfully. Japan has always been a place where outside and inside influences are twirled into one.

Unusual instruments

Toshihiro Akamatsu 赤松敏弘 – vibraphone

http://vibstation.net/

Vibraphonists are rare everywhere, but especially in Japan. After studying with Gary Burton at Berklee, he's the pre-eminent vibe player in Japan. Listening to him in his live shows and on record, he makes you feel every other group should have vibes too.

Robert Belgrade – clarinets, sax, tabla

https://www.facebook.com/BringBelgradeBack/

After studying tabla and vocals with Ali Akhbar Khan, he spent years in Japan, returned to the States, and resettled in Japan. A multi-instrumentalist, he writes for and plays in world music groups like Tatopani, with strikingly original compositions in various time meters.

Tony Guppy – steelpan

https://jp.tonyguppy.com/

A serious steelpan player from Trinidad and Tobago, he's settled into the Tokyo music scene and has been invited to play with a range of musicians, both live and on record. Steelpan never sounded so jazz-like. He's expansive and delightful.

Christopher Hardy – percussion

https://christopherhardymusic.com/

He's a percussionist who adds polyrhythms, textures, shapes, and energy to every group he joins. He's busy almost every night of the year, and for good reason—he's like the salt of every show. Check out the CDs to which he's added his eclectic and earthy sound!

Bruce Huebner – shakuhachi

https://www.shakuhachibruce.net/

A master of the shakuhachi, a traditional Japanese bamboo flute with an otherworldly sound, he's never let himself stay confined to boundaries. He can improvise with any jazz group but sounds especially nice in acoustic settings.

Yukihiro Isso 一噌幸弘 – Noh-kan, dengakubue, shinobue

https://issoyukihiro.com/

The Noh-kan is the traditional wooden flute played in Japanese Noh. That's where he started, but he's journeyed through Western classical music, world music, and jazz. He moves between these worlds, but it's a fascinating blend when he plays improvised music. The many flutes he's mastered add a unique voice to different groups.

Koichi Makigami 巻上公一 – voice, theremin

http://www.makigami.com/

Theremin seems one of the least likely—and yet when you hear it, most likely—of instruments to add to an avant-garde jazz group. He brings a cornet with him, but the theremin fascinates audiences and adds a spectral sound to the proceedings, along with his Tuvan throat singing.

Miya – modular flute, synthesizers

https://miya-music.com/

Talented and exploratory, she's created a series of recordings that use her flute with a unique synthesizer setup. The result is ethereal improvisational music. But when she sits down with a more traditional jazz group, she sounds just as impressive.

Yoichi Okabe 岡部洋一 – percussion

https://okabeyoichi.com/

A central pillar of the Latin jazz community, he plays a full range of percussion that sounds just as good for hard-driving jazz as it does for salsa dancing. If you want clave-ful polyrhythms, he's the guy.

Hideki Sato 佐藤英樹 – conga

https://mk741852963.wixsite.com/hidequisato

He is a conga player who ups the level of the many groups with his full-on style that he partially acquired in time spent in Cuba. He's also traveled in the Caribbean and South America, bringing back those rhythmic treasures to Tokyo's best Latin groups.

Yoshiro Suzuki 鈴木ヨシロー – timbales, drums, percussion

https://yoshirosuzuki.wixsite.com/website

Another Latin musician who has played all through the Caribbean with some of the most famous musicians in the salsa world. He's a dynamic player who seems to breathe in polyrhythms and has added his virtuoso playing to a wide range of bands.

Eiji Taniguchi 谷口英治 – clarinet

https://taniguchi-eiji.com/

The clarinet is not rare in jazz history, but in the current age, it's rarely on stage except for a change of pace. But he's made a career of it. Though he's impressive on an old Count Basie or Duke Ellington tune, his elegant tone and serious approach are not stuck in the past, but are pristine contemporary jazz.

Michiyo Yagi 八木美知依 – electric 21-string koto, 17-string bass koto, electronics

http://michiyo-yagi.cocolog-nifty.com/

Adding modern electronics and traditional koto seems an unlikely match, but it becomes a powerful expression of musicality in her hands.

Playing with some of the best free jazz and improv players, her koto powers the music with deep tones and complex harmonies, but the way she plays also adds delicacy and nuance. It has to be heard to be believed. She's one of my favorites—her groups always impress.

Reiko Yamamoto 山本玲子 – vibraphone

https://reikoyamamoto.net/

Vibes always sound sleek and cool with a late-night musical vibe, and she follows that tradition with verve. Her CDs have excellent sound recording, so you can hear each note ring out as she wants it to. Live, she's dynamic and entertaining, creating compelling jazz.

Masaki Yoshimi 吉見征樹 – tabla, kanjira, matka

https://sound.jp/tablin/

He is a percussionist who adds, shapes, and expands the groups he plays with. His tabla playing is impressive enough for some of the jazz world's best players to make new projects just to play with him.

Yoshino 与之乃 – Satsuma biwa, vocals

https://x.com/yoshinobiwa

Traditional and avant-garde, she plays with smaller ensembles, usually with a very progressive approach to creating soundscapes and new blends of musical approaches. Biwa has the image of delicacy and grace, and that's true, but she adds dynamism to every note.

Singers

Introduction

Good jazz singers are rarer than might be expected in Japan. There's a long tradition of entertainers who draw on the Great American Songbook, and many places feature singers as entertainers. Since I'm more of an instrumental jazz guy, I lean into those singers who are more on the jazz side of the spectrum.

When I teach jazz to my students, they always ask me, "Don't they have words?" I tell them to imagine the words or even to go beyond words and try to let the music touch them more intuitively and humanly, deep inside their emotions.

The singers here are singers like that. It's hard to sing in a language other than your native tongue. The phrasing, rhythm, and intonation are tricky to get right. A few singers I've heard sing wonderfully in English don't speak much English. Others, of course, have spent years overseas or had their education in English, so singing in English is as easy as singing in Japanese.

Other singers have made a career of singing jazz standards in Japanese. Most songs in the great American songbook have been translated into Japanese, often with accepted versions. However, a few singers have done their translations with even better results. Translating English to Japanese is hard enough, but try fitting the words in Japanese onto the chords, rhythms, and harmonies!

If you're a fan of singers, probably the best place to hear jazz singers in Tokyo is the jazz club Naru Yoyogi. https://yoyogi-naru.com/. It's the sister club to Naru in Ochanomizu, but Naru in Yoyogi focuses entirely on vocalists. It's an intimate venue with small groups or just a pianist and a wonderful place to hear the best jazz singers.

Many other jazz clubs also have singers, but not every night. It's no exaggeration to say those vocal nights are busy, especially around holidays like Christmas or Valentine's Day. Many hotel bars also feature singers from both Japan and abroad. But here, I'm sticking to singers who perform in the jazz-focused clubs.

Singers

Akiko

https://www.akiko-jazz.com/

She got her start in the smallest of small jazz clubs but has since developed a bigger audience and larger venues. She's explored big band singing, pops, ukelele, and swing. She has great musicians backing her on record and on stage.

Chie Ayado 綾戸智恵

https://www.chie-ayado.com/

With a huge following, she's moved beyond the small confines of clubs and regularly fills larger venues with her piano playing and singing. She covers not just jazz, but also jazz-ified soul, rock, pop, and J-pop songs in Japanese and English. She reaches audiences with her gravelly voice, nuanced interpretations of well-chosen songs, and great backup bands.

Charito

https://charito.com/

Straight-ahead, soulful, and satisfying on every stage she graces, she's a singer who holds the audience in the palm of her hand. Originally from the Philippines, she's toured Asia, recorded in America, and made her home in Japan. She performs regularly and is on the bill at every jazz festival in Japan. Reserve early—I've never seen an empty chair at her live shows.

Andrea Hopkins

https://www.instagram.com/androlita/

A tasteful singer whose recordings have not received the appreciation they deserve. Live, she can front a big band with ease, and often does, but it's the intimate shows, with a small band or just piano as accompaniment, where you can hear the real beauty of her singing and her roots in Georgia, USA.

Hikari Ichihara 市原ひかり

https://hikariichihara.com/

Also included in the trumpet section, she's a marvelous singer who controls her voice like a trumpet. The rare female trumpeter in Japan, she has the tone and creative improvising to back up any praise, and she is just as nuanced when singing as playing trumpet.

Eri Kamiya 神谷えり

https://erikamiya.bitfan.id/

Singing from inside the jazz canon does not seem enough for her. But even when she reaches out for a rock or pop tune, she makes it her own and sings it jazz-like, even without straight jazz backing. I especially like that she sings in Japanese. When that aligns, it's beautiful to hear.

Shiho

https://www.facebook.com/friedpride.shiho

A talented singer who started as a duo with a guitarist called Fried Pride, she quickly gained a broad following and moved more to the pops side of the spectrum. She still has her jazz chops, but she's been popular ever since. She has a strong sense of rhythm, melody, and scats with creative arrangements and unique turns of phrase.

Shun Sakai 酒井俊

https://shunsakai.net/

Some singers are easy to appreciate, and others are easy to fall in love with. She's both, and in both English and Japanese. With a series of recordings dating back to 1990, she's been busy in clubs and still regularly tours. She records with her pick of the best jazz musicians. Her husky voice and knowing phrasing are always appealing.

Junko Sumi 澄淳子

https://www.facebook.com/sumi.junko.9/

She has long been one of my favorite singers. Her CD "Gingin, Giragira" caught my ear when I first came to Japan. On that recording, she took the children's songs and nursery rhymes of Japan and turned them into jazz with all the love and the beauty of a childhood melody. Her jazz vocals are accomplished and passionate.

Akemi Shoomy Taku 宅Shoomy朱美

https://x.com/shoomy_note

A fine pianist and vocalist, she sings with a unique vocal style ranging from jazz to whatever music interests her. She sings in Japanese and English, with the occasional Portuguese take on Brazilian standards, but always done in her inimitable style.

Tamao 木村玉緒

http://kimmtamm.html.xdomain.jp/

She always has a great band behind her, which is needed to support her soaring vocals and compelling onstage presence. Her Japanese vocals are always mesmerizing, as is how she translates American standards into Japanese. She also sings standards in English with great energy and style.

Tea

https://www.tea-music.com/

A relative newcomer to the Tokyo jazz scene, she left her native India to perform worldwide, finally settling in Japan. She has a voice that sends chills down your spine. She moves effortlessly from jazz arrangements of pop songs to jazz standards, but always sounds like herself. She knows how a song can be delivered most beautifully.

Toku (flugelhorn)

https://www.tokujazz.com/

Also included in the trumpet section, Toku loves to sing as much as splash out on an extended flugelhorn solo. He's a great performer—brass or voice—no matter what instrument he's on. His singing is especially sensitive and strong.

Michiko Yoshino 吉野美知子

https://michiko-yoshino.com/

A jazz vocalist who returned from studying in America to perform regularly and also to teach jazz vocals. Her style is straightforward, with unadorned honesty in each song. She sings from the heart with a real dedication to the beauty of a song.

Geila Zilkha ギラ・ジルカ

https://www.geilajazz.com/

She's spent her life moving between cultures, but her real nationality is the world of jazz. Japan was lucky enough to finally be chosen as her home base. Her recordings are a mix of standards and pop songs, and she sings both with vitality and energy. She also pulls together great backing bands who add their talents to her high-energy, spot-on singing.

Big Bands

Introduction

Japan is home to many big bands—and I do mean many! This tradition has held its ground against the onslaught of expensive jazz clubs, music company strangleholds, and the call of other musical styles. The big bands are the beginning of most jazz musicians' careers, giving them the experience, skill, feel, and flow of jazz.

To understand the predilection, you need to go no further than the Yamana Big Band Jazz Contest. This annual event pits university big bands against each other in a contest judged by Japan's top professionals. It's an event that reveals the depths of big band passion. Yamano Big Band contest website is here: https://www.yamano-music.co.jp/ybbjc/ Go if you can!

Or check out the Yokohama Jazz Promenade's junior high and high school big band shows. Watching kids as young as thirteen get ready on outdoor stages around Yokohama, you want to cheer them on before they even play a note. Yokohama opens up its streets and venues once a year, which is always an opportunity to hear these young people and old pros. Yokohama Jazz Promenade website is here: https://jazzpro.jp/.

Japan is inundated with amateur big bands. My former editor at The Japan Times plays in one, and it's a joy to see people from all walks of life join together in an admittedly small room to play for friends, family, and fans. The annual Someday Jazz Club's Big Band Festival (usually in May) brings in the pros for a week-plus of big bands, with some musicians playing in several. Big Band Festival at Someday: http://someday.net/

There are many reasons for the love of big bands in Japan, some of which I discuss in this book's History and Culture section, but almost any week of the year, a big band is playing somewhere. Considering also how hard it is to organize, that's surprising. Where do you find one that is big enough in the expensive practice rooms of Tokyo? And with all the musicians so busy, when?

One big band leader told me he practiced section by section and paid taxi fares home in the middle of the night. It was the only time to get people together and find an affordable practice room. Most musicians are great at sight reading, so they sometimes see the chart for the first time just before the gig.

So many people in Japan have started from brass bands, gone on to big bands, and then become musicians, pro or amateur, or alternately become devotees or plain old fans longing to be more involved. Big bands are a large part of why jazz remains so firmly ingrained in the musical psyche of Japan.

In this section, I list the best big bands that regularly play in the Tokyo and Yokohama area. I list the leader of the band, and their site, though not all bands have a dedicated site.

Big bands

923 Big Band, leader Kohata Mitsukuni 木幡光邦

https://x.com/kunizobb

The name "923" comes from his nickname "Kuni san," which is those three numerals in Japanese. He's selected the hardest-playing musicians, ones with drive and energy. When they come on stage, they come to play hard, fast, and funky.

Satoko Fujii Orchestra, leader Satoko Fujii 藤井郷子

https://satokofujii.com/wp_site/satoko-fujii-projects/satoko-fujii-orchestra-tokyo/

An edgy, experimental, adventurous orchestra with two incarnations, one in Tokyo and the other in New York. The same charts work differently in both places. Still, that schizophrenic musical approach is perfect for creating a free jazz big band that is as unexpected, intense, and compelling but also warm, inviting, and full of humor.

T.P.O. Funk Orchestra はぐれ雲永松

https://tpoinfo.com/

Shift the letters around, and you get T.O.P. (Tower of Power), and if you know the Tower, you will know their sound. The impressive solos by band members go together with the funky undertow. A band that knows how to have a good time and has a following.

C.U.G Jazz Orchestra, leader Yasuhiro Kohama 小濱安浩

https://www.cugjazz.com/

A classic big band situated deep in the tradition of big bands. Their charts cover classic jazz numbers from "Over the Rainbow" to "Green Dolphin Street" to rock arrangements. The members are drawn from the cream of the jazz crop.

Irie Amigos Big Band Latin Jazz, leader Shinichiro Irie 入江新一郎

https://irieamigos.com/music/

A top-notch, Latin big band whose charts rocket over clave rhythms. The members have had experience playing or studying in the Caribbean and South America. The songs are sometimes pop or rock tunes transformed by Cuban rhythms. Expect dancing and brilliant solos.

Banda Caliente Grande, leader Katsunori Fukay 深井克則

https://www.facebook.com/Katsunorindo

A spot-on fun band led by a dynamic pianist who became captivated by Latin rhythms and devoted his career to the same. He leads a trio, a small group, and this grande version. The charts are carefully arranged, and the band members choose to play those charts to the max. It's dance-ready jazz clave and muy caliente!

Yoshinobu Inagaki & his Big Band, leader Yoshinobu Inagaki 稲垣貴庸

https://www.facebook.com/people/稲垣貴庸/100020032443608/

This finely tuned band deeply loves big band music in its classic, pristine state. The charts are based on advanced harmonies and complex textures. The layering of sections is done exceptionally well. Of course, the band members are drawn from the top tier of Japanese musicians—it's how it should be done.

One Night Jazz Orchestra Fusion, leader Masahiro Kobayashi 小林正弘

https://www.facebook.com/masahiro.kobayashi.566/

They offer a fresh, modern take on big band music without fear of electric instruments. Their fusion-ish approach to making dynamic music is strong and appealing, and it fills the room. The get-up-and-jam spirit resides here, along with an appreciation of the classic big band style.

Tokyo Big Band, leader Jonathan Katz

https://www.jkatz.net/tokyo-big-band

This big band shows the importance of the members meshing to create tensions and resolutions and form a just-right mix. He picks the best, so Tokyo Big Band has that dynamic and then some. Add fascinatingly well-written charts by leader Katz, his originals, well-arranged Japanese songs, and the occasional updated pop number, and you have a big band that takes the tradition into new territory—a personal favorite.

New Herd Big Band, leader Toshiyuki Miyama 宮間利之

https://newherd.jp/

It is an unapologetically devoted tribute to Woody Herman's The Herd, but with its take on that classic big band sound. You can get the vibe from the website (only in Japanese), which explains why big bands are so amazing, with charts, diagrams, and explanations. It's less about instruction, though, more about passion. The New Herd has plenty of both.

Eric Miyashiro's EM Big Band, leader Eric Miyashiro,

https://www.ericmiyashiro.com/

As much of a virtuoso with his big band as on trumpet, this band doesn't play often enough, but when they do, they deliver high-energy, fresh music. With so much energy all around, the band always leaves audiences exhilarated. EM doesn't scrimp on the solos, either, which makes the shows exciting.

Junko Moriya Orchestra, leader Junko Moriya 守屋純子

https://www.junkomoriya.com/

Constantly innovative, creative, and dynamic, this big band has plenty to say in their tight ensemble work and the lovely solos. Whether playing her originals, an arrangement of a Thelonius Monk piece, or an updated Count Basie jam, her band is spot-on with playing, soloing, and jazz sense. With a half-dozen exceptional recordings, she also travels the country to help amateur bands push their level up. Plus, she won the Thelonious Monk Jazz Composers award.

Yoichi Murata Orchestra, leader Yoichi Murata 村田陽一

https://x.com/YoichiMurata

His big band features fiery charts and feisty soloing. He brings out the soul in his band members and uses it well. The electric guitar, bass, and keyboards don't stand out, but blend harmoniously into the funky flow. This is a muscular, driving band that digs deep.

Tetsuya Tatsumi Big Band, leader Tetsuya Tatsumi 辰巳哲也

https://www.facebook.com/tetsujazz/

With a well-selected collection of members and well-written arrangements, what could go wrong? Nothing, it all goes right. This band has the controlled looseness that makes for the best jazz. It's a great band that doesn't play often enough.

Tokyo Nettai Jazz Rakudan 熱帯JAZZ楽団, leader Carlos Kanno

https://www.facebook.com/nettaijazz/

Taking their love of Latin rhythms and high-energy performances, this big band can fill an auditorium and play to a stadium of fans. The rhythms are intense, and the shows are fun, but it's a serious big band that has gained popularity with a wider audience and for the right reasons.

Sun and Moon Orchestra, leader Mark Tourian,

http://www.marktourian.com/marktourian/webpages/index-m.html

After playing bass with most of the best names in jazz, he can call on those players to fill out his big band, and he does. A progressive, tightly formed band that brings modern jazz sounds to this older form. The contemporary jazz compositions are especially elegant, and he gives ample time to all the soloists.

Kenichi Tsunoda Big Band, leader Kenichi Tsunoda 角田健一

https://tsunokenband.jp/

This is a pristine, classic big band with a traditional sound that isn't all that traditional. Celebrating 35 years, this big band is one of the longest-running big bands in Japan, and for all the right reasons.

Hammond B3 Organ Players

Introduction

Tokyo is Hammond B3 Heaven, but once you get addicted, you realize there should be more. And yet, try carrying a vintage Hammond B3 and Leslie speakers down the basement stairs of a Tokyo club, and you'll see why there's not more. One club, Sometime, used to host a Hammond B3 festival, but carrying those heavy wooden cases down the stairs and set in place was too much. Not to mention getting it back up the stairs.

Fortunately, thanks to technology, the Hammond B3 portable models are available and affordable, and many jazz clubs have dedicated evenings to them. As a fan of Jimmy Smith, Joey Defrancesco, Jimmy McGriff, Dr. Lonnie Smith, and others, it pleases me that the B3-drums-guitar or sax combo is still a feature in many clubs' monthly schedules.

One club, Organ Jazz Club, is devoted to the instrument and the style. That club has two organs ready and waiting, and a mirror is set on the wall to reflect the keyboard so you can see how the organists' hands move over the keyboards and foot pedals. They have organ-less jazz on some nights, but when the players in this section show up, the music cooks.

Hammond B3 groups are appealing for their funkiness, earthiness, and groove. Other Japanese jazz musicians sometimes understate these elements in their approaches. They don't have to be present all the time, but with Hammond B3 players, they are front and center.

Even in regular jazz clubs, the following players sound great in the often-confined spaces of Tokyo's clubs. It's been nice for me to lay back and groove to such soulful music on many nights. Hearing jazz steeped in soul, funk, and blues and played with such dedication is heartening. Many of the organists have formed trios and written compositions that genuinely impress.

Hammond B3

Atsuko Hashimoto 橋本有津子

https://www.facebook.com/atsuko.hashimoto.165/

She swings hard with a lot of soul. That's the highest compliment you can give a Hammond B3 player. She's unapologetically old-school and has played abroad at festivals, on tours, and various clubs, far from her home in Osaka. A fiery and rootsy player who I wish played more in Tokyo.

Yuta Kaneko 金子雄太

https://aquapit.amebaownd.com/

With one hand on the old-school keyboard and another on a forward-looking set of keys, he's got a style and sound that is all his own. His trio Aquapit is a winner and one of the best B3 trios in Japan. His technique is exceptional, proficient, and practiced, but without losing any of the groove—one of my favorites.

Daisuke Kawai 河合代介

http://www.daisukekawai.com/

He always commands the stage with a full-on attitude that rockets along. He drives other musicians' groups too. He plays with some of the funkiest musicians, whether sax, drums, or guitar, and is always a welcome addition. Like all great B3 masters, he's a band all on his own.

Akio Sasaki 佐々木昭雄

https://www.facebook.com/JAZZORGAN.SASAKI/

Pleasingly old-school and deep in the Hammond B3 tradition, he plays organ with an easy-going manner that belies plenty of zeal. Even when he's slowing down for a ballad, there's bubbling energy in his two hands and his feet. He's keeping the B3 flame alive.

Hal Tsuchida 土田晴信

https://haltsuchida.com/home

With extensive overseas experience, having lived in the US for over a decade and Germany for a few years, he learned keyboard technique from Tony Monaco, among others. He knows how to lock into a groove and keep the melody spinning like a dancer. It's good that he's resettled back in Japan. He creates soulful sounds with compelling solos.

Akiko Tsuruga 敦賀明子

https://www.akikojazz.com/

An Osaka native who's made New York her home, she's been lauded by Lonnie Smith, among plenty of other accolades from the press. She swings hard on her albums with stellar musicians at her side. She doesn't play in Japan often enough, but she plays regularly in New York and tours Europe.

Blues, Salsa, Brazilian, and other music

Introduction

It would be impossible to fully convey the variety of musical forms played every night in Japan. However, I am always impressed by all the musicians, including those who've dedicated themselves to other styles of music. So, I wanted to include some of the musicians who play music that is not so far from jazz.

Jazz has traditionally been a music that incorporates other forms easily. In my musical tastes, I follow that lead. Listen to everything and find what feels the best. Many musicians move outside the limits of jazz to add their playing to recordings and other bands, and not out of economic necessity so much as having "big ears" (as musicians often say) for all kinds of music. That is to say, jazz is a complex music, but every form of music is complex in some way.

Jazz purists might want to skip this chapter, but most jazz lovers like all sorts of music. So, let me include a few of the nearest musical forms—blues, salsa, samba, and ambient improv. Each of those forms has its devotees, with numerous websites covering them. Each of them has a lively scene in Tokyo and Yokohama. I won't go into rock, punk, or the myriad pop styles this time, as that would lead this guide too far afield.

But I want to include musicians who would appeal to big-eared jazz readers. I'd be remiss not to include a few who have impressed me over the years, and lit up an evening out. This section also helps position jazz along the larger spectrum of all the music played every night in Japan.

Blues and other

Samm Bennett
Singer and songwriter, percussion, multi-instruments

https://www.polarityrecords.com/

An eclectic and engaging musician, he plays percussion, drums, and single—and triple-stringed instruments and is mean on squeaking duck. A lyricist with tremendously creative and poetic power, he leads an open mic event called Drunk Poets See God and the King Cake Baby trio, sometimes a quartet, specializing in Professor Longhair and other New Orleans music. His other groups are eclectic and fascinating.

Hiroshi Eguchi 江口弘史
Blues bass

https://the-bassification.jimdosite.com/

Rock-solid bassist who anchors the best blues in Japan and accompanies visiting blues musicians, leading their backing groups. He toured America for years with some of the biggest names like Mavis Staples, Honeyboy Edwards, and Sugar Blue. He made me understand that the Japanese can understand the blues profoundly and fully.

Morgan Fisher
Keyboard, composer

http://www.morgan-fisher.com/

More rock and roll than jazz, he's also a proponent of ambient and long-form improvisation. He ranges among keyboards (from his extensive collection) of more kinds than could ever fit on a single stage. He hosts a marvelous musical "salon" where you can hear musicians up close. And did I mention he played with Queen and Mott the Hoople in his younger, wilder years? A fascinating musician.

Steve Gardner

Blues guitar, vocals, harmonica

http://www.ramblingsteve.info/

Mississippi misses him, but he's become a regular fixture in Japan's blues scene, often playing with his partner-in-blues, Felix Sonnyboy. He plays acoustic blues that can sound as electric as any amped-up guitar and knows more blues tunes than a Google search. He brings all the ferocity and passion of Delta blues to Tokyo.

Kenji Koyasuda 小安田憲司

Blues guitar, vocals

https://www.facebook.com/kenji.koyasuda

He is a blues guitarist who knows what he plays from the inside out. He has a knack for tight riffs and how to construct a solo like his blues guitar heroes. Ask him for the list! He's the force behind Sun Alley, one of the longer-running blues bands in Tokyo. One of my favorites.

Lisa Ono 小野リサ

Vocal

https://onolisa.com/en/top-en

It's impossible to imagine anyone in any audience who wouldn't love her. She radiates positive energy and emotional depth just walking on stage. Born in Brazil, she established her career in Japan, but is popular everywhere. Her dozen albums have reinterpreted and promoted bossa nova, jazz, and whatever else she turns her attention to. She sings, plays guitar, and composes. She's one of everyone's favorites.

Orquesta de la Luz

https://www.laluz.jp/

I'm not sure if anyone wants to call this jazz, but a lot of the band members are jazz players, and anyway, it's one of the best salsa bands, not just in Japan but in the world. Led by the indomitable Nora, they've recorded and played worldwide since 1984. They have fans from the heart of salsa countries just as much as from Japan. They often veer toward jazz, but with their most recent release celebrating their fortieth anniversary, they are back to complete salsa, with plenty of extended solos to turn up the heat.

Saigenji サイゲンジ

Guitar

https://www.saigenji.com/

A powerhouse of a performer, even with only an acoustic guitar in hand, his playing impresses. He can command a festival stage as easily as a small club. His singing is strong, calm, and sure, and he moves easily between Portuguese, Japanese, and English. His vocal percussion makes you look around for the rest of the band, but it's just him, scatting with fervor and originality. He impresses not just with technique, but with heart and soul.

Son Reinas

https://sonreinas.com/biography.php

All-woman salsa bands, orquestas femininas, have been an important part of salsa history and contributed significantly to the development of the Afro-Cuban style in jazz. Japan only has one big one like this one, but that's all it needs. They've been together, with various personnel, since 1993, when leader Izumi Muramatsu traveled to Cuba and returned with the holy salsa grail. She has been touring, playing, and recording ever since.

Arisa (Alisa) Sunaga 寿永アリサ

Vocal

https://www.facebook.com/sunaga.arisa

A Latin singer who moves from Japanese to Spanish to English. She's a performer who can front a big salsa band and get the audience on their feet. Her singing graces many Latin jazz and salsa bands in Tokyo and helps keep the salsa scene alive in Japan.

Where to Jam, Hang, and Shop

Jam sessions

Introduction

Jam sessions are integral to keeping the jazz scene flourishing. All over the country, jam sessions run by pros are open to amateurs who want to join in and hone their skills.

At most places, there's a charge or minimum requirement for a drink. Considering the high rent in Tokyo and Yokohama, it's a bargain. For most club owners who run jam sessions, it's a labor of love.

Jam sessions are very welcoming. They are happy to have new people come and join in. Just show up with your instrument, wait your turn, ask for a song you know, and you'll get a supporting band.

And you'll enter a community!

Other participants know other jam sessions, good shows, and places to go. Ask them. They will point you in the right direction.

But make no mistake, the level can be very high at some sessions, and they are almost always run by one or two professionals, who take time away from their schedules and career scrambles to help bring up musicians still working on their playing.

It's also a pleasure to listen. When I've gone, I'm always surprised to hear how good some up-and-coming musicians are. It's also comforting to listen to mistakes, hesitations, and misdirections. It's a reminder of how hard jazz is and how much of a pleasure it is because of that high level of difficulty.

So, here's a list of jam sessions. I haven't gone to every single one of these. But I wanted to include this as it gives a larger view of how much jazz is going on and because people always ask about this.

Some of these sites are all in Japanese, but mostly, you can see which nights have jam sessions. "Session" sometimes carries a different meaning from "jam session." It can sometimes refer to pro musicians playing with a new group or arrangement without the open atmosphere of a "jam session." So, be sure "jam" is in there.

Always check ahead on the price and requirements. Every place has its procedure, order, and plan. It's good to know beforehand and be ready to play with others according to how they do things at that place. Some of the websites are only in Japanese too, so if you don't read Japanese, you'll have to make do with translation apps. That should work, but be sure to double-check before you go. And be flexible when you're there. Enjoy!

Listing of sessions

Jazz spot intro

ジャズスポット　イントロ

The granddaddy of all jam sessions.

B1 NT Bldg., Takadanobaba, Shinjyuku-ku, Tokyo.

03-3200-4396

〒169-0075 東京都新宿区高田馬場2-14-8 NTビルB1

Takadanobaba Station (Yamanote Line, Tozai Line, Shinjuku Line)

Jam sessions are every day except for Monday. Friday night is a midnight session from 23:00 - 03:00. No music charge, just a drink charge.

https://jazzspot.intro.co.jp/

Dolphy

ドルフィー

The best place in Yokohama to go for jamming.

Daiichi Nishimura bldg. 2F, 2-17-4, Miyagawa cho, Nakaku, Yokohama-shi

(045)261-4542

〒231-0065 横浜市中区宮川町2-17-4 第一西村ビル2F

Hinode-cho Station (Keikyu Line), Sakuragicho Station (Negishi Line, Blue Line)

Jam Session is on the 4th Monday, from 19:00. Charge is 1,400 yen.

https://dolphy-jazzspot.com/jamsession.html

Bright Brown

ブライトブラウン

Blues you can use in a stripped-down, easy-going space

2F Yuzawa Daini Bldg., 5-59-9, Nakano, Nakano-ku, Tokyo

(080) 3366-1130

〒164-0001 東京都中野区中野5-59-9 湯澤第二ビル2F

Nakano Station (JR Chuo Line, Sobu Line, Tokyo Metro Tozai Line)

Blues jam session on Thursdays from 20:00 to 23:00. 800 yen, plus one drink order.

https://brightbrownnakano.wixsite.com/brightbrown/session

https://brightbrownnakano.wixsite.com/brightbrown

Art x Jazz M's

(アート×ジャズ　エムズ)

Warm and welcoming spot for jazz and jamming

B1 Myojo Bldg., 2-7-5, Honcho, Kokubunji-shi, Tokyo

(042)325-7767

〒185-0012 東京都国分寺市本町 2-7-5 明星ビルB1

Kokubunji Station (JR Chuo Line, Seibu Kokubunji Line, Seibu Tamako Line, Narita Express)

Jam sessions are from 19:30, except for the Sunday jam session from 15:00 to 21:00. The charge is 1,500 yen to 2,000 yen, depending on the event. Jam session days are every Sunday and Monday. 3rd Saturday is a vocal jam session. Even-numbered months' second Sunday is a jam session for beginners. Also, there are special jam session events.

https://www.ms-artjazz.com/

Yokohama Jazz First

(横浜ジャズ・ファースト)

A great space with a serious dedication to jazz.

1F Second Yoshida Building, 9-chōme–140 Chōjamachi, Naka Ward, Yokohama, Kanagawa, 〒231-0033

045-251-2943 from 18:00〜

045-252-8414 daytime from 09:00〜

〒231-0033横浜市中区長者町9-140 第二吉田ビル1F

From the Hinodecho Station on the Keikyu line, it's a 3-minute walk. Also, a 10-minute walk from Sakuragicho or Kannai Stations

Even with an outstanding line-up of performers, this fantastic club turns its stage over to jam sessions once a month. It is a great place to meet other musicians and to jump into the jam.

    First Saturday Jam is held every first Saturday of the month. Jam sessions start at 16:00 and go until everyone gets tired. Participants are Y1,900 plus two drinks, and listeners are Y1,500 and two drinks.

https://jazz-first.com/

https://www.instagram.com/yokohama.jazz.first/

Jazz Bar Soultrane

ソウルトレーン

東京都 台東区花川戸1-13-16 浜松ビル2F

Hamamatsu Building 2F, 1-13-16 Hanakawado, Taito-ku, Tokyo

From Asakusa Station, about a 4-minute walk north along the river.

Their jam sessions are on various nights, so checking the calendar carefully is best. They have afternoon and evening jam sessions in and among the occasional live shows.

https://soultrane.jp/calendar

Cafe Cotton Club

カフェコットンクラブ

BF-3F, Sounds building, 1-17-14, Takadanobaba, Shinjuku-ku, Tokyo

03-3207-3369

〒169-0075 東京都新宿区高田馬場1-17-14 SOUNDS bldg. BF-3F

Jazz live shows and jam sessions every Friday from 18:30.

The music charge is from 3,500 yen.

https://www.cafecottonclub.com/jazz/

Every Swing

エブリィスイング

B1F, Ueno Est Building, 3-15-14, Higashi-Ueno, Taito-ku, Tokyo

(03)5818-3513

〒110-0015　東京都台東区東上野3-15-14ウエノエストビルB1F

Ueno Station (JR Yamanote and many other lines, Tokyo Metro Ginza Line and Hibiya Line.)

Jam Session on Tuesday from 19:30. The music charge is 2,500 yen.

http://every-swing.com/

Giee

ギー

Sanko Building, Basement floor 1, Honcho 2-3-9, Kokubunji-shi, Tokyo
(042)326-0770

〒185-0012東京都国分寺市本町2-3-9 三幸ビルB1

Kokubunji Station (JR Chuo Line, Seibu Kokubunji Line, Seibu Tamako Line, Narita Express).

Jam sessions are mostly on Sunday, usually from 13:30 to 17:00, but sometimes in the night.

https://giee.jp/

https://giee.jp/info/394018

In F

インエフ

3F, Tsuda Building, 3-4-19, Higashi-Oizumi, Nerima-ku, Tokyo

(03)3925-6967

〒178-0063東京都練馬区東大泉3-4-19津田ビル3階

Oizumi Gakuen (Seibu Ikebukuro Line)

Jam session day is about once a month, usually on Saturday.

https://in-f.live/site

Into the Blue

イントゥー ザ ブルー

4F, Kiyokawa Building, 1-18-14, Nakamachi, Machida-shi, Tokyo

(042)850-9378

〒194-0021東京都町田市中町1-18-14きよかわビル4F

Machida Station (JR Yokohama Line, Odakyu Line)

Jam sessions are held irregulary.

The charge to participate in a jam sessions is about 2,700 yen, and 1,700 yen to listen.

http://intotheblue.info/schedule

J-flow

ジェイ・フロー

2F, Iwasaki Building, 3-13-6, Kamezawa, Sumida-ku, Tokyo

(03)5637-7577

〒130-0014 東京都墨田区亀沢3－13－6岩崎ビル2F

Jam sessions or workshops everyday. Closed on Tuesday.

Music charge from 2,300 to 3,200 yen.

https://j-flow.net/2018sessionfaq/

https://j-flow.net/schedule_session/

Jack and Suzie

ジャック&スージー

3-30-2, Kameari, Katsushika-ku, Tokyo

080-7713-4192

〒125-0061 東京都葛飾区亀有3-30-2

Kameari Station (JR Joban Line)

Session schedule is usually from 13:00 to 16:00 (daytime), 19:00 to 21:30 on weekdays, and 18:00 to 21:00 on weekends. The charge is around 2,500 yen.

https://jackandsuzie.tokyo/

Jazz Bar Fill In

ジャズバー　フィルイン

4F, ICL building, 19-24, Aizumi-cho, Shinjuku-ku, Tokyo

(03)3358-4885

〒160-0005 東京都新宿区愛住町19-24アイシーエルビル4F

Akebonobashi Station (Toei Shinjuku Line)

Vocal sessions on Tuesday and Thursday, sometimes on Saturday. The session day charge is from 2,000 yen.

https://www5.hp-ez.com/hp/fillin/page1

Ko-Ko from sonoka

ココ フロム ソノカ

2F, Himawari-building, 2-26-5, Dougenzaka, Shibuya-ku, Tokyo

03-3463-8226

〒150-0043 渋谷区道玄坂２－２６－５ひまわりビル２階

Jam sessions from 19:00 to 22:30. The charge of Tuesday jam session is 2,900 yen.

https://jazz-koko.com/

Manhattan

マンハッタン

3F, Kiraku Building, 2-2-7, Asagaya-kita, Suginami-ku, Tokyo

(03)3336-7961

〒166-0001 東京都杉並区阿佐谷北2-2-7喜楽ビル3F

Jam sessions on Thursday and on Sunday. Music charge is from 3,000 yen.

http://www.ateliermw.com/manhattan/livesch.html

MJSmile

エムジェイスマイル

2F, 2-4-15, Minami-cho, Kichijoji, Musashino-shi, Tokyo

(0422)24-6541

〒180-0003 東京都武蔵野市吉祥寺南町2-4-15-2F

Kichijoji Station (JR Chuo Line, Sobu Line, Keio Inokashira Line)

The music charge varies depending on the host musician of the jam session.

The schedule of jam sessions depends on the week, so please check the club's calendar.

https://www.mjsmile.com/event-schedule/

Ogikubo Rooster

荻窪ルースター

Kyoritsu Dai 51 Bldg. B1, 1-24-21, Kamiogi, Suginami-ku, Tokyo

(03)5347-7369

〒167-0043 東京都杉並区上荻1-24-21 協立第51ビル B1

Ogikubo Station (JR Chuo Line, Sobu Line, Tokyo Metro Marunouchi Line)

Blues sessions are held irregulary. The charge is 1,000 yen to participate, and there is no charge to just listen.

http://www.ogikubo-rooster.com/north/session.html

Somethin'

サムシンジャズクラブ

1-8-8, Ikebukuro, Toshima-ku, Tokyo

(090)3875-1320

〒170-0014 東京都豊島区池袋1-8-8

Jam session everyday, except for the most Mondays.

Beginners can participate without registration, but from the second time, member registration is essential.

https://www.somethinjazz.com/jp/

Sunny Side

サニーサイド

2F, RICOS Building, 3-28-1, Nishi-Waseda, Shinjuku-ku, Tokyo

(03)5272-6119

〒169-0051東京都新宿区西早稲田3-28-1　RICOSビル2F

Nishi-Waseda Station (Tokyo Metro Fukutoshin-Line)

Vocal sessions mostly on Saturday, and jam sessions mostly on Sunday. Closed on Monday.

https://www.sunny-side.jp/

Jazz Kissaten

Introduction

For the price of a cup of coffee, you can hear the best-recorded jazz in the world in Tokyo and Yokohama. Just head to a jazz *kissaten*, or jazz coffee shops—*jazzu kissa* for short—find a good chair, order a coffee, and relax.

These havens of jazz culture are the real ports of entry for jazz into Japan. Since at least 1933, when the famed jazz kissa Chigusa opened in Yokohama, Japanese have flocked to these coffee shops for a pleasurable education in the latest jazz on vinyl and now on CD.

Jazz kissaten are unique to Japan. Other countries have coffee shops that play music, but Japan's are aimed at listening to jazz more than at drinking coffee. In some, talking is forbidden. All ears are pointed towards the speakers. There's no talking, usually, certainly no dancing, inside. It's a very internal-looking space where you listen to music and spend time with yourself.

Jazz kissaten provided a communal space where people who lived in tiny apartments, often with paper-thin (literally) walls, could go to turn up the volume. Jazz kissaten served as shared living rooms, where you could bring your vinyl records if you so chose, request those from the *master*'s collection, or sit back and soak in whatever was playing. If you see the word "jazz" written on the sign of a shop, there's a jazz kissaten inside.

DUG was my first favorite place. When I first arrived in Japan, I spent Friday afternoons there reading and prepping classes that I taught in the evening. I also frequented another place in Jinbocho, Hibiki, which is now gone, and another in Akasaka, which is also gone. Many, though, have survived.

In the '90s, I spent every Thursday afternoon at Meg, in Kichijoji, reading, writing, correcting my students' homework, and occasionally dozing off. All the while, jazz was playing loud enough to prohibit talking. I wonder what grades my students would have received if I'd done my marking in a different place.

These days, lunching at Eagle in Yotsuya, where I change trains on the way to work, is a breather in the working day, a shot of musical energy more wakening than caffeine.

Once you go in and order, you can stay as long as you like. The places are always comfortable and inviting (except one with an English "No Talking" sign that flashed if you talked). For many people, they are like a second living room or an outside office.

Afternoons are mainly for coffee, but at about five or six p.m., alcohol starts to be served. Whiskey was long associated with jazz and still is, but these days, drink lists are more extensive, though not by much.

Jazz kissaten served many purposes. When vinyl records were still hard to get and good stereos beyond the budgets of most Japanese, these spaces provided both. They were central spaces to share the love of improvised music without bothering anyone else.

All things Western were shut down during World War II, but with the American occupation, they opened back up. American service members helped supply the vinyl records that made these small spaces thrive. One serviceman, Don De Armand, who was stationed in Yokosuka, wrote me that he sent vinyl records to the owner of Chigusa for many years after he returned home.

In an interview, the famous pianist Toshiko Akiyoshi told me she learned to play by listening at Chigusa and other spots in Ginza. When she knew the master well, she would ask him to pick up the needle and put it back so she could figure out a particularly tricky section to play in her evening gig.

From the 1950s through the 1970s, Japan was really into jazz, and these coffee shops served as centers for disseminating all things jazz-related. By the early 1960s, they featured in films by directors like Koreyoshi Kurahara, whose "Black Sun" (1964) and "The Warped Ones" (1960) featured soundtracks featuring Max Roach and Clifford Jordan.

For the alienated youth tired of Japan's reconstructed and booming economy, the cafes were centers of information about jazz, with books and magazines available for customers to read. Even now, flyers for live shows, concerts, lectures, new releases, jam sessions, and everything related to jazz are piled on shelves or racks by the door. A few places have lectures by jazz specialists who play recordings with their talk.

In a fascinating study of kissaten by researcher, professor, and pianist Mike Molasky, some 500 jazz cafes opened around Japan in the middle of the 1970s. As Japan's economy improved, the choice of records continued to expand, and the need to have a space separate from one's apartment to listen to recordings continued. Japan's many record stores are still inundated with a great selection of used vinyl.

The jazz kissa that remain today continue the tradition, and it can be too crowded to get a seat on some evenings. The older places that remain, such as Shinjuku's Dug (opened in 1961), Yotsuya's Eagle (opened in 1967), Kichijoji's Meg (opened in 1970), Shinjuku's Old Blind Cat (opened in 1965) and Samurai (opened in 1965) still play vinyl. However, CDs are much more common these days.

A feeling of sanctity still reigns in most jazz cafes. They are privileged, sacred spaces for chilling out and listening to jazz. Most cafes are not as strict about talking as they once were (very few places now flash "No Talking" signs), but a calm serenity lingers.

If you want to request something, don't hesitate. There are no corporate-approved playlists with a CD to buy at these places. They play what they like and what customers are interested in. The cafe may not always have what you want, but it won't hurt to write it down on paper if they use that system or ask the wait staff. Most jazz kissas also offer light meals, sandwiches, or a special pasta for lunch, and drinks are usually very affordable.

Be forewarned, though, that some owners are not particularly interested in attracting a large number of customers. Foreign customers have swamped some places and driven out regular customers. These are local places that survive on a local clientele. While the global travel industry has its positive aspects, one of the negatives is over-tourism at cherished venues. So, please, if you do go, respect the vibe, don't disturb other patrons, and enjoy the sound of jazz on vinyl.

Some places charge a 500-yen table fee, especially in the evening or after 5 pm, so don't be surprised. Ask them or look at the menu closely. Whatever you pay, jazz kissaten is a slice of jazz history unique to Japan and a wonderful experience. This section covers a few, but not all, of the many jazz kissaten. They're a dying breed, sad to say, though the ones that remain are special places.

Also, many of the jazz clubs are open as jazz kissaten in the afternoons. Some have afternoon live shows at a reduced price. Check the information in the Jazz Clubs section for times. Many offer a lunch set or coffee set with great jazz laying to wash it down.

Jazz Kissaten

Chigusa

ジャズ喫茶ちぐさ

Nogecho 2-94 Naka-ku, Yokohama, Kanagawa

070-8348-8409

神奈川県横浜市中区野毛町2-94

Sakuragicho Station (JR Negishi Line, Yokohama Subway Blue Line)

About a three-minute walk from Sakuragicho Station. An eight-minute walk from Hinodecho Station. Open 12:00 to 22:00. Music charge at night.

jazzchigusa@gmail.com

http://noge-chigusa.com/

https://www.jazzinjapan.com/clubs-and-venues/chigusa

https://www.instagram.com/nogechigusa/

Though its status is somewhat in limbo, with plans to open it as a jazz museum, this is an important place. Recheck its status before going as it may or may not be open. The oldest jazz kissaten coffee shop in Japan, Chigusa was started in 1933. It's been in operation spinning records ever since. Despite the loss of records, the deaths of owners, and the usual economic pressures, Chigusa has survived. To put it into perspective, the Village Vanguard, New York's jazz club, started in 1935, according to the Guinness Book of World Records.

Who's oldest doesn't matter as much as who's most influential. Vinyl records are an essential part of how jazz spread around the world. The jazz kissaten was founded when the soundtrack of cosmopolitan life around the world was jazz. Chigusa is a pilgrimage spot for anyone who loves jazz. It's just a room, but what a room!

For Japan, Chigusa was where musicians like Toshiko Akiyoshi, Sadao Watanabe, and other famous players went to hear the latest record in their early years. They would spend hours memorizing new riffs and chords from the vinyl imported by owner Mamoru Yoshida.

Check out my interview with Toshiko Akiyoshi where she talks about putting the needle back on a record at Chigusa to hear one riff over and over.

https://www.jazzinjapan.com/interviews-posts/toshikoakiyoshi

Check out my interview with Don De Armond, who was stationed in the service in Japan in the mid-1950s. He helped Chigusa owner, Mamoru Yoshida, get records after World War II. You can hear his love of jazz in Japan in this interview. The photos below are his, taken years ago. I thank him again for sending those.

https://www.jazzinjapan.com/interviews-posts/dondearmond

Chigusa is a great place to visit, to hang out, to soak up the long history of jazz in Japan, a country which has become one the most important homes for jazz. In large part, that's due to Chigusa. It's a place that truly deserves the overused term "global."

Long before globalizing was even a concept, the beauty and power of jazz played on vinyl records at Chigusa was enlivening listeners, opening up musical minds, and helping educate a generation of musicians. It's great to stop by and see where all that happened, and to feel it still happening.

Yokohama Down Beat

横浜ダウンビート

2F, Miyamoto Bldg. 1-43 Hanasakicho, Naka-ku Yokohama-shi, Kanagawa-ken

045-241-6167

〒231-0063 神奈川県横浜市中区花咲町1-43 宮本ビル2F

Sakuragicho Station (JR Negishi Line, Yokohama Subway Blue Line)

About a three-minute walk from Sakuragicho Station towards Noge area.

Hours: 16:00-23:30 Closed on Monday.

http://www.yokohama-downbeat.com/

One of the granddaddies of the jazz kissa world, the posters are smoke-stained, and the atmosphere is out of a film noir. It's a nostalgic gem saved in amber. The vinyl is well-worn and well-listened to. Drinks are standard issue, and food, enough to nibble on, but it hardly matters, you'll be overwhelmed by all the photos, old record covers, paintings, newspaper clippings, and knick-knacks that cover the walls, floor, ceiling, and counters. It's a real axis mundi of jazz in Yokohama.

DUG Jazz Cafe & Bar

ジャズカフェ&バー・ダグ

3-15-12, Shinjuku, Shinjuku-ku, Tokyo.

(03)3354-7776

〒160-0022 東京都新宿区新宿3-15-12（アドホック隣）

Shinjuku Station (JR Yamanote Line, Chuo Line, Sobu Line, Saikyo Line, Shonan Shinjuku Line, Tokyo Metro Marunouchi Line, Oedo Line, Toei Shinjuku Line, Odakyu Line, Keio Line, Narita Express, and more lines)

　　From the East Exit of JR Shinjuku Station, head to the large Yasukuni Dori (the wide street with many lights), which is right next to the sports shop Adhoc and near Shinjuku Piccadilly Cinema.

Hours: cafe 12:00-18:30, bar 18:30-23:30

http://www.dug.co.jp/

https://www.facebook.com/jazzdug

https://www.jazzinjapan.com/clubs-and-venues/dug

https://www.instagram.com/dug_jazz.cafebar/

Perhaps the jewel in the crown of jazz kissaten in Japan, DUG, is smaller than it once was. The once-upon-a-time three full floors of jazz, plus two nearby spaces, have shrunk to a basement space. But no matter, the brick walls, wood furniture, and great music make DUG one of the coolest places in Tokyo. It's been that way since it was opened in 1961 (when it was called DIG, so, technically, DUG started in 1967).

Vibe and history aside, the selection of music comes first here. The vinyl and CD collection was put together over the years by the owner, Hozumi Nakadaira. He's a fascinating character whose fantastic jazz photos hang on the walls. Take a look, and you'll see the photos he took when John Coltrane, Thelonius Monk, Miles Davis, Archie Shepp, Bill Evans, Tommy Flanagan—most of the American jazz greats, and all the Japanese jazz greats—came through Tokyo.

Many of those famed musicians played at DUG back when it had space for live performances. Nakadaira-san met them, photographed them, and helped to make Japan the jazz-loving country it is today. If the photos on the wall are insufficient, ask to see one of Nakadaira-san's books, a copy of which is usually somewhere around the bar.

Like most jazz kissaten, the afternoon is quiet and calm, without much talking, though that rule is not strictly enforced here. It gets noisy and lively in the evenings, and the volume's raised. The well-worn wood of the tables and chairs is a testament to the number of customers who have stopped by over the years. DUG is a well-known place, which is as it should be. It should be a stop on every jazz fan's list.

Café Bar Eagle

Café Barいーぐる

1-8, Yotsuya, Shinjuku, Tokyo

(03)3357-9857

〒160-0004 東京都新宿四谷1-8

Yotsuya Station (JR Chuo Line, JR Sobu Line, Tokyo Metro Marunouchi Line, Tokyo Metro Nanboku Line)

It is a one-minute walk from JR Yotsuya station. From Yotsuya Station, head along Shinjuku Dori (the large street) toward Shinjuku. Eagle is downstairs on the right-hand side, not far from the large intersection.

Hours: weekdays 11:30-23:40, Friday 11:30-23:50, Saturday 14:00-23:40 (15:30-23:40 on the day of Asahi Culture Center class). Closed on Sundays and public holidays.

http://www.jazz-eagle.com/

https://www.jazzinjapan.com/clubs-and-venues/eagle

https://x.com/jazz_eagle

https://www.facebook.com/jazzeagle1967

Eagle is one of the longest-running jazz kissaten in Tokyo. Its calm, sleek interior has been there since 1967. The sound system is spectacular, with large JBL speakers, a choice of two CD players, a pre-main amp and power amp, a Yamaha record player, and Denon cartridges. In the old days, you could bring in your own cartridge to test it out, but it depends on who runs the shop. Regardless of the equipment, though, the sound is stellar.

Seats are comfortable and graciously set apart. You can hear well anywhere, even with people eating the simple, substantial daily lunch set. There is pasta, fried potatoes, meat pie, quiche, and small pizza in the evenings. But as with the best jazz kissaten, the music is the reason to go.

The choice of jazz here tends towards the most straight-ahead, but the selection thoroughly covers the '60s to the present day. The staff choices are excellent, so it's easy to kick back without worrying. The record jacket or CD cover is always placed upright on the counter so you can hear what's playing.

Be sure to respect the rule of being quiet until 6 pm. Many jazz kissaten in the past were as strict as a library about no talking. Music deserves to be heard in the best possible environment for calm reflection and solitary experience. After 6 pm, it's OK to talk, and the place becomes more of a jazz bar. But even at night, most people go there to breathe in rather than breathe out. It's easy to say why the café has been running for 50 years.

Bar&Kitchen Funky

吉祥寺 Funky

1-7-3, Honcho, Kichijoji, Musashino-shi, Tokyo.

(0422)21-1464

〒180-0004 東京都武蔵野市吉祥寺本町1-7-3

Kichijoji Station (JR Chuo Line, Sobu Line, Keio Inokashira Line)

A four-minute walk from Kichijoji Station, in the lane that runs along the back of Parco.

Hours: Lunch & Cafe time 11:30～17:00 (Saturday, Sunday and Public holidays),

Dinner time 18:00～24:00 (Saturday, Sunday and Public holidays), Dinner time 16:00～24:00 (Weekdays), Closed on Monday, the 2nd and 4th Tuesday.

https://www.sometime.co.jp/funky/

https://www.facebook.com/mugi.funky/

https://www.instagram.com/kichijoji_funky/

https://x.com/funky211464

Head upstairs for the jazz vinyl collection and a superb selection of cocktails. They have music other than jazz here, so don't get upset if they aren't playing what you want. Just ask, and they're usually glad to accommodate any requests you might have. The food is great here, too.

Jazz Bar Samurai

Jazz Bar サムライ

5F, 3-35-5, Shinjuku, Shinjuku-ku, Tokyo.

(03)3341-0383

〒160-0022 新宿区新宿3-35-5 守ビル5F

Shinjuku Station (JR Yamanote Line, Chuo Line, Sobu Line, Saikyo Line, Shonan Shinjuku Line, Tokyo Metro Marunouchi Line, Oedo Line, Toei Shinjuku Line, Odakyu Line, Keio Line, Narita Express, and more lines)

It's a two-minute walk from the southeast exit of JR Shinjuku Station. Head downstairs and walk down the alley along the raised street. The building has a small entrance about three buildings down from the corner. It's close, but can be hard to find. Read all the signs opposite the raised street, and you'll find it.

Hours 18:00-25:00. Jazz time every Saturday 17:00-18:00. Last Sunday 15:00-18:00 free jazz jam session. Sometimes, there are live shows or events.

http://samurai.favy.jp/

https://www.jazzinjapan.com/clubs-and-venues/samurai

https://www.facebook.com/Jikenx/

It's hard not to fall in love with Samurai. The room is packed with hundreds of *manneki-neko*, "welcoming cats," for one thing. But around those cat figures are hundreds of photos, dozens of mismatched lamps, hanging scrolls, dried flowers, figurines, vases, and knick-knacks. You are bopped visually as well as aurally.

Despite the hundreds of cat eyes looking down on you, Samurai is a serious jazz hangout. Their slogan says it best: "Drinkin' Listenin' Relaxin.'" All three of those come easy here. Samurai has a looser, wilder view of jazz than many traditional jazz kissaten. It is more of a "jazz bar" since it's mainly open in the evening, but ultimately, it's beyond simple description.

The vinyl collection includes a lot of free jazz and improvised music. The "master" has excellent taste, so fans of free jazz should ask him for recommendations or kick back and listen. His collection of straight-ahead music is just as substantial, making it possible to switch between styles.

Samurai also hosts a free jazz session on the third Sunday of the month from 15:00 to 18:00. Call to ask for details, but this is unique, as most jazz jam sessions tend towards the traditional.

Food and drinks are reasonable, with pizza, fried noodles (*yakisoba*), potatoes, salad, and pilaf as the primary comfort foods. Drinks are beer, whiskey, and the usual suspects. Try his unique homemade liquors for something special.

Samurai is the most unpretentious, otherworldly space you can imagine, which makes it easy to sink into the excellent sound system and unique vibe. The hundreds of lucky porcelain cats beckon and welcome you into the world of jazz in just the right way!

Jazz Bigboy, Jimbocho

(ジャズ・ビッグボーイ)

1-11, Jimbocho, Chiyoda-ku, Tokyo.

(03)3233-4343

〒101-0051東京都千代田区神保町1-11

Jimbocho Station (Tokyo Metro Hanzomon Line, Toei Shinjuku Line, Toei Mita Line)

Right outside of the A7 Exit of Jimbocho Station.

Hours: 13:00-17:00, 19:00-22:30 (Tuesday – Friday). Closed on Saturday, Sunday, Monday and public holiday.

http://jazzbigboy.sakura.ne.jp/

Perhaps the only jazz kissaten with windows, this sleek little corner spot in Jinbocho, the bookstore neighborhood of Tokyo, is welcoming, calming, and yet lively with music. The sound system is exceptionally good, and the coffee is drip-filtered. CDs tower in the corners, and vinyl lines the shelves and spills onto the counters. A serious collection of jazz and all you need to lay back and enjoy it.

Jazz Union

ジャズ・ユニオン

4-28-8, Jingumae, Shibuya-ku, Tokyo.

(03)5770-5472

〒150-0001東京都渋谷区神宮前4-28-8

Harajuku Station (JR Yamanote Line), Meiji-Jingu-Mae Station (Tokyo Metro Chiyoda Line, Fukutoshin Line)

Walking away from JR Harajuku Station towards Omotesando, turn left on the second street after the large Meiji Jingu-Mae crossing. It's just a short walk, five minutes or so, with a turn down a small street on the left.

Hours: 13:00-20:00 (-21:00 on Wednesday and Thursday). Closed on Tuesday.

http://jazzunion.jp/

https://www.jazzinjapan.com/clubs-and-venues/jazzunion

https://x.com/jazz_union/

https://www.facebook.com/jazzunion7/

@jazz_union

The Jazz Union Café is truly an oasis in the heart of Harajuku. This cozy jazz cafe is ideal for healing the mind, body, and soul. The flurry of shopping and fashion outside disappears as you sink into the chairs and wrap yourself in great jazz.

    The owner, Doctor Kuwasaki, is a big jazz fan. He opened the cafe on top of his Harajuku Mental Clinic in collaboration with Disk Union, one of the biggest record chains in Japan. Every other month, Disk Union brings around 600 new CDs and LP records, from classic jazz to new releases, to be played in the Café. The turnover means there will always be something new and something old to hear.

    Anyone can request the music from their selection, which contains around 800 recordings. The state-of-the-art sound equipment comprises custom-made JBL speakers and a custom-made pre-amp, run through McIntosh vacuum tube amplifiers. A small red upright piano fills one corner and is played at the two monthly live shows. That's about it for decoration, but that's all that's needed since the café is about listening, not looking around.

    The menu offers a select variety of coffees and teas. There is no alcohol or food, but you can bring your favorite snack. There is free Wi-Fi. This is a wonderful spot devoted to hearing jazz in perfect conditions.

MEG

ジャズ喫茶メグ

Kichijoji Honcho 1-31-3, Musashino-shi, Tokyo.

武蔵野市吉祥寺本町1-31-3

(0422)21-1421

Open: 13:00-16:00 and live events 18:30 -22:00. Times may vary, so check the site.

http://otokichi-meg.net/

Head out the north exit (the Sunroad Exit). Turn right and walk along the train tracks (east), past a *Koban* police box, through an intersection. Three streets past the intersection, turn left. It's three buildings down on the right, on the second floor.

With a fantastic stereo set-up for vinyl records and CDs, the sound here is one of the best in the city—and that's saying something. Gearheads can ask about the record player, cartridge, equalizer, amps, control amps, power amps, speakers, and all the rest. Still, when it comes down to it, the space washes the music over—and into you—with volume, attention to detail, and, of course, passion.

Most evenings have live shows, so it sometimes closes at about five p.m. for the musicians to set up. Management changed in 2019, but jazz moves forward, and fans stay fans. The crucial function of playing great music for serious listeners has endured.

Some evenings and weekend afternoons also sometimes host CD and LP talks by renowned jazz music buyers and specialists. Those talks are in Japanese, but the music takes center stage, so it doesn't matter. Meg is a place that is passionate about jazz and expresses that passion in all the right ways.

Nardis

ジャズ喫茶ナルシス

Y.O Building 2F, 1-13-6, Kabukicho, Shinjuku, Tokyo

(03)3209-6900

〒160-0021 東京都新宿区歌舞伎町1-13-6 Y.Oビル 2F

Shinjuku Station (JR Yamanote Line, Chuo Line, Sobu Line, Saikyo Line, Shonan Shinjuku Line, Tokyo Metro Marunouchi Line, Oedo Line, Toei Shinjuku Line, Odakyu Line, Keio Line, Narita Express, and more lines), Shinjuku West Exit Station (Tokyo Metro Oedo Line)

Five minutes walk from Shinjuku Station, or seven minutes walk from Shinjuku West Exit Station.

Hours: 18:00-22:30. Closed on Sunday.

There's a jazz club called Kashiwa Nardis in Kashiwa, Chiba. Please don't get them confused. Kashiwa Nardis is a great live house, but the Nardis jazz kissaten is located in Kabukicho, the nightlife (red-light) district of Tokyo. It's a delightful, unassuming spot in the middle of it all, with an excellent vinyl collection, basic drinks, and sometimes lovely ikebana flower arrangements at the end of the bar or on the shelves. It's a great place to hang out.

The Old Blind Cat

（ジ・オールド・ブラインド・キャット）

Konwa Center B2, 3-26-3 Shinjuku, Shinjuku-ku, Tokyo

050-5462-1628

〒160-0022 東京都新宿区新宿3-26-3コンワセンタービルB2F

Shinjuku Station (JR Yamanote Line, Chuo Line, Sobu Line, Saikyo Line, Shonan Shinjuku Line, Tokyo Metro Marunouchi Line, Oedo Line, Toei Shinjuku Line, Odakyu Line, Keio Line, Narita Express, and more lines), Shinjuku 3-Chome Station (Tokyo Metro Marunouchi Line)

From the east, central east, or southeast exit of Shinjuku Station, The Old Blind Cat is close, but a little tricky to find. Check the map out and keep your eyes open for the sign. Look for the one-eyed green and black cat. You'll find it on the pedestrian street, one corner from the station.

Hours: 18:00-24:30. Closed on Sunday

https://theoldblindcat.foodre.jp/

https://www.jazzinjapan.com/clubs-and-venues/theoldblindcat

https://x.com/theoldblindcat

https://www.facebook.com/theoldblindcat

https://www.instagram.com/theoldblind_cat/

The Old Blind Cat is a quintessential Tokyo jazz bar. Head down the two flights of stairs (so steep they are more like a ladder), and you enter another world—of jazz. The small space feels like being in a submarine, but after the music starts sinking in, it's a place to unwind—cozy, calming, and filled with jazz.

Drinks are standard bar fare but high-quality. Whiskey is the standard order out of tradition, but plenty of other choices are on offer. There are nibble foods along the counter, perfect for the drinks.

Vinyl records are the order of the day here, but recently, video screens around the space offer some visuals. And why not? The sound system is excellent, and if you ask for vinyl, you can hear almost any track you can think of from the extensive collection.

The big pleasure is leaning back into the well-worn wood (the place was founded in 1965), drink in hand, and floating off into the music. The music plays from seven in the evening to whenever it seems time to stop. Be sure to save energy to get back up the two flights of stairs.

Scratch

(スクラッチ)

2F, Marco Polo Building, 1-8-14, Honcho, Kichijoji, Musashino-shi, Tokyo.

(0422)21-1969

〒180-0004 東京都武蔵野市吉祥寺本町1-8-14 マルコポーロビル2F

Kichijoji Station (JR Chuo Line, Sobu Line, Keio Inokashira Line)

It is about a three-minute walk from Kichijoji Station. Head out the north (Sunroad) exit. Walk down the covered Sunroad shopping promenade. Take the second (uncovered) pedestrian alley to the left. Walk past the Coppice Department Store and turn right before the sizeable four-lane street. It's the second building down on the right, second floor.

Hours: 11:30-22:00 (Monday, Friday, Saturday), 11:30-17:30 (Tuesday, Wednesday, Thursday), 11:30-20:00 (Sunday, Public Holiday)

Scratch is a pleasant and comfortable jazz kissaten with a great selection of vinyl and a serious sound system. They still allow smoking, which might be a deal-breaker for some fans, but smoke aside, the interior of well-worn benches, cushion-covered chairs, and wobbly tables is classic. It's a kissaten in the day and a bar in the evening. There's a small music charge in the evening.

The music is straight-ahead, but they will accommodate requests. Overall, they have a great selection of music, and the place's acoustics are solid. There's no restriction on talking, and colleagues, couples, and old friends fill the place with conversation under the low lights.

Drinks are what you'd expect, but the food is way above average, so it's worth checking out. Many people come here to eat. The walls are lined with classic album covers, and the mirrors struggle to make the place look larger than it is. It's easy to fit a large group along the tables, which is rare enough to warrant attention.

It's a cozy, well-run jazz spot.

Vagabond

バガボンド

1 Chome-4-20 Nishishinjuku, Shinjuku City, Tokyo 160-0023

(03)3348-9109

〒160-0023 東京都新宿区西新宿1-4-20

Shinjuku Station (JR Yamanote Line, Chuo Line, Sobu Line, Saikyo Line, Shonan Shinjuku Line, Tokyo Metro Marunouchi Line, Oedo Line, Toei Shinjuku Line, Odakyu Line, Keio Line, Narita Express, and more lines), Shinjuku West Exit Station (Tokyo Metro Oedo Line)

About two minutes walk from Shinjuku Station, or right out of the Shinjuku West Exit Station.

Hours: 17:00-23:30, 17:00-26:00 (Friday)

https://www.vagabond-shinjuku.com/

A funky bar with decent food, good drinks, great music playing always, and the occasional live performance. Once inside, you're inside the world of jazz. They call themselves a "jazz izakaya," the best of two worlds. Founded in 1976, they know what they're doing.

Record Stores

Introduction

Vinyl is addicting and alluring. There's no two ways about it. For those wanting to check out the vinyl stores in Japan, I've compiled a short list of the larger and easier places to find jazz vinyl records.

For those people who are old enough to have had vinyl records when that was all there was, know how fascinating they are. For those people in the just-past "CD Age" and the present "Streaming Age," vinyl is an easily acquired taste. It sounds better, more authentic, retro, nostalgic, or cool. It's certainly how generations of listeners and musicians have experienced, learned, and lived with jazz.

Whatever your relationship with the platter is, or wherever you stand on the buying continuum, you will find good vinyl record hunting in Tokyo. There are many stores, so you can always find surprisingly good purchases and bargains if you have time, energy, and money. Vinyl stores still carry a rich trove of music and are fascinating to look through.

Jazz kissaten, though, is the most critical place I listen to records. Many of them have deep collections that would be hard, if not impossible, to duplicate, not to mention their great stereo systems and listening spaces. Like many things in Japanese culture, records have never really disappeared. They still carry meaning and value.

Japanese are very careful with possessions like records, so you can be sure that the ratings given to the quality of the discs are almost always accurate. You can find some very well-cared-for vinyl and more used ones priced accordingly. I've listed a few places to get you started, but there are plenty more in different city areas.

I've stopped my vinyl addiction because of space and sanity, and I like to listen broadly. Also, I've come to love live shows more than recorded music. But I get the idea, and I still have plenty of friends who listen to records zealously.

This list will steer you to most of the well-known places. But be forewarned, record stores change their offerings all the time. That's part of the fun. A jazz vinyl fan can buy up all the jazz, and it will take the store a while to refill the jazz section. Some places only have a small jazz section since hip-hop, R&B, reggae, or house music comprise most of the offerings. For that reason, I haven't written much about the stores, but I'm sure vinyl lovers will figure it out.

Happy shopping! Happy listening!

Coconuts Disc Kichijoji

ココナッツディスク吉祥寺店

2-22-4 Honcho, Kichijoji, Musashino-shi, Tokyo

(0422)23-1182

〒180-0004東京都武蔵野市吉祥寺本町2-22-4

Kichijoji Station (JR Chuo Line, Sobu Line, Keio Inokashira Line)

12:00-21:00

Open throughout the year.

http://coconutsdisk.com/kichijoji/about/

Big Love

(ビッグ・ラブ)

3F-A, 2-31-3, Jingumae, Shibuya-ku, Tokyo 150-0001

(03)5775-1315

〒150-0001 東京都渋谷区神宮前2-31-3 3F-A

Harajuku Station (Yamanote Line)

14:00-20:30, Closed on Monday.

http://www.bigloverecords.jp/

Darumaya

だるまや

2F, 1-36-5, Higashi-Ikebukuro, Toyoshima-ku, Tokyo

(03)5992-7385

〒170-0013東京都豊島区東池袋1-36-5 笹屋ビル2F

Ikebukuro Station (JR Yamamote Line, Saikyo Line, Shonan Shinjuku Line, Tohokuhonsen Tokkyu-Line, Tokyo Metro Fukutoshin Line, Tokyo Metro Marunouchi Line, Tokyo Metro Yurakucho Line, Seibu Ikebukuro Line, Tobu Tojo Line)

12:00-21:00. Open throughout the year.

http://darumaya.to/

Discland JARO

ジャロ

26-6, Udagawa, Shibuya-ku, Tokyo 150-0042

(03)3461-8256

〒150-0042 東京都渋谷区宇田川26-6

Shibuya Station (Yamanote Line, Saikyo Line, Shonan Shinjuku Line, Toyoko Line, Denentoshi Line, Inokashira Line, Ginza Line, Fukutoshin Line, Hanzomon Line)

Open throughout the year, except for new year's holiday.

12:00-18:00 (Friday, Sunday)

13:00-18:00 (Saturday)

http://www1.ttv.ne.jp/disclandjaro/

Disc Union Shinjuku Jazz Shop (CD and Records)

ディスクユニオン新宿ジャズ館(CD/レコード館)

3F, 3-34-1, Shinjuku, Shinjuku-ku, Tokyo

(03)5379-3551

〒160-0022　東京都新宿区新宿3-34-1 ジュラクツインBビル 3F

Shinjuku Sanchome Station (Fukutoshin Line, Marunouchi Line, Shinjuku Line)

11:00-21:00 (weekdays), 11:00-20:00 (Sunday and public holidays). Open throughout the year.

http://diskunion.net/shop/ct/shinjuku_jazz

Disk Union Jazz Rare Groove (Shibuya)

ディスクユニオン渋谷ジャズ/レアグルーヴ館

BF, Antenna 21, 30-7, Udagawa-cho, Shibuya-ku, Tokyo

(03)3461-1161

〒150-0042　東京都渋谷区宇田川町30-7アンテナ21 BF

Shibuya Station (Yamanote Line, Saikyo Line, Shonan Shinjuku Line, Toyoko Line, Denentoshi Line, Inokashira Line, Ginza Line, Fukutoshin Line, Hanzomon Line)

11:00-21:00 (weekdays), 11:00-20:00 (Sunday and public holidays)

http://diskunion.net/shop/ct/shibuya_jazz

Disk Union Jazz Tokyo

（ディスクユニオンジャズ東京）

2F, 2-1-45 Kanda Surugadai, Chiyoda-ku, Tokyo

(03)3294-2648

〒101-0062　東京都千代田区神田駿河台2-1-45　ニュー駿河台ビル2F

Ochanomizu Station (Chuo Line, Sobu Line)

11:00-21:00 (weekdays), 11:00-20:00 (Sunday and public holidays)

http://diskunion.net/shop/ct/jazz_tokyo

HAL's

(ハルズ)

B-306, 7-10-17, Nishi-Shinjuku, Shinjuku-ku, Tokyo

(03)3364-1577

〒160-0023 東京都新宿区西新宿7丁目10-17 新宿ダイカンプラザB館306号

Shinjuku Station (Yamanote Line, Chuo Line, Sobu Line, Saikyo Line, Shonan Shinjuku Line, Marunouchi Line, Oedo Line, Shinjuku Line, Odakyu Line, Keio Line, Narita Express, and more lines)

12:00-20:00. Open throughout the year.

http://www.hals-jazz.com/

HMV Record Shop, Shibuya

HMVレコードショップ渋谷

Noa Shibuya 1F/2F, 36-2 Udagawa, Shibuya, Tokyo

(03)5784-1390

〒150-0042　東京都渋谷区宇田川町36-2 ノア渋谷1F/2F

Shibuya Station (Yamanote Line, Saikyo Line, Shonan Shinjuku Line, Toyoko Line, Denentoshi Line, Inokashira Line, Ginza Line, Fukutoshin Line, Hanzomon Line)

11:00 - 21:00

https://www.hmv.co.jp/recordshop/news/shibuya

HMV Record Shop, Shinjuku

HMVレコードショップ新宿

6F Alta Shinjuku, 3-24-3, Shinjuku, Shinjuku-ku, Tokyo

(03)5362-3360

〒160-0022東京都新宿区新宿3-24-3 新宿ALTA 6F

Shinjuku Station (Yamanote Line, Chuo Line, Sobu Line, Saikyo Line, Shonan Shinjuku Line, Marunouchi Line, Oedo Line, Shinjuku Line, Odakyu Line, Keio Line, Narita Express, and more lines)

11:00-21:00

https://www.hmv.co.jp/news/article/1911271052/

HMV Record Shop, Kichijoji

HMVレコードショップコピス吉祥寺

2F A Copicce Kichijoji, 1-11-5, Kichijoji Honcho, Musashino-shi, Tokyo

(0422)29-1130

〒180-0004 東京都武蔵野市吉祥寺本町1-11-5コピス吉祥寺A館2F

Kichijoji Station (JR Chuo Line, Sobu Line, Keio Inokashira Line)

10:00-21:00

https://www.hmv.co.jp/news/article/1911271054/

Jazzy Sport

(ジャジー・スポート)

3-17-7, Gohongi, Meguro-ku, Tokyo

(03)6452-3916

〒153-0053 東京都目黒区五本木3-17-7

Gakugei-dai Station (Tokyu Toyoko Line.)

15:30-19:00, Closed on Saturday, Sunday, and public holidays, but it depends on each month (schedule information is on the blog).

https://jazzysport.shop/

http://www.jazzysport.com/blog/diary.cgi

Jet Set Records

(ジェット・セット・レコーズ)

201 Yanagawa Bldg., 2033012 Kitazawa, Setagaya-ku, Tokyo

(03)5452-2262

〒155-0031東京都世田谷区北沢 2-33-12 柳川ビル201号

Shimokitazawa Station (Keio Inokashira Line, Odakyu Odawara Line).

12:00-20:00

https://www.jetsetrecords.net/location/tokyo/

http://www.jetsetrecords.net/

Manhattan Records

マンハッタンレコード

10-1, Udagawa-cho, Shibuya, Tokyo

(03)3477-7166

〒150-0042 東京都渋谷区宇田川町10-1 木船ビル

Shibuya Station

12:00-20:00

http://manhattanrecords.jp/

Technique

テクニーク

2F, Kubo Bldg., 33-14, Udagawa-cho, Shibuya-ku, Tokyo

(03)5458-4143

東京都渋谷区宇田川町33-14 久保ビル2階

6 minutes from Shibuya Station.

12:00-21:00

http://www.technique.co.jp/

Universounds

(ユニバーサウンズ)

202, Plaza U, 3-46-9, Koenji-Minami, Suginami-ku, Tokyo

(03)3314-5185

〒166-0003 東京都杉並区高円寺南3-46-9 プラザU202

From Koenji Station (JR Chuo Line, Sobu Line).

14:00 - 19:00. Closed on Wednesday

http://www.universounds.net/

Akaru Records

アカル・レコーズ

103, 3-21-11, Kikugawa, Sumida-ku, Tokyo 1300024

〒130-0024 東京都墨田区菊川3-21-11レジデンス須賀菊川 103

13:00-19:00 (Tuesday-Saturday)

Closed on Sunday, Monday, and public holiday.

https://akaru-records.com/

https://www.instagram.com/akarurecords/

Tower Records Shibuya

タワーレコード渋谷店

1-22-14, Jinnan, Shibuya-Ku, Tokyo

03-3496-3661

〒150-0041東京都渋谷区神南1-22-14

11:00-22:00 Open everyday, otherwise noted.

https://towershibuya.jp/

Upstairs Record and Bar

アップステアーズレコーズ&バー

3F, 3 Chome-27-1 Kitazawa, Setagaya City, Tokyo

03-6754-1052

〒155-0031 東京都世田谷区北沢3-27-1 YSビル 2F

21:00 to 25:00 or later. Open everyday. (Irregular closed days will be noted on Instagram.)

https://www.instagram.com/upstairsrecordsandbar

Flash Disc Ranch

フラッシュ・ディスク・ランチ

2F, Misuzu Building, 2 Chome-12-16 Kitazawa, Setagaya City, Tokyo

03-3414-0421

〒155-0031 東京都世田谷区北沢２-12-16三鈴ビル2F

12:00-20:00 Closed on Wednesday.

https://www.facebook.com/flashdiscranch/

https://x.com/Flash_Tsubaki

Dub Store Record City

ダブストア　レコードシティ

Misuzu Bldg. 1F, 7-8-3 Nishi-shinjuku, Shinjuku-ku, Tokyo

〒160-0023 東京都新宿区西新宿7-8-3ミスズビル 1F

13:00-20:00 Open every day except for the year-end and new-year holidays.

https://www.recordcity.jp/en

Shinjuku store is the largest, but they have other locations.

When and Why
—History and Culture

A brief history of jazz in Japan

Japan has a long history of jazz, almost as long as jazz itself. Though this history is less well known than in other countries, jazz took root in Asia in the 1920s, about the same time as it did in jazz's homeland—the United States. At that time, booming port cities like Shanghai, Hong Kong, Singapore, Kobe, and Yokohama were becoming urban centers of culture, trends, and globalized culture. From the early beginnings of jazz in those Japanese cities, jazz has continued to be part of Japan's urban culture. Re-infused over the decades by records, bands, concerts, and musicians, as well as Japanese musicians traveling abroad to study, the jazz scene in Japan has remained vibrant.

The following article gives a brief overview of jazz's history in Japan. For more detailed insights, historical details, and fuller explanations, please read the other articles later in this section. They discuss different aspects of the Japanese jazz scene in more detail. This article will get you started by positioning jazz more clearly in the historical sweep of cultural changes and exchanges.

The beginnings in the 1920s and 1930s

In the days when large ocean liners traveled from port to port throughout the world, swinging bands serenaded passengers on board. In Asia, musicians from the Philippines were famed for their musical skills, and they helped transport the new style of jazz worldwide. What was famous in New York City or London or Shanghai was just as famous in Yokohama or Kobe, at least among the well-off and trendy in those far-flung cultural hubs. Jazz served as the music of the times and was played everywhere that wealthy cosmopolitan dancers, music-lovers, or nightclub habitues congregated or traveled by ship.

The first Japanese jazz recording is often attributed to the Nitto Jass Band. Recorded in 1925, it was called "Walla Walla" and sounds much like American recordings of early jazz at the time. (You can listen here: https://www.youtube.com/watch?v=j3nfSGMCKsI). It sounds very much like recordings in the US, and the singing is in English. As in many places in America, especially New Orleans, Japanese bands at the time had busy schedules. They would play in the newly built fashionable department stores during the day, then move to tea parties in the afternoons and dances in the evening. They played various music, but jazz venues allowed them to play more freely and freshen up standards when the audience was right.

Jazz mainly took root in port cities like Kobe and Yokohama, but gradually, the mercantile center of Osaka, and later the capitol city, Tokyo, started to embrace whatever was new and exciting. Through the 1920s and 1930s, young people, *mo-ga* modern girls in bob cuts and heels and *mo-bo* modern boys in dandified outfits searched for a more international and cosmopolitan lifestyle. The arrival of jazz imported not only new music but also a set of cultural values that challenged traditional values and musical traditions. Jazz was exciting, new, and modern.

One *New York Times* correspondent who reported on traveling the "jazz latitude" around the world in 1922 described the jazz played on board and in port cities such as Honolulu, Yokohama, Kobe, Shanghai, Hong Kong, Manila, Singapore, Nice, Monte Carlo, London, and of course, New York City. Jazz was the music for that era's cosmopolitan culture, as global trends, fashions, music, and cuisine spread worldwide, at least at a certain level of affluence. But more than in many cities, jazz continued to thrive in Japan.

The war years, the late 1930s to 1940s

The only hiatus in jazz's tenure in Japan was during the Second World War. As Japan ramped up its control over the Pacific region and increased control at home in Japan, military authorities started to shut down all forms of cultural expression and institute strict regulations on public and private behavior.

Dance halls, where jazz was played around the clock through the 1930s, were shuttered. Anything with Western influence, whether music, fashion, leisure, or literature, was increasingly censored. Even the *jazz kissaten* that sprang up alongside the dance halls fell under surveillance by military authorities as potential breeding grounds of dissent. By the mid-1940s, when World War II was at its worst, jazz was completely banned as a subversive Western influence.

After the war, the late 1940s and 1950s

That ban on jazz was swept aside when American forces invaded Japan and occupied the country. With the Occupation of Japan by the American military from 1945 to 1952, jazz, and indeed all things American, created a fervor with Japanese ready to move past the tragedies of the war years. All aspects of Japan were upended, and considerable social conflict ensued as Japan started to search for new forms of society, daily life, leisure time, and culture, not to mention government.

The post-war excitement for change created a demand for new forms of entertainment. Much of it was Americanized. Sports such as baseball, cinema, and music again flooded into Japan, particularly from the United States. Government, laws, rights, and social values were changing. Jazz had never really left, but interest in it re-emerged from the war years with special fervor.

Pianist Toshiko Akiyoshi, who got her start then and went on to lead her famed big band in the US and Japan, noted that there were three kinds of dance halls at that time: for American officers, for American enlisted men, and for Japanese. In an interview, she said she preferred the officers' clubs because there were fewer fights.

Japanese musicians who could play the hard-driving swing music of the time for dancers and listeners in those clubs were in demand. Jazz was entertainment more than an art form and was fanatically loved. Most Japanese musicians of the time tried to emulate American musicians, like Fumio Nanri, "the Japanese Louis Armstrong." Jazz was emulated. Gradually, though, Japanese musicians developed their own voice and way of playing, internalizing and mastering the complex musical practices of jazz.

Though many jazz musicians were among the American servicemen, Japanese jazz players primarily learned jazz through recordings. They couldn't afford records, much less expensive stereo equipment, so they convened at coffee shops where they could smoke, drink coffee, request songs, and exchange knowledge.

Servicemen who went to the jazz coffee shops facilitated the import of vinyl records. Though restrictions remained on films, magazines, and newspapers through the American military board of censorship, the authorities generally gave jazz a free pass.

Because of Japan's generally tight quarters and close living arrangements, playing loud music in apartment buildings or neighborhoods was not an option. Inside the sacred space of the jazz kissaten, though, they could listen freely.

Alienation and free jazz in the 1960s

From the post-war period through the 1970s, Japan was a regular stop on the international jazz circuit. All the great musicians of that golden era came through Japan. One need no more evidence of that than the walls and photo books that adorn the jazz kissaten, Dug, in Shinjuku.

Dug owner and photographer Hozumi Nakadaira befriended and took photos of the greats, who often played in his kissaten/club. John Coltrane made a famed trip in 1966, while musicians like Miles Davis, Cannonball Adderly, and Art Blakey, among many others, toured regularly.

Shinjuku and Shibuya became centers for young people eager to hear new, challenging sounds in music and who could afford the price of a drink to listen to it. Film directors, most notably Koreyoshi Kurahara, featured jazz soundtracks for his tales of youthful rebellion and social malaise. Kurahara used jazz kissa in the Shibuya area of Tokyo as settings for several of his films, including *Black Sun* (Kurahara 1964) and *The Warped Ones* (Kurahara 1960). Jazz, especially free jazz, began to be associated with youthful attitudes of rebellion and escape from the increasing strictures of Japanese society.

As Japan became increasingly business-minded and conformist, many young people started to protest, as they did around the world in the 1960s. College students barricaded themselves inside campuses to protest the government, the economy, the school system, and the control of everyday life. In particular, they were against the revision of the agreement allowing American bases to remain in Japan (in 1960) and the government's support for the Vietnam War (in 1968). Jazz kissaten and clubs became spaces where the music was not just for fun, but part of a revolutionary mindset.

As elsewhere worldwide, jazz became divided between progressive free jazz and old-style jazz as entertainment. However, both thrived in Japan as the country's economy and standing developed rapidly. Free jazz and free improvisation influenced jazz playing as more people became interested in jazz as a distinctly different form of music from the burgeoning world of pop, folk, and rock music. By this time, jazz had settled in as an essential cultural form, or rather forms, since diversity of expression became a large part of how musicians and fans started thinking of the music.

Jazz also became part of Japanese nightlife. As rock and pop took over as dance music and Japan's economy started to take off, jazz became music to contemplate at a more profound level. It became an object of study and veneration for dedicated fans who bought records, magazines, and concert tickets. Many of the best-known jazz spaces, like Dug, Eagle, or Airegin, got their start at the end of the 1960s and are still in business today.

The 1980s bubble years

When Japan's economy moved into the so-called bubble years of the 1980s, jazz clubs were often a place for socializing in the evenings. With land prices and the stock market soaring, company expense accounts were generous, and *salarymen* used them for entertaining clients, often lavishly.

Living here and going to hear jazz in the late 1980s, I was always a bit startled by salarymen spending their evenings at jazz clubs. Drinks flowed freely, and that was after dinner and before more drinks before catching the last train home. Jazz clubs proliferated, with many offering a "bottle keep" system, where customers could buy a bottle of whiskey from the club, write their name on it, and then buy ice and mixers each time they came. That kept customers coming back and kept the jazz clubs full. (I used to keep a bottle of vodka at Dug and Sometime. I thought I'd arrived.)

During those years, jazz magazines had tremendous circulation. Jazz festivals sold out, and touring jazz bands filled large halls and auditoriums. Jazz was a sophisticated pastime for those with enough cash, education, and interest.

At the same time, many jazz musicians started traveling abroad. Toshiko Akiyoshi had already studied at Berklee College of Music, and many others, like Sadao Watanabe, followed her to study and soak up the music by playing wherever they could with American jazz groups.

At the same time, jazz education expanded inside Japan. Senzoku College of Music established a full jazz course in 1996, with sister school status to Berklee College in Boston. Many of the traditional classical conservatories in Japan added jazz courses as well. Schools such as Shobi Music University, Kunitachi College of Music, Showa University of Music, and Koyo Conservatory in Kobe have become well-known for their full-fledged jazz programs.

In addition to these larger schools, smaller *senmon gakko*, specialty schools, for jazz and music in general, became popular with young people. Professional jazz musicians gave lessons to aspiring young musicians at these schools.

Importing jazz from abroad became much easier, and jazz records, CDs, and instruction books were easier to acquire.

According to The Asahi Shimbun, Swing Journal had a circulation of 300,000 at its peak around 2000. The 70,000 readers of Jazz Hihyo and 100,000 readers of Jazz Life were likely the same people. However, those major jazz magazines folded after the arrival of the internet and online radio stations.

Those magazines and many others aimed at studying how to play better jazz formed a continuous force for numerous aspects of jazz. The magazines had a profound effect with articles of criticism, reviews, interviews, and how-tos.

However, when the bubble collapsed in the early 1990s, such profligate spending ended, and many clubs suffered or closed. This also changed the kind of music they offered. Instead of catering to businesspeople, they started catering to fans who came more for the music. More clubs opened near smaller stations, providing a neighborhood listening spot for people living nearby.

The musicians who came back from abroad no longer wanted to imitate Western approaches, but instead developed their own way of playing jazz based on their own experience, interests, and points of view. Through the 1990s and 2000s, the jazz scene broadened and deepened.

The large clubs remained, but many smaller clubs closed. However, a surprising number remained. New ones opened with modernized sound systems, upmarket service, and as much devotion to jazz as ever.

Nowadays, well over 100 clubs play live jazz nightly in Tokyo and Yokohama, along with those in the surrounding prefectures of Chiba and Saitama. While the number of people in the larger metropolitan area is huge, the number of clubs is an impressive testament to how much jazz is loved in Japan. Most of those clubs offer live music nightly. Outside Tokyo and Yokohama, every large city has a jazz club, multiple jazz coffee shops, schools, amateur bands, and record stores. It's easy to lament the closures, but the opening of new clubs shows the demand still exists.

This brief historical overview leaves out a lot, but it shows the staying power of jazz over the past century. Jazz has remained a dynamic art form widely present in Japan. Even with the devastating effect of the COVID-19 pandemic, it has continued, showing no sign of fading away anytime soon.

The other articles in this section detail why jazz has remained popular in Japan. They also examine the process of cultural integration and explain why and how jazz fits into Japanese culture.

How jazz fits Japanese culture

Jazz's roots in the African-American experience and culture seem an unlikely transplant into Japan's long history and complex culture. It's confusing how a spontaneously creative, freedom-loving art form fits so well into a culture with relatively formalized patterns of interaction and rigid social hierarchies.

But on the other hand, what better place?

Still, it's surprising that one of the most potent and expressive African-American cultural art forms, combined with European musical elements, could find such a welcome home in a traditional social structure. Jazz met welcoming traditions, values, attitudes, and needs in Japan.

So, is jazz like film or baseball, two other successful imports from the West? No one would consider Japanese film to be different from other film traditions, though its characteristics feel distinctly different from classic Hollywood or French new wave cinema.

Or, could jazz be considered an artistic set of techniques that can be used to express any feeling, theme, or story (if one gets good enough)? Or does jazz contain specific, inviolable rules and a depth of localized experience that doesn't transplant?

Is jazz open to innovation in new hands from new places? Or can it only be copied? Is it a culturally dependent set of patterns, or can it adapt to a different cultural soil? Is jazz's adaptation to Japan—and vice versa—a happy accident? Or does it reveal the universal human qualities of the music itself?

In this essay, I'll try to give some broad thoughts on how and why jazz continues to flourish in Japan and what welcoming factors might be involved. The fact that jazz thrives in Japan reveals a lot about Japan and a lot about jazz.

Virtuosity and craft

First, Japanese culture has long valued three of the essentials of jazz—virtuosity, authenticity, and spontaneity. Let me take each of those in turn. They are indigenous elements that have helped smooth the import and growth of jazz in Japan.

The high level of control and craft necessary to perform jazz is part of the striving for perfection inherent to Japanese culture. In Japan, virtuoso performance is rooted in the master-pupil tradition of arts and crafts such as sword-making, pottery, sushi, kabuki, painting, and architecture. Jazz has a master pupil system too, with critics, if not musicians, noting lineages and examining who influenced who.

While Western jazz tends to reject strict hierarchies and exact influences, in Japan, discipleship is often a source of pride. For most jazz musicians in both cultures, a certain period of apprenticeship or discipleship is essential to obtain the high level of skill needed to play the music and express oneself individually. The respect for virtuosity makes the transition from jazz in America to jazz in Japan much smoother.

Japan's tradition of arts and crafts places a similar importance on technique, skill, and control over tools—or instruments—as jazz does. It takes years to learn the skill of jazz, just as it does that of pottery or swordmaking. Japanese culture's high valuation of attention to detail is also integral to jazz practice. The long hours of honing technique needed to play jazz are just as essential when learning traditional Japanese art forms.

I don't mean to suggest that sword-makers are abandoning their craft and turning to jazz. Instead, the framework for acquiring a high level of performance and the mindset of working towards the perfection of craft are already well established. Those conditions welcome jazz.

Authenticity and personal voice

One key element of jazz culture is a deep respect for authenticity and individual expression. All jazz players strive to develop their sound, which may be derived from tradition and the jazz masters. Jazz musicians want to sound like themselves. Japan is often accused of being a culture of imitation, but individuality is highly regarded at the highest levels of art.

One of the tensions in jazz that make it so fascinating is that a deep immersion into tradition allows one to be free of that tradition by evolving a personal style and an individual approach. While commercial music mimicking other countries' trends and styles is pervasive in Japan, the value of authentic self-expression persists in art, fashion, film, and literature. Jazz places special emphasis on authentic expression, and so do serious Japanese cultural forms.

Indeed, Japan's jazz scene was inspired by America and historically involved adulation of the West, especially of America during the American Occupation after World War II. But even then, it was the authentic, original voices of so many jazz greats that were influential. More interestingly, perhaps, African-American musicians were being idolized, not the entire American society or culture.

When I first started listening to Japanese jazz, I did compare musicians here to those I'd heard in America. I needed to place new music in terms of what I knew. After years of listening, I realized that Japanese musicians strive for a unique voice, just as jazz musicians do everywhere. Developing a singular voice depends on acquiring experience, understanding, and plenty of practice. That seems universally understood.

Spontaneity and improvisation

Overall, Japan is not a place that values great variation in expression or interaction in daily life or the working world. Yet, when everyday interactions conform to expected patterns, the rigidity of Japanese daily life pushes many people to break away from those pre-set forms. Improvisation is all the more highly valued because it is so rare.

Jazz offers the breaking of bound energy in beautiful ways. It's not the drunken complaining type of catharsis, a stereotype of Japanese salaryman culture, but rather, jazz offers a controlled catharsis. Like many artistic experiences, live jazz involves an engagement that restores and rehumanizes the individual. Jazz provides a way to incorporate spontaneity into art, experience it as a listener, and perform it as a musician. Because of jazz's unique way of achieving that experience, jazz helps revalue and reemphasize the importance of spontaneity in human life, where it is often in short supply.

That sounds similar to Zen Buddhism, one of Japan's most enduring and unique contributions to world culture. Zen's silent meditation and stillness may seem very different from jazz's audible, dynamic expression, but they often aim for the same thing—natural spontaneity. Ironically, spontaneity does not come from discarding all rules, restrictions, and structures. Instead, it comes from having internalized the rules and structures thoroughly enough to transcend them—in both jazz and Zen.

Counterparts to America's jazz culture and practice exist in Japan, though they may appear as oppositions or tensions that set up a dynamic, not a simple one-way reaction. I'd argue that the underlying dynamics of Japanese culture, usually unspoken or unnoticed, serve as fertile ground for jazz to flourish. Let me point out what a few more of those dynamics involve.

Group thinking

Like other Asian cultures, Japanese culture is said to be group-focused. In my experience, consensus is crucial, and awareness of others is highly valued. This often slows down meetings or negotiations and makes conformity to the group the easy way out. However, it also builds resentment against group pressures.

Other people are noticed and considered, often too much so, whether in a working group or public spaces. This feeling for others in the group comes from early training in Japanese schools and runs through intense company training in the first years of employment. Meetings are often less about solving tasks and more about establishing harmony.

Strangely, harmony sounds like the interactive dynamics of the best jazz groups. Jazz is primarily a group activity demanding close interaction between individuals. The best jazz groups have always had a kind of extrasensory perception, as in Miles Davis' album title, "E.S.P." The intensity of jazz group interaction fits well with the psychosocial experience of Japanese group thinking and sensitivity to others.

In Japan and in jazz, individualism is primarily expressed as a member of a group. Of course, there are solo recordings in jazz and loners in Japanese society, but when playing in a group, jazz solos arise with help from what others are playing. The individual can shine with the support of the group. That way of thinking is common in Japanese society.

Rebellion and counterculture flair

Though group thinking is the default mode of Japanese society, rebellion against conformity is also part of Japanese psychology. The pressure to conform in Japan is very powerful. The middle-class values of maintaining a secure job, family, home, and way of life hold sway over most Japanese.

However, many Japanese rebel against or avoid the pressures of those expectations through their hobbies. Jazz is one of those outside pursuits, one that often rises to the level of obsession.

Japanese consumer culture powerfully promotes the latest trend, style, band, concoction, or catchphrase. When I teach music, students always ask, "Is he or she famous?" Fame and mass approval become the mark of acceptability. J-pop boy bands and girl groups are everywhere—on billboards, TV shows, advertisements, and store racks. You can't escape them.

But many people *want to* escape them—and do. Far from the reach of corporations, Tokyo and Yokohama have thriving club scenes with live music of all kinds. Young people distribute self-made recordings, swap indie styles, and keep music alive by word of mouth. That applies to jazz just as much as to other genres.

In personal life, dropping out of the corporate lifestyle or the dominant consumer culture is an enormous leap for most Japanese. If you drop out, you can't go back. But for an evening, the pressures of the corporate and consumer world are lessened or forgotten in jazz clubs, jazz coffee shops, and in the music itself. New sounds, improvised activity, and sensory pleasure take over.

Jazz is a sophisticated pleasure, engaging enough to keep the mind going while letting the mind unwind. It's counter-culture and subculture, more like reading a controversial book than getting your nose pierced. It's not that jazz is conservative or fits a conservative lifestyle, but instead that it offers a respectable escape. A counter-culture vibe is part of jazz and gives it high social value. So, jazz carries social cache and respect. My students call it "adult music."

Even when jazz doesn't serve rebellious purposes, it rejects mass consumer culture. Jazz values quality over quantity. While Japanese consumers are often pushovers for corporate products, a large percentage are savvy consumers with highly developed tastes. Jazz is one of those.

In the oversized, alienating, and commercial spaces of Japan's giant cities, jazz clubs provide small pockets of intensely human focus where creativity is on display, far from the dictates of the workplace or trendy consumerism. If jazz weren't here in Japan, you'd have to invent it.

Urban Music

Jazz also fits into Japanese culture because of its urban nature. Jazz is city music, and one thing Japan has is cities. Japan's urban spaces are large and expansive enough to support multiple subcultures.

Jazz fits into the vast cosmopolis of the greater Tokyo area and other large cities not just because urban areas are large enough to support many different kinds of countercultures, but because urban cultures involve a degree of complexity and literacy. Jazz can be a hobby, a lifetime passion, a leisure pursuit, but a complicated one. Its very complexity is part of the appeal. The Japanese populace is highly literate, not only in terms of the written word but also about food, art, and music. At one point, it was claimed that Japan had the largest number of symphony orchestras of any country. I believe it.

Like America and Europe, Japan has a tradition of Bohemian counter-culture linked to jazz. The specific patterns and values might differ, but the straight life and *mizu shobai*, the floating world of night entertainment, is just as big a contrast in Japan as in America or Europe, and perhaps even greater. Moving between the Bohemian night world and the "straight life" daytime world has always been common in Japan. Jazz is night-time urban music.

Jazz involves a degree of *otaku* (slightly obsessive) behavior too. Jazz fanatics delve into details, collect autographed CDs, line their homes with vinyl records, frame memorabilia, and argue on internet message boards. For many fans, jazz is an urban obsession with romanticized allusions and multiple meanings. That doesn't mean their interest is superficial. Just the opposite, Japanese jazz fans are some of the most knowledgeable and sophisticated in the world. The jazz world becomes a place to escape even while the day job remains a grind, but it also is an escape that is melded into the urban culture.

Zen and Shinto

Jazz also neatly fits into two threads of traditional Japanese culture—the Zen side and the Shinto side. These two religious and cultural traditions can be seen in many different aspects of Japanese culture. Zen aesthetics are sleek, serene, and minimalist. Shinto aesthetics are rootsy, wild, and raucous. The bare quiet of a rock garden is Zen. Shouldering a portable "mikoshi" shrine through the streets with drunken, barefoot neighbors is Shinto.

Jazz culture has both the bluesy side of Mingus's "Better Get Hit in Your Soul" and the refined side of Miles's "Blue in Green." Japan has cerebral and refined aesthetics as well as corporal and explosive aesthetics, which correspond roughly to the contrasting Zen and Shinto aesthetics.

In that sense, jazz's continuums find an analogy in Japan's continuums. When jazz expresses a search for the ultimate minimal configuration, the simplest modal structure or pedal point, it fits neatly into Japan's Zen taste. And when jazz cuts loose into free jazz or a looser, wilder way of creating musical energy, Japan's Shinto side emerges.

Cultural parallels can always be found between cultures, but religious patterns and practices are ingrained in Japanese society. With jazz, the cultural universals have neatly synced to create synergy. Once jazz established itself, like many cultural memes, it persisted and was passed on from generation to generation.

Global thinking and democracy

Japanese culture is deeply conservative. It preserves attitudes, practices, values, and structures and keeps them viable for much longer than most other cultures. However, the conservative, traditional mindset is balanced by the openness, adaptability, and receptivity of an internationalized city life. In other words, Japan is flexible enough to accept one of the most flexible styles of music.

Although the Japanese are often considered inward-looking, their interest in jazz reflects a global mindset. Jazz has become arguably the most international music, so when Japanese listeners hear it, they express their outward-looking side. While jazz fits into traditional Japanese categories, jazz provides a contrast, an escape, and an answer to the conservative elements in Japanese life. It is different and appealing for that reason.

The interdependence and respect between musicians within a group express a basic urge toward equality and fairness, both in the group and in the quality of playing. In jazz, if you're good, you're good. It doesn't matter where you are in the social hierarchy, jazz erases the hierarchy and creates a new one based on ability, taste, creative power, and artistic expression. Despite ongoing authoritarian tendencies in politics and pockets of society, most Japanese accept democratic values and put those into practice—nowhere better than in jazz.

I've used broad strokes in this essay, but after listening to Japanese jazz for several decades, I've kept wondering why and how jazz has carved out such a significant niche in Japan. While some clubs and jazz kissaten have closed, new clubs, bigger vinyl stores, local festivals, jazz schools, background music, and younger fans keep appearing.

There is much more to say on this cross-cultural analysis, but all this musing shouldn't distract from the music. I hope it enhances appreciation of jazz in Japan and gives a framework for experiencing it more deeply. The ideas outlined above offer ways to consider the surprising persistence of jazz in Japan. It's certainly lured me in. I didn't come to Japan for the jazz, but it's undoubtedly one of the reasons I have stayed.

The Process of Cultural Integration

Introduction

The jazz scene in Japan is a notable example of the complex blending of cultural values across widely different traditions, contexts, and conditions. The arrival of jazz in Japan, at several stages in the 20th century, entailed an integration of widely divergent approaches in conceptions of music's inherent characteristics, expectations about performance, and social attitudes towards music. Jazz spread throughout Japan, as it did around much of the world, most noticeably in the 1920s and 1930s when modernism was recreating cultural expression of all kinds and urban cosmopolitanism spread worldwide.

That movement of jazz continues today, though much of the cultural circulation is hidden away, unstudied, and unconsidered. In the otherwise interesting book by Stuart Nicholson, *Is Jazz Dead? Or has it Moved to a New Address?*, Japan barely gets a mention (Nicholson 2005). However, Japan has consistently been one of the main scenes outside of the United States for the promulgation and performance of jazz. Now, too, Japan is a place for preserving jazz as a living, breathing nightly experience. Hundreds of jazz clubs dot Japanese cities and continue to provide a place for jazz to be heard alive and well.

Jazz took root in large, quickly expanding cities throughout Asia, but mainly in port towns such as Shanghai and Hong Kong, where large ships could dock. Those passenger ships featured jazz onboard and were instrumental in helping to spread jazz across the world and making jazz part of the burgeoning entertainment industry. In the colonial-structured cities on the circuit of travel through Asia, such as Singapore or Hong Kong, jazz was *the* music of those entertainment centers until the Second World War constrained recreational travel.

In Bangkok, the King of Thailand began to play jazz trumpet, became highly accomplished, and helped promote jazz throughout Thailand and Southeast Asia. He composed many jazz pieces, performed widely, and encouraged music study with programs, grants, and live performances with touring musicians. In the Philippines, especially in Manila, the long tradition of live music easily merged with the influence of jazz as America annexed the islands. Jazz gained popularity again after World War Two throughout most cosmopolitan areas in Asia.

This spread of jazz through diverse cultures means that jazz in Asia can be explained by examining many interlocking factors. It is important to examine the "power dynamics attending any particular combination of cultural forms," as Charles Hersch argues in his interesting study of early jazz, *Subversive Sounds* (2007). More revealing and appropriate to the complex dynamics of jazz, though, is to examine jazz in Asia through the practices and attitudes of jazz musicians themselves. The power dynamics influence the performance and conception of jazz in any context. Still, those influences become subtle and obscure once inside Japanese culture, mainly because of Japan's long tradition of craft-based cultural forms and highly structured social hierarchies. The historical and political relations with America further complicate the issue.

Jazz in Asia in general, and in Japan in particular, can be fruitfully examined by looking at several key features of jazz: the demands of playing the music, the conceptual changes the music entails, and the challenge of integrating the music inside a different cultural context from America.

Japanese challenges

Tokyo, Yokohama, and Kobe were Japan's leading centers for jazz before and after the war. Those cities were already at the forefront of social changes, with cosmopolitan lifestyles that embraced whatever was new and exciting. Those three port cities were open to importing products, practices, and cultural forms of all kinds.

The arrival of jazz imported a different set of cultural values that confronted pre-existing values far beyond the confines of musical tradition and liberated and expanded others that might have remained dormant. As in most places, jazz was translated into Japanese culture through complex negotiations and adaptations. The first focus of this paper will be on how jazz projected and promoted international, cosmopolitan values, and very complex ones. The explanations here draw on E. Taylor Atkins' seminal *Blue Nippon* but diverge from his framework in many details (Atkins 2001). That cultural adaptation started in the 1930s but expanded when Japan was under the occupation of America. Jazz was quickly associated with non-traditional values and alternative lifestyles that emerged in Japanese culture after World War Two. During the American occupation of Japan and through the 1960s, jazz could be considered an importation of a foreign practice, one with great appeal.

But, the second focus of this paper will be on the next stage of the process, which took place with the second generation of jazz musicians who emerged in the late 1990s and early 2000s. Bringing jazz thoroughly into Japanese culture took much longer than an examination of the post-war era alone could reveal. The second wave of establishing jazz in Japan started in the 1990s and continues to the present. In Japan, it took time to absorb the skill of improvisation and intra-group interaction. Still, this internalization was just as important, and even more so than the first importation of cultural values and jazz practices.

So, the second part of this paper will examine how the concepts of improvisation and interaction of jazz became a new form of artistic and cultural practice more fully rooted in the Japanese experience starting roughly around 2000. This section will argue that the integration of jazz improvising and group interacting took longer than the importation of cultural values in the post-war era.

In this paper, I'll focus on two different moments in the history of jazz in Japan: the 1950s, when jazz's cultural values began to spread, and the present moment, meaning the last ten to twenty years, when jazz can be seen as embedded in Japanese culture as a common cultural practice.

The *longue durée*, as historians from the French Annalists School would term this approach, is one helpful way to examine how jazz entered, spread, and took root in Japan. It also helps to consider and clarify how new meanings were attached to jazz in Japanese culture and how new practices became accepted. The interplay between the technical demands of playing the music and the reception of the music into cultural categories created a unique dynamism that is both an integration and disruption of cultural attitudes and musical practices.

1950s Japan imports a culture

The generation of Japanese jazz musicians after the war was noted for high-level technique, ability to emulate American players, a sense of jazz as entertainment, and individualized expression. Musicians were often called "the Japanese Louis Armstrong" or "the Japanese Coleman Hawkins." That habit has long since disappeared, but it was part of bringing in cultural attitudes as much as trying to copy a particular style or method of playing. It was also a way of keeping the culture outside the authentic Japanese culture and presenting the music as less threatening to traditional cultural values. Jazz was present, even adored, but not yet fully internalized.

At that time, Japanese musicians learned to play jazz by listening to records, imitating the jazz musicians who came through Japan on tours, and playing with the bands formed by servicemen in the occupying forces. Japanese musicians from that generation learned to play from recorded music at "jazz kissaten," or jazz coffee shops. These coffee shops were instrumental in establishing jazz in Japan. One of the oldest, *Chigusa*, in Yokohama, opened in 1934.

Several of Japan's most famous jazz performers, notably Toshiko Akiyoshi and Sadao Watanabe, heard the latest Bud Powell or Charlie Parker recordings in Chigusa's tiny space in the post-war years. In an interview, Toshiko Akiyoshi said:

I was so interested in everyone's playing, and the only way to learn was to listen to records. I used to go to copy the records in those jazz coffee shops. Those were very important places to learn new tunes. Chigusa is still there in Yokohama, and there was another one in Yurakucho called Combo. They had many records. If I asked the owner to play that particular little bit again, he would pick the needle up and drop it there again. So, on some LPs, that particular little place on the record would get worn out. That was a very important place for me. (Akiyoshi 2005)

Other *jazz kissaten* drew steady clientele of fans and musicians. The excellent Down Beat opened in 1956 in Yokohama and still stocks over three thousand LPs, plus CDs. The walls are plastered with smoke-stained back issues of the jazz magazine, Down Beat, and this "jazz kissaten" continues to perform its function of providing a relaxed and comfortable place to sink into the analog vinyl sounds of jazz on a top-quality sound system, even though musicians no longer go there to learn how to play.

During the Occupation, Yokohama's pride in being the most progressive city in Japan was affirmed through jazz. Jazz became symbolic of issues related to a newly evolving sense of national identity. At the same time, the post-war obsession with American culture in general broke up the power of traditional Japanese cultural values and practices, supplanting them with concepts of freedom, self-expression, and equality imported from American culture. Yokohama was also closer to many of the American military bases.

According to Atkins, the post-war years in Yokohama were crucial to developing the democratic attitudes and improvisatory skills that bebop, in particular, demands. By email, he commented:

This period was absolutely pivotal for Japanese jazz musicians. There seemed to be a greater concentration of clubs catering to African-American G.I.s than elsewhere, and thus Japanese who leaned more toward bebop than swing and dance music seem to have gravitated to Yokohama. (Atkins 2007)

Jazz was at that time two slightly different things: a dance music that could earn musicians a livelihood playing in clubs and a means of asserting their individuality in a very distinct art form from those of traditional Japan. In some sense, the Japanese musicians who emerged with their own style and approach to jazz at that time were considered culture heroes. They were instrumental in changing the attitude towards music, both in how it was played and how it was received. Musicians such as Sadao Watanabe (born 1933), Terumasa Hino (born 1942), and Toshiko Akiyoshi (born 1929) brought jazz fully into Japanese culture.

As "culture heroes," Japanese jazz musicians had a ready and willing audience for the values and practices they began to master. Japan was largely receptive to the import of cultural values after the devastation of the war. Everything about jazz was different from the traditional values of Japanese culture, such as respect for authority, duty to country, social harmony, and positioned hierarchy. Many Japanese believed an over-emphasis on these values led to the war. These values were particularly rejected by many artists at the time, as well as by large parts of Japanese society that were intent on rebuilding the country into a democracy. Jazz was one of the most positive assertions of anti-traditional values. Jazz was linked to the attitude of internationalism and served as part of the ongoing criticism of militaristic, Japan-centric values that had dominated during the war years.

At the time, it must have seemed easier to set aside the Japanese values that had led to war and instead import American cultural values wholesale. So, it was not until the late 1970s and early 1980s that Japanese musicians started exploring their Japanese roots and finding ways to blend traditional Japanese music with jazz. That includes not just using Japanese melodies but finding a feeling for the music that is both Asian and Western at the same time. Yosuke Yamashita (born 1942) is one musician, and one of the first, to include Japanese elements into his music. He has worked with traditional *taiko* Japanese drummers and musicians trained only in traditional Japanese music. When asked why he so often includes Japanese melodies and feeling into his works, he said, "Yes, why is that? I'm not sure exactly. Jazz is an American music, but I'm not a Japanese who wants to become an American. I always feel like a Japanese" (Yamashita 2005). Yamashita explained how he originally studied Western classical music but continued to find ways to bring jazz together with Western classical and Japanese music. His search was less to find the right mix for his music than to find the best ways of making his vision of jazz as rich and complex as possible.

Yamashita's attitude and approach, which were widely shared by other musicians, marked the beginning of the fuller integration of jazz into Japan. They were no longer copying and importing wholesale but using jazz to think. Mixing diverse musical forms was a way of creating and improvising, which reveals a deeper internalization of jazz concepts and practice. Even with open-minded and jazz-savvy musicians like Yamashita, it took longer for a fuller integration of jazz values to take place more broadly. Yamashita's 1990 recording, *Sakura*, is an excellent, early example of how internalizing jazz practice and values could lead to a fuller integration with Japanese musical culture (Yamashita 1990). Still, it took another decade or two for such approaches to become more common in Japan.

Following the war, through the 1960s, jazz was considered wild, rebellious, and freeing, an attitude similar to its reception in many countries. It was also an escape from the ennui of the time and an escape from the traditional values that began to reassert themselves after the occupation finished. Japanese society, politics, culture, and economics gradually became more independent from American influence. Jazz was an embrace of "western-ness" and a refusal to be Japanese in the traditional sense of conforming to pre-set values. At the very least, jazz allowed a setting aside of Japanese-ness to pursue another set of norms and goals and to bring those norms, practices, and attitudes into Japanese thinking.

That sense of jazz being an alternative pathway, of stepping outside the more conformist approach to life, is still the same now. Current alto sax player Seiji Tada, one of the leading jazz players in Tokyo, described his break from a typical life to becoming a musician this way.

I always played since college, but in 1988, I came to Tokyo. Before that time, I had been a banker. I quit after five years. I went to an economics university and after graduation, worked at one bank for the whole time. During that time, as an amateur, I played at live houses once a week or so, but not professionally. When I turned pro, it was extremely difficult to quit a good, respectable job. My parents were totally opposed to it. And we fought about it. Fiercely. But I had decided, so I was determined to leave. (Tada 2007)

Such artistic conflicts are universal, of course, but became aggravated in the 1960s as Japan's economy took off based on conservative corporate principles, and the corporate culture of large companies became a dominant ideology and lifestyle.

In the 1950s and 1960s Japanese culture, jazz served as a way to express individuality, adopt cultural values such as self-interested freedom, and to put distance between oneself and the conformist patterns of Japanese society.

Improvisation and interaction

However, the younger generation of jazz musicians is quite different from that first post-war generation. They tend to focus more highly on improvisation as a practice and group interaction as a core value. Having a strong, dominant group leader became less critical. The younger players have grown up focused on jazz as a potential, if not easy, career choice. That choice increased with the Senzoku Gakuen College of Jazz, which started a major in jazz music in 1996 and then established an exchange program with the Berklee College of Music in Boston.

Jazz programs at conservatories and private schools of music have continued to expand. Professional jazz musicians in Japan consider teaching jazz not just a way of paying the bills but a way of continuing and strengthening jazz culture. The jazz scene has also continued to expand so that younger musicians can easily find jam sessions to practice, amateur gigs, and plenty of big bands to hone their skills. Universities have jazz "circles," extracurricular groups who invite their alumni-turned-pros to teach and mentor.

Mostly, though, there is a shift in attitude to the importance of developing skill at improvising while remaining carefully and meaningfully integrated into the group. Long, selfish solos are out; jazz as a conversation is in. Jazz textbooks imported from Berklee and other American schools, many of which are translated to Japanese, have also influenced the way of teaching and learning jazz. An entire curriculum has been developed for learning jazz inside Japan based partly on those imported books, techniques, and practice methods. Many jazz musicians who come to Japan to play also run workshops and master classes.

But at the same time, a broader view of how to create improvised music has taken hold. Many of the top jazz musicians in Tokyo and Yokohama who teach have developed varied approaches to getting students to enter the mindset needed for good improvisation. Seiji Tada, who teaches and mentors many younger musicians, explained his advice for younger musicians this way:

Students always say, "Can you please give me some advice?" That's really hard, but the thing I usually say is to just relax more. They often ask me about their sound, too. "How was my tone?" is a common question. Or, they ask, "Was I swinging?" At the jam sessions, there are some pros, but you also have students, amateurs, and all levels of musicians. You have really skilled people and some who have not developed so far yet. Every different level of playing has its own problems and its own set of worries. So, really, that's why I almost always say, "Just relax." (Tada 2007).

Relaxing may be easier said than done since degrees of relaxation and tension are highly determined by culture. Japan's culture expects more tension, both physical and mental, in public. America, especially for jazz, tends to be the opposite.

Other musician/teachers note that they have to get students to learn more about culture, film, art, poetry and other forms of expression, and to understand how art forms and cultural expressions interconnect and mutually influence each other. Perhaps most relevant is the tendency to see jazz improvisation as a craft and skill that must be learned from a master, practiced over years during an apprenticeship period, and taken in as a set of physical, body-based activities, much like the older traditions in Japan of learning pottery, sword-making or any of another series of traditional crafts. The broader view among younger musicians in the last fifteen years or so is that they must develop themselves as artists with a broad view of life if their technique is genuinely going to be useful.

That is, jazz improvisation takes on much of the traditional approach to developing skills that have long been part of Japanese culture. Jazz education is also positioned inside a broad range of attitudes, understandings, and personal attributes. The tradition of craft apprenticeship and mastery in Japan has remained surprisingly vital. The way of handing down traditional techniques from generation to generation adapts easily to the world of jazz. Ironically, then, Japan's conservative cultural practices become redirected towards a countervailing form of imported cultural practice – jazz improvisation. It becomes a way of meditating, focusing, and breaking free, but also of acquiring a set number of specific, detailed performance practices that encourage improvised expression.

However, it is important to note that traditional learning of craft in Japan also focuses on the broader development of the self. One could not just acquire pottery techniques; one had to become a potter. The same applies to jazz. Technique must be acquired through study with a master, but a jazz musician's existential, ethical, individual, and spiritual development is now considered just as essential. That shift from acquiring technique to becoming a jazz musician in a more holistic sense is evidence that jazz has integrated into Japanese culture much more deeply and permanently than in the 1960s.

While improvisation is the most challenging element all aspiring jazz musicians need to learn, equally important is the ability to interact well with different jazz groups. The Japanese jazz scene encourages and facilitates the development of the skill of interactive give-and-take on the bandstand in many ways. The post-war generation may have learned jazz by listening to records. Still, the current generation has learned it by sitting in with a variety of different groups and learning by playing. The number of jam sessions at the amateur level has continued to be an essential part of the jazz scene in Tokyo and Yokohama. Many clubs, such as Naru in the center of Tokyo, have regular jam sessions at a nearby sister club. Shinjuku Pit Inn, another long-running club, has afternoon sessions for younger musicians to acquire comfort with live performance, spontaneous interaction, and improvisation on stage.

Younger jazz musicians also place a heavy emphasis on jazz as a group conversation. Big bands are central to most jazz musicians' experience in Japan, starting as early as junior high school. The annual Yamano Big Band Jazz Contest, now in its 46th year, brings together the best college bands from across the country to be voted on by professional jazz musicians. The traditional groupthink mentality of Japanese culture contributes to the big band's central position in the jazz experience. The sensitivity to the presence, opinions, and concerns of others in a group is a traditional value in Japanese society. Even well-established Japanese jazz musicians keep their chairs inside one or even several big bands. One pianist, Junko Moriya, as well as many others, supports her own bands and projects by writing big band charts and running clinics for amateur big bands all over Japan.

In addition to the chart-reading, tight ensemble type of big band, another kind of large ensemble, what might be called a jazz collective, has emerged in recent years. Of course, there are bands with set members who often play together, but at the same time, there are large bands that get together in a loose configuration of flexible membership. Most bands play "sessions" to try out new combinations of players and find the right connections. These sessions are try-outs, practice, and relaxed jamming, but in some ways, they can be more interesting than the more organized sets of bands who stick to their own fully formed repertoire. The sessions often incorporate the spontaneity of jazz more fully, letting the process more than the product come to the fore.

These collectives have a looser, more casual character than the tighter, focused groups of the past. They emphasize group dynamics and a more open approach to rhythm, soloing, and arrangements. Free jazz, groove rhythms, and extended solos, often in group soloing, are common. The best-known example is Shibusa Shirazu, a large collective that often brings *butoh* dancers, fire-eaters, mimes, and other performers on stage with them. The members of the collective vary each time, with some regulars, but basically, they maintain a rotating cast of musicians. They rarely perform from charts but have enough regulars on stage to kick off the playing, as everyone else joins in and follows along, something like a hip, earthy Suzuki method violin class. But there are many other collectives like Shibusa Shirazu as well. Pianist Takeshi Shibuya leads one of the best of such flexibly organized groups. His seven to 12-piece group, called the Shibuya Takeshi Orchestra, can be heard on his 2003 release *Zutto Nishi-Ogi* and his 2000 release *Tamasa* (Shibuya 2000 and 2003). Live, though, the charts direct the group, but towards a free expression as soloists and contributors to the group sound.

These large, shifting collectives of musicians play together in many different configurations, substitute for each other, and know each other's work closely. Their approach to jazz takes something from Charles Mingus, focusing on a limited set of head arrangements or even simply melody lines and a basic groove. Several of them work with Latin clave rhythms, with a Latin music rhythm section that lets the lead instruments jam for as long as they like. This looser approach to jazz evinces a more complete internalization of jazz principles and practices and the surrounding values of jazz.

The jazz made by these collectives has even been termed "Chuo Line jazz," after the train line connecting the funky, laid-back clubs where most musicians play. This style of jazz stays open and loose, forming a counterpoint to the tighter, more planned approach of jazz groups through the 1990s. Those earlier groups followed the patterns set by record companies and producers of more commercially oriented jazz, even while moving towards playing in their own individual voice. The jazz collectives record live shows and now use YouTube but rarely, if ever, work with large music companies. The improvisation-heavy, unpolished element of these loose collective groups is interesting, unique, and new. They have an unformed and unfinished aspect that recalls late-night jam sessions as much as a polished consumer product. These groups have released jazz from commercial pressure in order to find a greater range of individual variation in voice, style, and approach.

The development of this looser, more exploratory approach to collective improvisation is an important development in Japanese jazz. It evinces a more thorough internalization of the core elements of jazz. Jazz is no longer an imported cultural practice used in the rebellious drama inside Japanese culture but has become a genuine part of the Japanese artistic culture. No one is copying American methods, but instead, they are creating a personal expression by applying jazz principles in their own way. The distinction is essential. The integration of jazz practice and the internalization of jazz's cultural values since the 1990s show how fully jazz is now embedded into Japanese culture.

Stepping just outside the dynamics of performance and reception of jazz in Japan, a series of questions arises. In an article on the "othering" of jazz within American culture, Nathaniel Mackey, taking a cue from Amira Baraka's work *Blues People*, argues:

'From verb to noun' means, on the aesthetic level, a less dynamic, less improvisatory, less blues-inflected music and, on the political level, a containment of black mobility, a containment of the economic and social advances that might accrue to black artistic innovation. (Mackey 514)

However, those aesthetic and political dynamics radically change when jazz moves into a distinctly different cultural and socio-political context such as Japan's. It is hard to understand how containment or misappropriation is part of any Japanese jazz musician's, or even the music industry's, concern inside Japan. That argument might have been relevant in the 1950s Japanese jazz scene, but it does not apply to the Japanese jazz of the past 20, and certainly the past ten years. Just the opposite, jazz in Japan has gone from noun in the 1960s to verb in the 2010s.

If anything, the attitude towards jazz is one of tremendous respect and devotion, of importing another country's and another subculture's traditional mode of expression with care, concern, and focused practice. At an aesthetic level, jazz in Japan has not continued to be a reduction of blues-based approaches to jazz but has become more improvisatory in both performance and conception. The ability to mix diverse cultural forms while remaining rooted in tradition and pushing boundaries shows how well integrated jazz has become in Japanese jazz culture. But beyond that, improvising with a depth of feeling and a naturalness of expression are challenges that all jazz musicians must face. Japanese jazz musicians now take on those challenges like other country's jazz musicians do.

When approaching jazz in other cultures, what is needed, then, are different aesthetic and socio-political approaches to discover and explain how jazz has moved throughout the world to other cultures and how jazz has mixed with other cultures in productive, creative, and meaningful ways. It is easy to argue that jazz has become an "international language" or even an "international art form," but it is much more difficult to trace the complex patterns of interaction, acquisition, adaptation, and exchange that keep jazz so vibrant and compelling in so many different places around the world. Equally difficult is to determine when and how jazz could be said to have become fully integrated beyond the initial conflicts of cultural importation. The looser collectives and internalized approaches of Japanese jazz in recent years give evidence that jazz has found an authentic cultural space and set of practitioners in Japan.

Works Cited

Akiyoshi, Toshiko. Personal interview. 2005.

Atkins, E. Taylor. *Blue Nippon: Authenticating Jazz in Japan*. Durham: Duke UP, 2001. Print.

Atkins, E. Taylor. Message to the author. 2007. E-mail.

Black Sun. Dir. Koreyoshi Kurahara. Eclipse, 1964. DVD.

Hersch, Charles. Subversive Sounds: Race and the Birth of Jazz in New Orleans. >Chicago: U of Chicago, 2007. Print.

Mackey, Nathaniel. "Other: From Noun to Verb." *The Jazz Cadence of American Culture*. New York: Columbia UP, ed. Robert G. O'Meally. 1998. 513-32. Print.

Nicholson, Stuart. *Is Jazz Dead?: (or Has It Moved to a New Address)*. New York: Routledge, 2005. Print.

Pinoy Jazz. Perf. Richie Quirino. Director Richie Quirino. 2006. Film. Online.

Shibuya Takeshi Orchestra. *Zutto Nishi-Ogi*. Rinsen Music, 2003. CD.

Tamasa. Carca, 2000. CD.

Tada, Seiji. Personal interview. November 2, 2007.

The Warped Ones. Dir. Koreyoshi Kurahara. Eclipse, 1960. Film. DVD.

Yamashita, Yosuke. Personal interview. 2005.

Sakura. Antilles, 1990. CD. Reprinted with permission from: "Jazz in Japan: The Process of Cultural Integration." *Jazz Cosmopolitanism: China's Perspectives of Jazz Music in the Internet Age*. Ed. Yu Hui, Tony Whyton. Zhejiang University Press (2016). (ISBN 978-7-308-16307-1).

Why Jazz Resonates so Far from Home

And now, Jazz is exported to the world. For in the particular struggle of the Negro in America there is something akin to the universal struggle of modern man. Everybody has the Blues. Everybody longs for meaning. Everybody needs to love and be loved. Everybody needs to clap hands and be happy. Everybody longs for faith. In music, especially this broad category called Jazz, there is a stepping stone towards all of these.

Dr. Martin Luther King, Jr,
On The Importance Of Jazz
Opening Address to the 1964 Berlin Jazz Festival.

How jazz travels

The extent to which the African-American music of jazz has taken root in Japanese nightlife has important cross-cultural implications. That spaces have been dedicated to the production and reception of jazz in all of Japan's urban areas and that jazz fans, jazz musicians and jazz industry workers are so many, and so devoted, can reveal a great deal about both Japan's globalized culture and about jazz's inherent adaptability as an art form. Except for a few years during World War II bans on all things Western, jazz has had an important presence in Japan for over a century.

Jazz travels well and works its way into cultures, like Japan's, where it would not in many ways appear welcome. By focusing on the practice and learning trajectories of jazz by Japanese musicians, the process of Japanese jazz musicians' and jazz fans' assimilation of the complexities of the music can be understood within a larger cultural context. Jazz has become part of Japanese culture because of new attitudes within the contemporary Japanese cultural context and the integration of the essentials of jazz practice with elements of Japan's traditional culture.

The present discussion explores this assimilation based on three areas of cultural transformation: first, the understanding of Japanese jazz musicians, based on their comments in interviews; second, elements and patterns of assimilation, based on an analysis of examples of jazz music; and third, consideration of the larger context of Japanese culture and historical changes, based on observations of jazz practice. By examining these three threads, the importation, assimilation, and transformation, jazz's resonance in Japan can be explored.

The process is immensely complex, but its foundation depends on an understanding of many interacting factors: the inherent characteristics of jazz, expectations about performance, social attitudes towards jazz, meanings of jazz, the practice of jazz, acquisition of technique, prevalence and accessibility of recordings, self-positioning vis-a-vis outside culture, and a basic understanding of jazz history and practice.

Jazz culture is not one thing but many, just as Japanese culture is not uniform. Both cultures have thrived in the postmodern age, at least in the urban spaces of large cities. From a global perspective, jazz spaces—the clubs, coffee houses, schools, practice rooms, and jam session venues—are interconnected by powerful transnational forces that bring them together. Jazz aficionados and musicians come together in jazz spaces as part of a globalized connection that, in many cases, is much more meaningful and binding than other connections inside Japanese culture. Japanese jazz fans very often revere someone like John Coltrane. This is more than just a matter of taste—it's an engagement with global culture.

To be sure, jazz was one of the most essential expressions of African-American culture beginning in the early twentieth century. However, the more accurate argument about jazz arriving in Japan would be that the universal elements of jazz culture, not the cultural locus of its origins, are what travel.

"Travel" is intentionally chosen here to capture how the movement from one culture to another is a simpler version of the fancier terms, importation, assimilation, and transformation. "Travel" and "traveler" are better terms because jazz has traveled inside people, inside jazz players and listeners. To trace the journey of jazz into Japan, it is essential to consider the people who have moved between cultural spaces, bringing the culture-hero fire of jazz across cultures.

Another argument that follows is that jazz, as a practice and as a culture or sub-culture, contains universal elements that mesh with local situations, beliefs, values, and practices. In that sense, jazz can be compared to baseball, film, or novels. A Japanese film is rarely considered to be made separately from the place of its origins. It doesn't raise the question of whether film can be viewed as a purely Western practice. Baseball perhaps retains more of the attributes of its origins, though sports are universal. Novels are considered even more flexible and adaptable since stories are part of most literary cultural traditions.

Jazz travels so well because improvised music, like stories, is part of most cultures. With that in mind, jazz seems readily adaptable to other cultures if considered a formal practice, such as film or novels. The idea in the present argument will rest on the assumption that jazz is a set of practices that are transportable, transferable, learnable, importable, exportable, and capable of being appreciated by people in many different cultures.

A third thread of argument is that jazz that travels draws more deeply on the universal cultural practices inside jazz culture. Improvisation and spontaneous creation over rhythmic and harmonic structures occurred in many cultures throughout history, not only in the African-American tradition. In musical cultures as diverse as Chinese opera, Indian ragas, and European classical composers were famed for their improvising ability. Improvisation has been essential in most of the world's traditional musical cultures. Tying jazz, and especially its advanced improvisatory nature, to its geographical, historical, and cultural origins is one way of praising the geniuses who developed jazz within the African-American culture of the early twentieth century.

However, another way of understanding American jazz is how those originators unlocked a universal form of expression that would liberate the practice, thinking, and experience. They pushed improvisation to new heights. In doing so, they opened improvisation to more potential practitioners. This opens a broader view of how jazz was imported to Japan. It will allow for a more inclusive, expansive, and meaningful view of jazz's global mobility. That implies that a more developed study of Japanese jazz can reveal much about jazz in a universal sense without losing a respectful understanding of jazz's historical origins. That isn't to say everything about jazz can be universalized, but it's interesting to see which parts can be.

How jazz imports

How jazz was imported, assimilated, and transformed into Japan involves not just a global narrative but many personal narratives as well. A historical narrative will be less of an objective factual history of a musical import and more of a cultural, affective, and subjective account of the importation within the experience of individual jazz musicians and a very receptive group of fans.

While most of the studies and theories of cultural construction and cross-border exchange have focused on colonial or postcolonial situations, it's hard to think how that applies to the case of Japanese jazz. Some writers, such as E. Taylor Atkins in Blue Nippon, argue for a sort of anxiety of influence from America (Atkins 2001) that applies to a particular point in the post-war period. That's undoubtedly true, but the consequent ongoing passion for jazz in Japan up to the present moment feels less like anxiety and more like genuine passion.

A more human-centered account of jazz in Japan can better consider the Japanese passion for jazz. The Japanese tendency to throw themselves into their hobbies, interests, and activities is well documented. That's also the case with jazz, especially in the experimental 1960s through the bubble years. Japanese jazz fans' passion keeps jazz a thriving cultural form in Japan. The musicians' words point this out in the interview clips that follow.

Jazz's existence and presence in Japan developed out of what could arguably be postcolonial contact during one period but can be better considered as an outgrowth of a globalized cosmopolitanism that spread worldwide during the 1920s and 1930s. Jazz was played everywhere wealthy cosmopolites congregated and traveled by ship. Atkins notes that Shanghai was a mecca for Japanese jazz musicians, calling Shanghai a "frontier" space where the contested exchange of cultures took place freely during the inter-war period. Atkins argues, "For Japanese musicians, Shanghai represented a rite of authentication and initiation into the jazz culture, an alternative experience, and a stepping stone to fame and fortune on the homeland's entertainment industry." (Atkins 1999).

While the cosmopolitan spaces of cities such as Shanghai, Paris, or Cairo in the inter-war period can be viewed as postcolonial, from the standpoint of jazz, a ground-level view would include more technical, musical, and cultural exchange than an analysis of cultural power dynamics. One New York Times correspondent traveling the "jazz latitude" around the world in 1922 wrote in the New York Times about Japan in this way:

> The Japanese have taken to jazz dancing with an enthusiasm that characterizes every Japanese adaptation of Western convention. Japanese men and women outnumber the Europeans on the floor during a dance at any of the large hotels in Yokohama, Kobe or Tokio.

(Hershey 1922)

Burnet's first-hand observations are steeped in cultural misunderstandings, but his writing is some testament to the early fascination with jazz in Japan. The article went on to observe jazz along a "latitude" in mainly port cities such as San Francisco, Honolulu, Yokohama, Kobe, Tokio (sic), Peking, Shanghai, Hong Kong, Canton, Manila, Saigon, Singapore, Bangkok, Calcutta, Bombay, Ceylon, Aden, Suez, Port Said, Cairo, Jerusalem, Nice, Monte Carlo, Paris, London and of course, New York. However, Jazz's omnipresence didn't mean it wasn't open to criticism. Hershey noted, "Japan really is the crossroads where jazz ends and ragtime begins" (Hershey 1922).

Except for the World War II years, when jazz and all things foreign were banned, jazz thrived in Japan. During the post-war years with the American Occupation, Japanese jazz changed to a different feeling and interpretation. One crucial point is that the jazz clubs, the negotiated spaces where jazz was assimilated, continued to be important and popular. Taylor Atkins has documented the jazz age of the 20s and 30s in Yokohama and Kobe in *Blue Nippon* (Atkins 2001). International jazz was built upon the concentration of wealth in cosmopolitan cities. This was a common thread worldwide, as the above list of jazz-loving port cities gives evidence. Those negotiated cultural spaces focused on jazz as dance music for the wealthy elite, performed by musicians drawn from various backgrounds, some of whom learned the music independently.

As in the West, jazz in the Japanese inter-war years supported dancing and provided background to other activities, including advertising. But it was not considered an expression of improvisation. By the time censorship was imposed during the wartime, jazz had yet to take on the focus on improvisation that it had after the bebop revolution in the late 1940s.

However, jazz in America had not undergone that transformation so fully, either, until bebop spread its revolutionary approaches and thinking. The powerful political implications of improvised music did not emerge in either country until much later in the 1960s. What is clear is that in the post-war years, jazz became one of Japan's most popular musical forms.

The spatiality of jazz

The *jazzu kissaten* were important spaces serving multiple purposes of importation and assimilation. The *jazzu kissaten* served as sites for a shared exchange. For players, they were schools, and for fans, they were places for shared information, examining cover art and liner notes, discussion with the owner and other patrons, and developing a critical consciousness.

By the end of the 1950s and the beginning of the 1960s, those *jazzu kissaten* evolved through broader expansion and deeper integration into the urban culture. These changes started to position the coffee shops and jazz as an outsider's music, a way for alienated and disenchanted young people to rebel against a rigidly hierarchical socio-economic system that valued material progress and social conformity. By this point, the change from importation to assimilation is well under way. Jazz has become a marker of social anomie.

This transformation from bright dance music in large dance halls to alienated listening text in small dark spaces has been well documented and examined in Molasky's work on *jazzu kissaten* (Molasky 2010). Focusing on the late 1960s in particular, Molasky argues that the *jazzu kissaten* helped import concepts and attitudes, especially those associated with 1960s free jazz, that expanded the scope of radical discussion of the time. The identification with the rebellious American 60s culture, especially African-American culture, Molasky argues, served as another influx of ideas contributing to Japan's 1960s protest movements.

These jazz spaces, from dance hall to *jazzu kissaten*, fit neatly into Edward W. Soja's "triple dialectic" of sociality, historicality, and spatiality. He points out, "a strategic awareness of collectively created spatiality and its social consequences has become a vital part of making both theoretical and practical sense of our contemporary lifeworlds at all scales" (Soja 1996). The jazz spaces thus have a "real-and-imagined character," to borrow Soja's term, that extends the spatiality into complex areas of human experience.

Beginning in the early 1970s, jazz records, affordable stereo equipment, and the jazz press expanded considerably, along with the growth of the domestic consumer market. Fans could listen at home, and musicians could express themselves in what was still an alternative musical form. Everyone began to see jazz as an element of and a reaction against Japan's increasingly consumerist values.

The musicians' attitudes and approaches began to evolve as the Japanese economy grew in the late 1970s and skyrocketing during the bubble years of the 1980s. Rather than listening at home, jazz clubs became places for businessmen to entertain clients. "Bottle keep" systems, where expense accounts purchased full bottles of expensive foreign whiskey, which were kept at the jazz clubs, were the expression of this return, though true fans never left, to the experience of live music.

Jazz identity and infinity

However, it must be remembered that jazz was imported and assimilated through the experience of individuals, particularly musicians, who, with a steady audience, could start to evolve Japanese jazz far beyond entertainment. With the power and energy of 1960s free jazz on board, in the minds of hardcore fans and musicians, jazz was no longer just for dancing or as a backdrop to business discussions. Jazz became a fully developed artistic form whose meanings, like its sub-styles, were potentially infinite.

The pianist Yosuke Yamashita exemplifies this trend towards more original expression beyond mimicking the West or the confines of entertaining.

I went to New York on my own. I wanted to try something new and create a new identity for myself. I was a newcomer and strongly felt the power and history of jazz there. So, I wondered how, as a Japanese person, I could participate in the history of jazz. Even though I was very much a devoted free jazz player, I wanted to try something new. Of course, I also wanted to do something for myself. I knew all these Japanese melodies. I started to think of Japanese instruments, such as the *shakuhachi* and *shamisen* and thought how that might translate to jazz. Jazz is an American music, but I'm not a Japanese who wants to become an American. I always feel like a Japanese. (Yamashita interview 2003)

His originality extends to nearly all of his work. Besides working with American musicians, particularly bassist Cecil McBee and drummer Pheeroan akLaff in their decades-long trio, Yamashita has also consistently engaged with traditional Japanese musicians, creating works that integrate Japanese and Western music. His consistent engagement with various types of music, including art, for example, his "Burning Piano" where he played a burning piano on a beach, shows how fully jazz came to be regarded as a flexible, impressive form in various combinations. His attitude would seem to be the very definition of assimilation and integration of the spirit of improvisation.

Other jazz musicians such as Takeshi Shibuya may have started by listening to American jazz, but his unique takes on American music, such as his essential Ellington series, show a complete assimilation of jazz in terms of technique, attitude, approach, and execution. The idea of moving from jazz as American music to jazz as improvised art is evident in the following quote from an interview with Shibuya:

When I first started listening to jazz, I liked the West Coast sound of people like Quincy Jones and Shorty Rogers. They had that mid-size group, and I kept it because I just liked the size itself. As a leader, I don't ask for any kind of sound. This sound is not my own sound. It's just fun. There is not a plan exactly, but rather, the relationship is good. Once the energy flows, then everyone can do what they like. (Shibuya 2002)

The increasing importance of developing one's own unique, identifiable sound, along with a loosening of approach, is another signal of jazz's integration into the Japanese consciousness of musicians in Japan. For those musicians growing up in the post-60s era, the need to develop one's own voice became increasingly essential for authenticity. Saxophonist Joh Yamada had this to say in an interview:

I'm not even really sure what jazz really is exactly, but the experience of every jazz musician is different. Basically, jazz is very individual, so the musician's specific sound is the most important point. I think that people want to play what they want to play, and for Japanese, their identity as Japanese is important and of course that affects the sound. For example, I think there is a Yokohama jazz sound. Musicians who play together often develop themselves together and maybe influence each other. That's natural. (Yamada 2005)

While Yamada, like so many others of his generation, went to America to study jazz, the spirit of their study was much more focused on developing a personal vision of jazz, expressed in a unique, individual voice. That attitude is not so different from what every American jazz musician holds.

Importing jazz consciousness

Musicians such as Satoko Fujii have taken this idea even further by pushing the boundaries of her take on jazz, or rather by erasing all boundaries, to think of jazz as aimed at a fuller pursuit of freely improvised music. Fujii said,

Jazz is a music which is still alive, you cannot find it in a museum. It develops all the time, and doesn't stay in the same place. Jazz is something which can take in everything. It has risk, so it still develops. Some people say jazz is a musical style with a certain rhythm or form, but I don't think jazz is like that. The most important thing in jazz is that kind of risk mentality. If music has that mentality, then I'd call it jazz, even if it doesn't have a jazz musical style. The most important thing is being exciting and interesting, not to play music as written, so to do that, we can do anything." (Satoko Fujii interview 2007)

Her comments show how deeply the jazz consciousness has sunk into musicians' conceptions of music and how jazz became seen less as a form or style than, as she notes, a "risk mentality." Fujii's comments also reveal how difficult it is to separate the importation of musical consciousness from assimilation. For jazz to be played authentically, something more than importation as imitation is required. These processes occur perhaps less as social or cultural shifts than in the minds of individual musicians.

By the end of the bubble era, Japanese jazz musicians like Fujii understood jazz consciousness. They understood, not just copied, the essentials of jazz—the emphasis on the improvisational moment, the balancing of the aleatory with control, the production of a genuine voice, and the understanding of musical limits and freedoms. That does not mean that the practiced building up of techniques and skills needed to play jazz is ignored, but rather that a building up of the jazz musician's consciousness is also needed.

That complexity, of course, leads to some degree of confusion and diversity, and it is perhaps where the fullest sense of jazz's assimilation to Japan can be found. Musicians such as the pianist Hiroshi Minami are aware of the undecided nature of jazz and how many other elements beyond the simply musical are contained within the idea of jazz. Minami's comments reveal what many Japanese jazz musicians struggle with: how to position their music within the larger frame of jazz historically, stylistically, and conceptually. Minami, who has written many books about jazz that include his own explanations of jazz, said:

The Japanese jazz scene could be classified into either straight-ahead bebop jazz or free-form jazz. There is no middle concept between these two styles. So, we need a postmodern jazz concept. I want to create jazz with intelligence, modesty, and a sense of cool. Before bop, everyone danced to jazz, like with Count Basie, but after John Coltrane, musicians played as intensely as possible. They started to express their libido, like this [screams]. So, I want some of that expression, and maybe the same basic concept as bebop, but well-dressed music that the audience can really sit down and listen to. (Minami personal email 2015)

The comments from these musicians, whose ages are roughly chronological in these past sections, offer insight into how the complete sense of jazz is evolving in Japan and how deeply those musicians understand that the sense of jazz could not evolve without a deeper understanding of jazz beyond the skills and technical elements of playing the music. That is one mark of the degree of assimilation.

Thirdspaces and jazz people

Tokyo and Yokohama have over one hundred venues featuring live jazz almost every night, and countless more 'live houses' where jazz, or jazz-like improvisational music, is played. It is important to remember that learning to listen, however and where it is done, is both a creative and participatory act. Japanese jazz's assimilation rests on a broad-based, informed, experienced, and capable audience.

Despite cuts to musical education and an educational system that is awash with a testing mentality, Japanese schools offer one boon to the jazz world—'circles,' or extracurricular groups. These circles, which are for everything from games to sports to music, meet outside the regular instructional day and typically have a set of practices rooted in the traditions and history of the circle itself. These circles are given room at the school for students to meet and learn from their *senpai*, or senior students, and usually have an advisor from among the teaching staff, or occasionally a graduate of the circle whose job is to help organize, supervise, and assist the circle. The brass band circle is where nearly every jazz musician in Japan got their start.

While most brass bands do not include improvisational elements and stick to tried and true works from film theme songs and classic big band songs, they provide the basis for group interaction and the acquisition of musical skills. The importance of this brass band experience cannot be overstated. Without it, there would be no jazz fans and many fewer musicians. Jazz bands and jazz music typically do not enter into students' experience until high school, though numerous junior high school bands sprung up after the success of the film "Swing Girls" (2004).

Those bands increasingly provide a more genuine experience of improvisation and more complex music from the jazz canon. Often, the circle members are much more than the traditional 16-piece jazz big band, so players exchange positions on various instruments so everyone can get a turn. Nearly every jazz musician credits this early experience with brass bands and big bands to their pursuit of a jazz career.

Leveling jazz up

Jazz musicians usually become involved with a group from their university's circle that becomes ever more serious about jazz. These circles have practice rooms on university campuses and serve as another *thirdspace* site to exchange information, listen to recordings, work on scores and lead sheets, and talk through attitudes. Many professional jazz musicians return to their university's circle to give workshops, lead jam sessions, and promote jazz education. It might be too much to say that all of this constitutes institutional support for jazz education, but given that practice rooms and private studios are extremely expensive in Japan's large cities, out of reach for most young Japanese, offering dedicated rooms for students to progress from junior high school brass bands to sophisticated jazz combos at universities shows that institutions at least are not stymying jazz.

From brass band to big band, one enduring jazz experience in many people's lives is the student big band, leading to amateur big bands. According to big band leader Junko Moriya, who travels the country leading amateur jazz big bands:

For *shakaijin* (working adult) big bands, I go to places like Nagoya, Osaka, and Hokkaido. The amazing part is that even in the smallest places, cities with 30,000 to 50,000 people, they have a big band. If you go to Osaka or Nagoya or Hiroshima, where they love *shakaijin* big bands, there are at least ten in each place. (Moriya 2017)

She noted that there were five or six alumni bands at her university, Waseda, some with a 60-year history. Those big band members also participate in jam sessions held nationwide. These jam sessions form part of the ongoing interest in jazz and contribute to jazz fans' continued interest in jazz as participants and listeners. Interestingly, many jam sessions take place at jazz clubs, of course, but also jazz kissaten, which operate as coffee shops throughout the day and convert to jam session spaces in the evening. The jam sessions are often hosted by professional jazz musicians with some connection to the owner, perhaps having gotten their start there.

In an interesting study, Novak had this to say about jazz kissaten, comparing them in some ways to the jazz loft spaces of New York.

Social spaces for listening can refigure musical meaning in ways that fundamentally alter the spatial and temporal trajectories of recordings – modern music's primary vehicle – and consequently change the meaning of their contents. While listening is sometimes glossed as a passive consumption of media, here I present it as a distinctly virtuosic and creative practice of circulation. Listening is not the final link of a chain of musical transmission, but the very crucible of musical innovation. (Novak 2008)

What's important to note here is that the 'chain of musical transmission' includes not just listening, as Novak notes, but also participating in different spaces from junior high school through adulthood. Listening, playing, consuming, and learning about jazz takes place not simply through reading the jazz press or listening at a well-informed jazz kissaten, but that the knowledge of and about jazz continues to be participatory. This continual active engagement, as player, listener, reader, and discussant, keeps jazz assimilating into Japanese culture. In Japan, the assimilation of jazz into the culture is thus not a single act in a brief historical period but is instead an ongoing process of engagement across a broad spectrum of people.

Assimilating jazz attitudes

The process of assimilating jazz does not simply occur inside the dense urban areas of Tokyo, Yokohama, Osaka, and Kobe, but is distributed throughout Japan, and includes a broader set of attitudes and cultural elements than jazz alone. The importance of these spaces for people outside the larger cities to learn about urban movements and cultural trends has been well examined by Molasky in his work on *jazzu kissaten*. He argues that the function of *jazzu kissaten* has changed from being a school in the 1950s to a temple in the 1960s, a supermarket in the 1970s, and a museum in the 1980s (Molasky 56-7). He is undoubtedly correct in this, but the function in each period has been retained to some extent in the succeeding one, piling up in postmodern accrual without entirely receding so that most jazz kissaten now serve all those functions.

The power of these spaces to contribute to the assimilation of jazz music and related values is evident in their continued presence. While other coffee shop chains have decimated the previously more significant numbers of kissaten of all kinds, they are making a resurgence in many urban areas for this reason. Still, *jazzu kissaten* have continued as distinct experiences with new shops opening up after the first onslaught of international chain coffee shops.

Schooling jazz and jazz media

Lastly, two more important elements of jazz assimilation must be mentioned: jazz schools and jazz media. The importance of specifically jazz-oriented schools must be mentioned, as jazz is now taught directly at numerous educational institutions. The most influential school since the 1960s was the Berklee School of Music, which was long seen as the best place for Japanese jazz musicians to study. To its credit, Berklee was instrumental in accepting and educating many of Japan's top professional jazz musicians. They brought back not just jazz chops but ways of teaching jazz. Most returning musicians began to teach at either the burgeoning departments of jazz in conservatories such as Koyo Conservatory in Kobe, Shobi Music University, Kunitachi College of Music, and Showa University of Music, but also at Sengoku Gakuen School of Music, the first college to offer a jazz course of study and a strong relation and exchange program with Berklee. In addition, *senmon gakko*, or specialty schools, offer jazz instruction.

Jazz assimilation has also been continually fueled by the jazz media in Japan, which remains dedicated, expansive, and influential. The major magazines have mostly folded with the arrival of the internet, jazz blogs, and online radio stations. At the peak readership around 2000, Swing Journal had a circulation of 300,000 (*The Asahi Shimbun* 2010), though the 70,000 readers of Jazz Hihyo and 100,000 readers of Jazz Life (*Ongaku Zasshi Ichiran* 2017) were likely many of the same people. Those magazines and many others aimed at studying how to play instruments and better jazz formed a continuous force for assimilating numerous aspects of jazz. The media's detailed CD reviews, interviews, reports of live shows, lead sheets, and how-to articles based on Japanese and foreign musicians form another aspect of the educative process and a central pillar of assimilation.

Taken together, the processes of assimilating jazz into Japan's musical culture are extensive and robust, even while in many ways jazz remains a rather specialized, if thriving, niche in the broader musical culture.

Transforming jazz or not

The issue of transformation is a more difficult one to ascertain. Determining how or if jazz has been transformed in Japanese culture involves considering what traditional and current cultural values jazz meshes with. It also entails discarding stereotypes of Japanese cultural acquisition. Transformation suggests the establishment of a sense of authenticity about the music. Transformation could mean changing the essential elements. Still, the issue of authenticity is more about the degree to which jazz is transformed or transplanted into Japanese culture and how jazz authenticity is defined. Is it the unique and individual imperatives of jazz? Or knowing how to play like past originators?

Jazz is a music that involves a deep commitment to authenticity. An authentic approach, voice, and technique is the essence of jazz. Evaluating that authenticity is inevitably a subjective undertaking that fits along a continuum. The somewhat stereotypical idea is that Japan is a quaint, isolated country that developed its social and cultural practices in isolation. That argument has some validity regarding many elements of Japanese culture, but in large part, jazz in Japan was developed as an antidote to and reaction against isolation. It was historically steeped in pro-democracy post-war attitudes. As with most of Japan's transformations of outside culture, the jazz world in Japan is highly internationalized and yet retains specifically Japanese qualities.

The recognition and respect accorded to the American originators of jazz does not mean there is deep anxiety about playing an American musical form. It is instead that Japanese identity can fit into that musical form. Japanese jazz musicians have chosen to make art in a form developed initially in America.

To return to the analogy to film, no Japanese film director worries about their identity as an auteur because they are using a technical narrative art form developed in America and France. Though that anxiety over identity makes a good academic study or dissertation topic, it is not part of the working world of most musicians' lives. Many Japanese musicians consider jazz an art form similar to printmaking, sculpting, or pottery. They bring their sensibilities, artistic sense, life experience, values, beliefs, and emotions to jazz. However, the practice of jazz, especially issues of voice and improvisation, are complex conflicts for all practicing musicians.

In that sense, jazz in Japan isn't any less authentic because it is created far from the source of its original social evolution. It is differently authentic. It's not "Do I sound like Miles?" but rather, "Do I sound like I want to sound?" Authenticity could mean following the historically original pattern, but it can also mean following creative impulses honestly. Musicians everywhere want to make authentic, honest music that reflects their values.

In many ways, Japanese jazz musicians nowadays are about equal distance from the jazz originators as many young learners in America might be. They all learn by listening to recordings and in schools at about the same historical and cultural distances. It is also important to note that Japanese jazz musicians are just as individualized as American or European jazz musicians because the music calls forth a response from Japanese culture and integrates elements of Japanese culture. Still, that call and response is as much an individual one for each musician as it is a generalizable expression of Soja's triple dialectic.

Concluding reflections

In considering the issue of the importation, assimilation, and transformation of jazz in Japanese culture, it is important to remember that the persistence of jazz in Japan says as much about jazz as it does about Japan. There is, of course, a deep and abiding respect for jazz's origins among Japanese musicians and fans. That sentiment is based on an awareness of history and a pride in being part of that history, of being part of one of the streams—a strong stream—of jazz history that flows outside American culture. It is essential to remember that the nature of jazz, having drawn on world cultures, remains flexible and adaptable to a wide variety of circumstances.

Jazz has continued to evolve in many different directions, so much so that the definition of jazz is still unresolved and unlikely ever to be resolved. Jazz has merged with many other cultures and musical practices. It has also drawn on a vast array of different cultures and somehow created a distinctive identity as a musical form. In that sense, it is no surprise that jazz has adapted to Japan, if that's the right word.

Music stores in Japan maintain separate sections for Japanese jazz from the rest of jazz, which reflects how Japan sees its relation to the world in general. However, this also speaks to an awareness of difference and identity that is more than marketing or sales strategies or store layout. Jazz's staying power in Japan involves many elements: assimilative practices, thirdspaces, individual importation, and various options for experiencing jazz.

Like Japanese culture, jazz culture is an intense blend of conservative and progressive elements. In jazz culture, the power of the past retains a hold on the present in ways unlike many other musical forms. One must know the jazz masters of the past to know how to play and, of course, why to play. At the same time, the progressive side of jazz keeps pushing the music forward into new combinations, deeper explorations of possibilities, and fresh transgressions of boundaries. That's what makes jazz so interesting.

A similar balance of conservative and progressive elements can also be seen in Japanese culture. The long-standing religious attitudes, historical practice of artisan crafts, and long-abiding beliefs of Japanese culture provide fertile ground for jazz's arrival. Japanese culture has a tight-gripping, backward-looking hold on the present in everything from education to politics to music. However, at the same time, the powerfully cosmopolitan nature of much of Japanese life brings on an attitude of searching for new experiences. The constant appearance of new fads and trends in everything from films to books, drinks, restaurants, activities, goods, and music is a defining element of Japanese economic and social culture.

Thinking of the conservative and progressive poles of jazz culture and Japanese culture, both cultures find new relevance in new contexts with a regenerative energy that conserves and preserves what came before. Thus, the questions about the importation, assimilation, and transformation of jazz to Japan are ongoing and unresolved. The overlap between them remains resonant with future possibility.

Works Cited

Akiyoshi, Toshiko. Interview by author. November 17, 2004.

Allen, Graham. *Intertextuality*. London: Routledge, 2000.

Atkins, E. Taylor. *Blue Nippon: Authenticating Jazz in Japan*. Durham: Duke University Press, 2001.

Atkins, E. Taylor. E-mail message to author. 2007.

Atkins, E. Taylor. "Jammin' on the Jazz Frontier: The Japanese Jazz Community in Interwar Shanghai. *Japanese Studies*, 19.1, 1999.

Derschmidt, Eckhart. "The Disappearance of the 'Jazz-Kissa'." In *The Culture of Japan as Seen through Its Leisure*, edited by Sepp Linhart and Sabine Fruhstuck, 303-15. State University of New York Press, 1998.

Dorin, Stéphane. "Editorial: The Global Circulations of Jazz." *Jazz Research Journal* 10, no. No 1-2 (2016). Accessed January 1, 2016. http://doi:10.1558/jazz.v10i1-2.29354.

Black Sun. Directed by Koreyoshi Kurahara. Performed by Tamio Kawaji and Chico Roland. 1964. DVD.

Fujii, Satoko. Interview by author. November, 2007.

Hershey, Burnet. "Jazz Latitude." *The New York Times,* June 25, 1922.

Hosokawa, Shuhei. "Shochiku Girls' Opera and 1920s Dotonbori Jazz." In *Music, Modernity and Locality in Prewar Japan: Osaka and Beyond*, edited by Hugh De Ferranti and Alison Tokita, 211-26. Burlington: Ashgate, 2013.

"Kaisai Gaiyo Dai 48 Kai Yamano Big Band Jazz Contest." Yamano Music. https://www.yamano-music.co.jp/docs/ybbjc/info/youkou.html.

Koyama, Kiyoshi. "Jazz in Japan." In *The Oxford Companion to Jazz*, edited by Bill Kirchner, 566. Oxford University Press, 2000.

Mackey, Nathaniel. "Other: From Noun to Verb." In *The Jazz Cadence of American Culture*, edited by Robert G. O'Meally, 513-32. New York: Columbia UP, 1998.

Martin, Denis-constant. "Can Jazz Be Rid of the Racial Imagination? Creolization, Racial Discourses, and Semiology of Music." *Black Music Research Journal* 28, no. 2 (Fall 2008). https://www.questia.com/library/journal/1G1-202513826/can-jazz-be-rid-of-the-racial-imagination-creolization.

Martinez, Dolores P. The Worlds of Japanese Popular Culture: Gender, Shifting Boundaries and Global Cultures. Cambridge: Cambridge University Press, 1998.

Minami, Hiroshi. Interview by author. 2005.

Molasky, Michael S. *Jazzu Kissa Ron: Sengo No Nihon Bunka O Aruku*. Tokyo: Chikuma Shobo, 2010.

Moriya, Junko. Interview by author. 2016.

Moriya, Junko. Interview by author. February 2017.

Nicholson, Stuart. Is Jazz Dead?: (or Has It Moved to a New Address). London: Routledge, 2005.

Novak, David. "2.5~6 metres of space: Japanese music coffeehouses and experimental practices of listening." *Popular Music*, Volume 27.1:15–34, 2008.

"Ongaku Zasshi Ichiran," 2017. An Advertising Agency: Horikoshi Corporation (Koukoku Dairi Ten: Kabusiki Gaisha Horikoshi), accessed January 2017. www.hrks.jp/ad_music/jazz/.

Pronko, Michael. "Power of Hope: Toshiko Akiyoshi Leaves Her Mark on the World of Jazz." *The Japan Times*, November 17, 2004. http://www.japantimes.co.jp/culture/2004/11/17/music/power-of-hope/#.WJ_T0xJ94UE.

Segawa, Masahisa. 1981. "Senzen no Nihonjin Jazu Shinga Tachi," Bessatsu Music Magazine: Record Collectors (May 1981), 30–39.

Shibuya, Takeshi. Interview by author. January 2002.

Shipton, Alyn. *A New History of Jazz*. London: Continuum, 2001.

Soja, Edward W. Postmetropolis: Critical Studies of Cities and Regions. Oxford: Blackwell, 2000.

Soja, Edward W. Thirdspace Journeys to Los Angeles and Other Real-and-Imagined Places. Massachusetts: Blackwell, 1996.

Swing Girls. 2004. directed by Shinobu Yaguchi. (Japan, 2004). DVD.

Tada, Seiji. Interview by author. November 2007.

The Asahi Shimbun. 2010. "Jazu Senmonshi Swing Journal Kyukan e Koukoku Shunyu Fushin." (May 17, 2010). www.asahi.com/showbiz/music/TKY201005170418.html.

The Warped Ones. Directed by Koreyoshi Kurahara. Performed by Tamio Kawachi and Eiji Go. 1960. DVD.

Yamashita, Yosuke. "Burning Piano 2008." March 8, 2008. https://www.youtube.com/watch?v=YpKT_eeCVNI.

Yamashita, Yosuke. Interview by author. September 2003.

Yoshimi, Shunya. "'America' as Desire and Violence: Americanization in Postwar Japan and Asia during the Cold War." Translated by David Buist. *Inter-Asia Cultural Studies* 4, no. 3 (2003): 434-39.

Yosuke Yamashita Special Big Band. *From the New World*. JamRice, 2016, CD.

"Zenkokuban Jazz Session." At Jazz: Jazz Portal Site. http://www.jazz.co.jp/LiveHouseSession/.

"Zenkokuban Live House." At Jazz: Jazz Portal Site. http://www.jazz.co.jp/LiveHouse/index.html.

Reprinted by permission from Springer. "Why Jazz Resonates So Far from Home," Michael Pronko. Music in the Making of Modern Japan: Essays on Reception, Transformation and Cultural Flows. Ed. Kei Hibino, Barnaby Ralph, Henry Johnson. Palgrave Macmillan 2021: 146-166. 3030738264.

Quiet About It Jazz in Japan

Japan is the largest home for jazz outside the United States. Though the number of musicians and venues for jazz in Japan is as extensive as those of any country or region, how jazz is received, learned, practiced, and regarded in Japan is much less known than in other countries. Stuart Nicholson's thoughtful survey of jazz outside the United States, *Is Jazz Dead?* (Rutledge 2005), offers only two passing mentions of Japan.

Alyn Shipton's monumental and otherwise inclusive *A New History of Jazz* (Bloomsbury 2001) mentions Japan not at all in its 900-plus pages. Yet, Japan can boast a century of jazz history and over 100 active jazz clubs in Tokyo and Yokohama alone. Jazz is one of Japan's most fully integrated, uniquely processed, and historically rooted cultural imports. Dorin argues that "the history of jazz can also be regarded as a multiplicity of stories, sometimes parallel, sometimes divergent, with different branches, linked to various places and social worlds in which jazz was listened to and played" (Dorin 2016). If so, Japan's story is an important one in the larger diaspora of jazz.

A brief survey of Japan's history and current scene shows how fully, if unexpectedly, jazz is importable, exportable, and capable of being treasured and created across cultures. Jazz became popular among the Japanese for many of the same reasons as in other countries, though distinctively Japanese attitudes and practices contribute to its flourishing. Jazz, it seems, can be played similarly, but felt differently. It can employ the same essential elements but generate quite different meanings. Perhaps no stronger argument for jazz's universality can be found than in the vibrant jazz scene of Japan.

Several key institutions, social conditions, and cultural forces have secured jazz's position in contemporary Japanese culture. First, the role of the jazz *kissaten*, or coffee shop, the past dance halls and current jazz clubs all contribute powerfully to jazz's enduring presence in Japan. Secondly, jam sessions, music schools, amateur big bands, and a vibrant jazz press have kept jazz from losing cultural ground, even gaining some.

Traditional cultural beliefs and practices, such as Zen and a strong craft tradition, have also contributed to jazz's status and popularity. The Japanese attraction to complex art forms that display a human touch draws musicians and fans towards the virtuosity, creativity, and authenticity that are central to jazz. In that sense, jazz's establishment in Japan as a cultural experience and dynamic practice is no surprise whatsoever.

Jazz Kissaten

The jazz coffee shops, or *jazz kissa* for short, have played an essential role in the unabated interest in jazz from the beginning of the twentieth century and are still central to Japanese jazz culture. Derschmidt notes that jazz started to spread around World War I, but "nowhere in Europe, and of course not in America, did an institution like the Japanese *jazu-kissa* evolve, a cafe, who's main, and as from the middle of the fifties whose sole, function was to provide a space in which to listen to jazz" (Derschmidt 1998).

The *jazz kissa* have a long and influential history and are arguably the central space for jazz's dissemination, study, and enjoyment. At *jazz kissa*, the music is the point, not the background to other activities. (Jazz was not the only music. Classical music *kissaten* are still running, along with a few tango and chanson *kissaten*. Blues and rock are available at evening bars.) There was never dancing, and jazz kissas were always more affordable, with just the price of a cup of coffee for hours of listening.

One of the longest-running *jazz kissa* is Chigusa in Yokohama. Founded in 1933, the famed owner Mamoru Yoshida ran his place with dedication and passion. Chigusa's history and space was, and still is, the standard for the hundreds of other *jazz kissa* throughout Japan.

Don De Armond, a serviceman stationed in Yokosuka during the American occupation, knew Yoshida well, sending him vinyl records from America after returning to America. Armond noted how Yoshida's and Chigusa's fortunes followed the times: "Mamoru Yoshida and his Chigusa were in business from 1937 to 1941; closed by military direction during the war years; demolished by the allied forces bombing of Yokohama in May 1945; rebuilt and reopened in 1946; and continued under his management until his death in 1994" (Pronko 2012). Chigusa is run by new owners, but the atmosphere is unchanged.

In the 1960s, jazz vinyl recordings gained even higher prestige but remained too expensive for most fans. *Jazz kissa* began to be spaces for young people rebelling against the stifling conformity and social oppressiveness of post-war Japan. They increasingly turned to free jazz.

According to Mike Molasky, in his fascinating study of the cultural meanings of *jazz kissa*, "There were over 500 jazz cafes reported in the magazine 'Jazz Nippon-retto' of 1976. What's more...the cafes which answered the questionnaire was 80 percent out of all cafes in Japan. There could have been over 600 jazz cafes in the middle of '70s" (Molasky 2010). The numbers have fallen off from that peak, but ironically, the international coffee shops edging them out now also play jazz as background music.

The *jazz kissa* that remain, and there are many, continue to be devoted to jazz. The walls of places such as Shinjuku's Dug (opened 1961), Yotsuya's Eagle (opened 1967), Kichijoji's Meg (opened 1970), Shinjuku's Old Blind Cat (1965), and Samurai (opened 1965) are all decorated with classic jazz LP covers. The shelves are filled with CDs, vinyl records, books, and magazines about jazz for customers to read.

Central to the room is the stereo system, which involves select, high-fidelity equipment. The *master* ("master," taken from English, is the word for the owner of small, individual shops, bars, or restaurants) chooses works from the collection, either vinyl or CD, though customers can also request specific songs or recordings. Some *jazz kissa* welcome regular customers bringing recordings to listen on the system, while others have evenings introducing recent releases. Every *jazz kissa* has a bulletin board with information about concerts, new releases, jam sessions, lectures, or other jazz activities, underscoring their community-oriented nature.

Customers can stay as long as they like, just as they would in a library. *Jazz kissa* were and still are privileged, dedicated spaces for listening to music on a sound system that individuals can not easily afford for their own apartments. Even if they could afford it, playing music loud would disturb neighbors. Under those conditions, jazz kissa became sanctuaries, with a respectful attitude from customers that recalls the propriety inside a Buddhist temple.

Dance Halls

Dance halls were the main venues where jazz was played and danced to in the early twentieth century. Jazz transferred easily to the wide-open entertainment districts of Tokyo, Yokohama, Kobe, Osaka, and other metropolitan centers in the 1920s and 1930s, especially the port cities. Mackie notes, "Such cities as Shanghai, Yokohama, Nagasaki, Hakodate, and Kobe were linked with international trading routes.... Ocean liners plied these routes, transporting tourists and traders, jazz bands and dancehall girls between the treaty ports" (Mackie 2013).

As well documented in E. Taylor Atkins' *Blue Nippon*, the jazz age in Japan started in the 1920s, a bit behind other world cities. Atkins notes, "The year of the stock market crash in America, which in many ways signaled the coda of Fitzgerald's Jazz Age, was the same year that witnessed Japan's most intense engagement with jazz to date" (Atkins 2001).

Ironically, at that time, Tokyo musicians appeared to have been too well-schooled to pick up the new music of jazz as easily. Segawa notes, "Tokyo musicians played semi-classical music with a lack of jazz taste. One of the reasons for this was that Filipino musicians arrived at Kobe along with their ship and often stayed in the port. Young merchants in Kansai were modernized and liked jazz music and adopted it as the dance music" (Segawa 1981).

Jazz in Osaka was also influenced by popular music, in particular, the Takarazuka Revue and the Shochiku Revue, all-female musical groups that are still hugely popular. Shuhei Hosokawa argues that early Dotonbori, the central entertainment district in Osaka, jazz was deeply influenced by the musicians, singers and popular style of these musical shows, and that musicians, Filipinos in particular, playing in the revues learned how to improvise from records and musicians somewhere between 1925 and 1927 (Hosokawa 2013). Jazz was an imported music, but it quickly blended with other musical performance styles and entertainment practices of the time.

Military and conservative forces eventually brought an end to such Westernized forms of music, leisure, and culture in Japan. Atkins states, "...by 1939, dance halls began closing for lack of business, as social censure effectively inhibited customers from patronizing them" (Atkins 2001). *Jazz kissaten* were under surveillance by military authorities as potential breeding grounds of dissent. By the 1940s, jazz was banned as a subversive Western influence.

Jazz was not heard again in Japan until the American Occupation, when it became the music played in dance halls and later at clubs, where dancing started to take a backseat to performance. The American bases were a generator of transformations of all kinds. Shunya notes, "Numerous powerful cultural influences —jazz, fashion, sexual culture— spread out from the American bases and took root very soon after the beginning of the occupation" (Shunya 2003). Jazz was again exciting and appealing to younger Japanese.

Japanese musicians started to play jazz under the tutelage of musicians stationed in Japan, and then to help transform it from dance music into an art form. Toshiko Akiyoshi, who played with Hampton Hawes when he was stationed in Yokohama after World War II, had this to say about that transitional period:

In 1959, I was playing at a nightclub in Ginza. There were a lot of beautiful hostesses, and everyone danced. I was one of the best-paid sidemen in Japan, but I just didn't want to do it. So, I quit and formed my own quartet called the Cozy Quartet. There were only the American service clubs and also a place in Yokohama called the Seamen's Club. It was a really rough place. Once a week, they would have a fight. But it was a place where I could play whatever I wanted to play. (Pronko 2004)

During and even after the Occupation, much of the attraction to jazz was also an attraction for the newly imposed democratic institutions. Japanese values, which many felt led directly to the war, were rejected. As Koshiro points out, "Amid the cultural and intellectual impoverishment of the Occupation and their weakening sense of esteem for the nation, the Japanese were desperately turning to the United States for cultural and intellectual stimuli" (Koshiro 1999).

However, the Japanese also became interested in jazz not just for its openness, otherness, and un-Japanese nature but as a musical form, style, and way of thinking that was valuable in and of itself. By the end of the Occupation in 1952, jazz clubs had become a central place for jazz culture. With the social strife of the 1950s and 1960s, as well as political turmoil and cultural rebellion, jazz became a place to escape conservative mainstream Japanese values.

Jazz Clubs

After dance halls disappeared, jazz clubs proliferated. Situated in small, underground spaces with a casual interior and excellent sound system, jazz clubs thrived because of increasing interest in jazz itself, jazz as a form of rebellion, and during the economic bubble years, jazz as a sophisticated backdrop for business entertainment.

Estimating the current number of clubs is difficult, but the website *At Jazz* lists 676 jazz clubs throughout Japan. That number, though, includes many places that feature live music only occasionally, and some are open sporadically. From a search of active websites, I found that Tokyo and Yokohama are home to over 100 clubs that offer live jazz nightly. The sheer number is a testament not just to the extensive nightlife of Japan's densely populated cities and the sophistication of music consumers but also to the Japanese passion for jazz.

The club scene is extensive and complex, spread widely over the greater Tokyo area with a diversity of venues. Musicians can try out new styles and approaches for eager listeners. The typical active jazz musician in the Tokyo area might play with anywhere from six to ten different groups in a month, at an equal number of other venues stretching from Tokyo to Yokohama and the surrounding prefectures of Chiba, Saitama, and Kanagawa.

That level of collaboration and cross-pollination serves important functions. Musicians are not only able to hear other musicians but also find those with whom they are like-minded. They must also stay flexible enough to fit into a new group with a different leader, style, and approach. Established musicians often lead "sessions," which, though sometimes paid, serve as tryouts for reshuffling personnel. More formal gigs use the band's or leader's name plus trio, quartet, or quintet.

Most of the better-known jazz clubs are found within the central Yamanote train line circle in the major entertainment hubs of Kannai-

Sakuragicho (in Yokohama), Shinjuku, Roppongi, and along the east-west Chuo Line. Many more clubs are located along the train lines that run out to the suburbs, with a friendly, neighborhood atmosphere.

The diverse locations allow musicians to play for different customers in each area. Of course, the individual character of each club, as well as the types and genres of music they feature, also helps to ensure that fans hear a rotating diversity of jazz and musicians have a chance to play for a different audience in different styles. Many clubs were hit hard after the earthquake in 2011, when many customers did not go out, but the majority have continued to do business as customers returned.

The jazz festivals that used to draw large summer audiences to beachside and mountain resort areas and large urban venues have dropped off in number. From the 1990s, with the economic downturn, the major festivals have all but disappeared. One enduring festival is the annual Yokohama Jazz Promenade, now in its 25th year. Yokohama promotes itself as the home of jazz in Japan, and the port city's festival in 2015 brought in over 150,000 people at 51 venues for 347 performances over two days.

Other smaller festivals have started to spring up, supported by local businesses and governments, such as the Asagaya Jazz Streets, held around Asagaya Station, just west of Shinjuku in western Tokyo. This cozy festival can be said to be truly of, by, and for the community. Students at the local elementary school design jazz-themed posters, mothers' groups act as volunteers, local businesses volunteer their showrooms, and tents are set up on streets by merchants for free shows. Famous musicians like Yosuke Yamashita play up close in the local school gymnasium, church, or community center. Jazz clubs and regional festivals are deeply integrated into Japan's nightlife and neighborhoods.

Learning Jazz in Japan

In the 1960s, many of Japan's top players went to America to study jazz. Since then, with each returning musician, more and more opportunities for studying jazz developed inside Japan. By the late 1980s, schools such as Sengoku Gakuen School of Music, the first college to offer a jazz course of study, emerged. Following Sengoku, Koyo Conservatory in Kobe established a jazz program in conjunction with Berklee, as Sengoku had done, and classical and traditional Japanese conservatories such as Shobi Music University, Kunitachi College of Music, and Showa University of Music expanded into complete programs of jazz study.

Just as important as formal schooling are the nearly 200 different jam sessions throughout Japan. (As listed on the *At Jazz* online site). These range from once-a-week open mic opportunities to sessions run by professionals. One of the most famous clubs devoted to jamming is Jazz Bar Intro in Takadanobaba. The club offers instruments, equipment, and a rhythm section house band. Most jam sessions are free, but others, especially those with professional instruction, cost a nominal fee.

No less important than learning how to play jazz is learning about jazz. Japan's jazz media remains dedicated, extensive, and influential. Three publications, *Jazz Hiyo*, *Jazz Life*, and *Swing Journal*, had impressively large readerships until the internet pulled readers away. At the peak of readership at the turn of the century, *Swing Journal* had a circulation of 300,000 (*The Asahi Shimbun*). Add onto that the 70,000 readers of *Jazz Hihyo* and the 100,000 readers of *Jazz Life* (*Ongaku Zasshi Ichiran*) and those reading about jazz in Japanese are much greater than the 70,000 English readers of *Down Beat* and 100,000 of *Jazz Times* in English (Mandel 2009).

Many other jazz magazines have come and gone in the past several decades. *Jazznin* was the first bilingual English-Japanese jazz magazine. Though *Swing Journal* ceased publication in 2010, other periodicals such as *Jazz Japan* and *Jazz Perspective* are still dedicated to publishing reviews, histories, interviews, and other jazz-related articles. "Mooks" (a Japanese neologism combining the "m" from magazine with the English word "book") with a specific focus, such as *Jazz Vocal*, *Jazz Bass Player*, and Guitar Magazine, continue to print on paper as other online jazz sites have sprung up. *At Jazz* is one of the most extensive, with listings of club dates, jam sessions, and everything jazz-related. The internet radio site, jjazz.net offers streaming along with information and reviews. *Jazz in Japan* is the most significant English language site, and *Tokyo Jazz Site* offers many different types of articles and a podcast. Other smaller sites have begun to spring up, filling in for the decrease in paper-based magazines.

Due to the sheer volume, estimating the number of books on jazz theory, scores and charts, playing techniques, history, interviews, and jazz-related topics is impossible, but the number published in Japanese is significant, as any search online or visit to a large Tokyo book, music, instrument, or CD and vinyl store will ascertain. Brick-and-mortar book, music, instrument, CD, and vinyl stores are still prevalent throughout Japan.

The Centrality of Big Bands

Most Japanese first learn jazz in big bands. A typical trajectory for Japanese jazz musicians and fans alike is to begin in the junior high or high school brass band and then progress to a big jazz band at university. That interest continues long past graduation. Many high schools started jazz bands after the popularity of the 2004 comedy film *Swing Girls*, directed by Shinobu Yaguchi. The popular film followed a girls' high school jazz band and inspired many to take up an instrument. Nowadays, 70 to 80 percent of colleges and universities have jazz big bands or jazz study "circles" ("circle," from English, is the name for college groups that focus on extracurricular activities). The circles can be quite formal and disciplined and are given space and support from the school.

Almost every one of the best players in Japan nowadays has participated in their university's jazz circle. Alumni who become jazz professionals take pride in returning and helping to mentor their former circle. The big bands offer a chance for many students to participate and serve a social function, but they also focus intensely on performance.

The annual Yamano Big Band Jazz Contest shows just how intensely. In its 48th year, the 2017 contest featured 35 college jazz big bands selected from all across Japan (Kaisai Gaiyo Dai). The contest auditorium is always standing-room-only. The winner is chosen by a panel of professional musicians, jazz critics, and teachers. Junko Moriya, long-time judge and leader of her own big band, said, "Every year, the contest is getting better and better because there are many more good teachers than ever before, who know what a great big band sounds like" (Moriya 2017).

After university, many *shakaijin*, (*shakaijin*, literally 'society person,' refers to working adults, not students) join local big bands and keep up their playing. The *At Jazz* site lists 591 *shakaijin* big bands all over Japan.

Moriya, who often travels to small towns to play as a guest musician, hold workshops and help the bands perform charts, including her own, said, "Big places like Nagoya, Osaka, and Hiroshima have festivals with at least ten big bands per city, but the amazing thing is even small towns, with only 50,000 population, in Yamaguchi-ken or wherever, will have a big band" (Moriya 2017).

University alumni big bands are often formed so graduates can continue to play together long after graduation. Big universities would have five or six alumni big bands all at different ages from their 20s through their 80s. Big bands allow individuals to participate in a group unrelated to the pressures and relations from their workplace. Many amateur big band musicians only love big bands, but others are complete jazz fans who find it a pleasure to not just listen to the music but to make it, too.

Big bands appeal to the general Japanese social orientation towards groups, but they also reveal an abiding interest in personal pastimes that continue throughout life. Japanese like pastimes that require studying specialized, even arcane, knowledge. Jazz serves as an engrossing, endless topic for leisure time that includes knowing history, culture, music, and, with big bands, performance.

Blending Cultures

Big bands are one of the most common lures for Japan's many jazz fans, but the fascination with the music comes from cultural as well as historical forces. It goes deep into issues of Japanese identity. As Shunya emphasizes, "During the course of postwar history, Japanese people reconstructed their own sense of national identity through the medium of desire and antipathy towards America" (Shunya 2003). That sense of identity was not based only on discarding traditional values but on acquiring a new blend of old and new, Japanese and Western values.

Zen Buddhism enormously influenced Japanese arts, aesthetics, and the daily life of present-day Japan. The Zen idea of art arising from a spiritual plane as a religious practice adapts easily to the complexities of jazz. The spare, spiritual nature of the traditional music of Japan, such as that accompanying Noh theater, rests on the Japanese concept of *ma*—the notion that sound can only exist in conjunction with silence. That may seem at odds with the often-densely complex structure of jazz, but at root, the idea is not far from the jazz concepts of playing the space between notes, laying out, and intricate rhythm.

Zen aims (without aiming) at establishing a mindset where selflessness allows genuinely natural movement. That is quite similar to the mindset needed for jazz improvisation. The attention to acting without conscious effort is both a Zen and a jazz ideal. Zen and jazz also depend on the body and breathing to focus, without effort, on creative, human action.

For many Japanese jazz players, the approach to jazz involves the same respect, devotion, and practice as Zen-influenced painting, flower arrangement, martial arts, and calligraphy. No Japanese jazz fan goes to a jazz show thinking they will be experiencing an exciting, new cosmopolitan form of music, as they would have in the 1920s, or that they are freeing themselves with a democratic American music, as many would have in the 1950s. Instead, jazz is a very high-level art form that speaks deeply to the inner self. This self is constructed through a confluence of traditional Japanese culture, international experience, and universal human values.

Another aspect of Japanese culture that contributes to respect for jazz is the Japanese craftwork tradition. The still-present traditional crafts of Japan, such as pottery, lacquerware, woodwork, sword-making, weaving, or dyeing, all demand an extensive period of apprenticeship under the supervision of a master. That these traditional crafts have survived under the pressures of a highly evolved consumer economy is a testament to the powerful forces of tradition. That force of tradition and personal artistic dedication transfer easily to jazz, with its similarly high demands of technical mastery and virtuosity.

As Martin argues, "The creative thrust that stimulated the invention and development of jazz and other African-American musics always operated as a practical negation of difference" (Martin). Yet at the same time, jazz for Japanese musicians and fans is less a transcending of the particulars of jazz's origins and much more of a way of meeting what Martin describes as "the emotional and aesthetic needs of people living in diverse societies around the world" (Martin 2008). In Japan, jazz is an intense experience where free play, creative complexity, wordless expression, openness to universal values, and improvisation can be experienced, felt, and hoped for.

The Future of Jazz in Japan

The oldest jazz record in Japan, "Walla Walla" (Nitto/King), was recorded in 1925 by the Nitto Jazz Band, whose members are now unknown. From this beginning to "Blues Suite No. 3" (Victor), recorded in 1962 by the Hideo Shiraki Quintet, almost all of the jazz in Japan was more or less imitative of the jazz heard on records. (Koyama 2000)

If that was the past, the future looks much less imitative. While almost all musicians still want to spend time at the source of jazz in America, the idea of originality and authenticity has evolved steadily since 1956, when King Records started to release full albums from Japanese jazz musicians. It is no longer "Do I sound like Miles?" but rather "Do I sound like I want to sound?" For Japanese musicians, no less than musicians in other countries, the drive to play well is an individual artistic one, even if tinged with collective cultural pride.

Because of that, the future of Japanese jazz looks bright. Several longstanding clubs have closed in the past two decades, but just as many new ones have opened. The audience is no longer chain-smoking, middle-aged business people with expense accounts. Instead, younger clientele interested in the music, a specific musician, or a certain style have begun to fill up clubs.

Jazz styles continue to diversify, with unique combinations of elements melding into a vibrant approach to music. Small festivals are dedicated to jazz manouche, Hammond B3 organ, free jazz, Latin jazz, and big bands. Musicians acquaint themselves with different styles before developing their own.

More women are playing jazz and leading their own bands. At the turn of the century, women primarily performed as singers or pianists, but now, musicians like trumpeter Hikari Ichihara and saxophonists like Ayumi Koketsu, Saori Yano, and Erena Terakubo are leading their groups. Traditional Japanese koto player Michiyo Yagi plays an electrified 21-string koto and a 17-string bass koto, complete with loopers and effects to expand the range of her sound.

Some musicians are turning to Japanese sources to find inspiration. Pianist Junko Moriya, who won the 12th Annual BMI/Thelonious Monk Jazz Composers Competition, released a CD based on the life and birthplace of Ieyasu Tokugawa on the 400th anniversary of his rule.

Pianist Yosuke Yamashita has blended his piano with shakuhachi and Kodo drummers. Inspiration comes from outside Japan, too, as more percussionists study and play in South American and Caribbean countries to pick up clave and other Latin rhythms at the source.

More and more groups expand the range of their material outside the great American songbook. Free jazz and free improvised music continue to be played by musicians as diverse as Satoko Fujii, Akira Sakata, and Eiichi Hayashi. Saxophonists Kazutoki Umezu and Naruyoshi Kikuchi, along with pianist Takeshi Shibuya, are masters of recombining genres into intense new forms. The future may not see the development of a purely Japanese style of jazz, but perhaps that's more genuine. Jazz is now more than ever a multicultural music, drawing on many sources and inspirations.

If one considers the larger diaspora of jazz, innovation, individuality, and authenticity in jazz were never entirely exclusive to a particular area, sub-culture, or ethnicity. Japan is not so far away as it once was, either, with the opening of borders, the ease of travel, and the global flow of information and culture. If thousands of people outside of Japan can become fans of Japanese manga, animation, design, sushi, films, and literature, will Japanese jazz be far behind?

Works Cited

Atkins, E. Taylor. *Blue Nippon: Authenticating Jazz in Japan*. Durham: Duke University Press, 2001. P. 67. 140.

Black Sun. Directed by Koreyoshi Kurahara. Performed by Tamio Kawaji and Chico Roland. Japan, 1964. DVD.

Derschmidt, Eckhart. "The Disappearance of the 'Jazz-Kissa'." In *The Culture of Japan as Seen through Its Leisure*, eds. Sepp Linhart and Sabine Fruhstuck. Albany: State University of New York Press, 1998. Pp. 303-315. Print.

Dorin, Stéphane. "Editorial: The Global Circulations of Jazz." *Jazz Research Journal* 10, no. 1/2 (January 1, 2016). doi:10.1558/jazz.v10i1-2.29354. Online.

"Gakusei Big Band." At Jazz: Jazz Portal Site. http://www.jazz.co.jp/SchoolBand/. Online.

Hosokawa, Shuhei. "Shochiku Girls' Opera and 1920s Dotonbori Jazz." In Ferranti, Hugh De, and Alison Tokita, eds. *Music, Modernity and Locality in Prewar Japan: Osaka and beyond*. Burlington: Ashgate, 2013. pp. 211-226. Print. P. 222.

"Kaisai Gaiyo Dai 48 Kai Yamano Big Band Jazz Contest." Yamano Music. https://www.yamano-music.co.jp/docs/ybbjc/info/youkou.html. Online.

Koshiro, Yukiko. *Trans-Pacific Racisms and the U.S. Occupation of Japan*, Studies of the East Asian Institute (New York: Columbia University Press, 1999), iii, http://www.questia.com/read/120080725/trans-pacific-racisms-and-the-u-s-occupation-of-japan. Online library. P. 67.

Koyama, Kiyoshi. "Jazz in Japan." In *The Oxford Companion to Jazz*, edited by Bill Kirchner. New York: Oxford University Press, 2000. Paper. P. 566.

Mackie, Vera. Alisa Freedman, Laura Miller, and Christine R. Yano, eds. "Modern Girls on the Go: Gender, Mobility, and Labor in Japan." Online Research Library: Questia. 2013. https://www.questia.com/library/120082648/modern-girls-on-the-go-gender-mobility-and-labor. P. 79

Mandel, Howard. "On Magazine's Circulation Figures." Jazz Beyond Jazz: Howard Mandel's Urban Improvisation. July 16, 2009. http://www.artsjournal.com/jazzbeyondjazz/2009/07/on_magazines_circulation_figur.html. Online.

Martin, Denis-constant. "Can Jazz Be Rid of the Racial Imagination? Creolization, Racial Discourses, and Semiology of Music." *Black Music Research Journal* 28, no. 2 (Fall 2008). https://www.questia.com/library/journal/1G1-202513826/can-jazz-be-rid-of-the-racial-imagination-creolization. Online library.

Molasky, Michael S. *Jazu Kissa Ron: Sengo no Nihon Bunka o Aruku*. Tokyo: Chikuma Shobo, 2010. Paper.

Moriya, Junko. Personal interview with Michael Pronko. February 2017.

"Ongaku Zasshi Ichiran." An Advertising Agency: Horikoshi Corporation (Koukoku Dairi Ten: Kabusiki Gaisha Horikoshi). http://www.hrks.jp/ad_music/jazz/. Accessed January 2017. Online.

Pronko, Michael. "Power of Hope: Toshiko Akiyoshi Leaves Her Mark on the World of Jazz." *The Japan Times* (Tokyo), November 17, 2004. http://www.japantimes.co.jp/culture/2004/11/17/music/power-of-hope/#.WJ_T0xJ94UE. Online.

Pronko, Michael. "Don De Armond Interview." Jazz in Japan. 2012. https://www.jazzinjapan.com/interviews-posts/dondearmond. Online.

Segawa, Masahisa. "Senzen no Nihonjin Jazu Shinga Tachi." *Bessatsu Music Magazine: Record Collectors*, May 1981, 30-39. Paper. P. 36

Shipton, Alyn. *A New History of Jazz*. London: Continuum, 2001. Paper.

Shunya, Yoshimi. "'America' as desire and violence: Americanization in postwar Japan and Asia during the Cold War.' Translated by David Buist. *Inter-Asia Cultural Studies*, Volume 4, Number 3. 2003. P. 439. P. 434.

Swing Girls. Directed by Shinobu Yaguchi. Japan, 2004. DVD.

The Asahi Shimbun. "Jazu Senmonshi Swing Journal Kyukan e Koukoku Shunyu Fushin.". May 17, 2010. http://www.asahi.com/showbiz/music/TKY201005170418.html. Online.

The Warped Ones. Directed by Koreyoshi Kurahara. Performed by Tamio Kawachi and Eiji Go. Japan, 1960. DVD.

"Zenkokuban Live House." At Jazz: Jazz Portal Site. http://www.jazz.co.jp/LiveHouse/index.html. Online.

"Zenkokuban Jazz Session." At Jazz: Jazz Portal Site. http://www.jazz.co.jp/LiveHouseSession/. Online.

Reprinted with permission from: *The Routledge Companion to Jazz Studies*, 07 Dec 2018, pages 271 - 280. ISBN-13: 9781315315805. DOI: 10.4324/9781315315805-26. Publisher: Routledge; Taylor and Francis

Outro

In Memorium

In Memorium 追悼の意を表して

Some great musicians and jazz people I had the good fortune to hear and report on have passed away over the years. I want to remember them as part of Japan's jazz world. They were a joy to listen to, talk with, and to be with on the same musico-physical plane. May they rest in jazz and peace.

Shoji Aketagawa 明田川荘之, ocarinist, pianist, owner Aketa no Mise (1950 – 2024)

Ryojiro Furusawa 古澤良治郎, drummer (1945 – 2011)

Chica Honda チコ本田, singer (1937 – 2024)

Takehiro Honda 本田竹広, pianist (1945 – 2006)

Fumio Karashima 辛島文雄, pianist (1948 – 2017)

Hiroaki Katayama 片山広明, sax (1951 – 2018)

Masabumi Kikuchi 菊地雅章, pianist (1939 – 2015)

Toshinori Kondo 近藤等則, trumpeter (1948 – 2020)

Norikatsu Koreyasu 是安則克, bass (1954 – 2011)

Koichi Matsukaze 松風鉱一, sax (1948 – 2023)

Dairo Miyamoto 宮本大路, bass saxophone (1957 – 2016)

Cecil Monroe, drummer (1955 – 2011)

Hoizumi Nakadaira 中平穂積, photographer, owner DUG jazz kissaten (1936 – 2024)

Takahito Mohican Seki モヒカーノ関/ 関恭史, pianist (1954 – 2013)

Ayako Shirasaki 白崎彩子, pianist (1969 – 2021)

Neil Stalnaker, trumpeter (1959 – 2020)

Hiroyuki Sugiya 杉谷宏幸, B Flat, owner (passed away in 2005)

Akira Suzuki 鈴木燿, B Flat owner (passed away in 2022)

Isao Suzuki 鈴木勲, bassist (1933 – 2022)

Kazuhiko Tsumura 津村和彦, guitar (1957 – 2015)

My other writing

If you're interested in Tokyo and Japan and enjoy detective mystery thrillers, check out my other writing. Detective Hiroshi unravels murder cases in the biggest city in the world.

An accountant turned detective who prefers spreadsheets to crime scenes, Hiroshi scours Tokyo's deserted alleys, jam-packed streets, and sleek skyscrapers to uncover the who and why of brutal murders with the help of old-school Takamatsu and ex-sumo wrestler turned detective Sakaguchi.

Dodging bureaucratic obstructions and political power plays, Hiroshi uses more respect than muscle, more savvy than protocol, to dig beneath the gleaming surface of a megalopolis resting uneasily in the grip of the global economy. At the end of the day, Hiroshi and crew don't mind washing away the grim realities and raging conflicts with a big bowl of ramen, a plate of yakitori, and bracing glasses of sake.

Detective Hiroshi Series

Shitamachi Scam (2023)

Azabu Getaway (2022)

Tokyo Zangyo (2021)

Tokyo Traffic (2020)

The Moving Blade (2017)

The Last Train (2017)

"Hiroshi is now as synonymous with Tokyo crime fiction as Harry Bosch is to LA noir."

Best Thrillers

"If there's a better crime series set in Japan, I've not yet read it."

Crime Thriller Hound

"The feel of classic noir imbued with Far East culture."

Indie Reader

"Pronko does as good a job of taking us on a trip through Tokyo—and a sweet and mournful journey it is—as Simenon does through Inspector Maigret's Paris."

Booklife by Publishers Weekly

And if you're interested in the daily life of Japan seen through one foreigner's eyes, check out the Tokyo Moments Series

Tokyo Moments Series

Tokyo Tempos (2024)

Motions and Moments (2015)

Tokyo's Mystery Deepens (2014)

Beauty and Chaos (2014)

The Tokyo Moments series contains collections of non-fiction pieces about life in Tokyo. Looking at the contradictions, intricacies, and enigmas of Tokyo, a city that is old and new, immense and intimate, indifferent and yet very humane, they take the reader on a journey into the heart of Tokyo.

"A poignant and passionate presentation of Tokyo as a city of contrast, not just a setting but a living entity."

Feathered Quill

"A charming, unaffected, and yet profoundly philosophical collection of essays on the colorful chaos that is Tokyo."

Independent Book Review

"The prose is beautifully weighted, a sense of place evoked, and telling details precisely set—not just the sights, but the sounds and the smells of the city. An impressive and rousing homage from a gifted storyteller."

SPR Review

"These aren't just snippets of Tokyo and the usual touristy accounts of the big attractions. Pronko takes a deeper look at what makes Tokyo hum."

Reader Views Five Stars

The Jazz in Japan Website

https://www.jazzinjapan.com/

And don't forget the website where you can read reviews of CDs, live shows, in-depth interviews, and essays, and check out the current calendar of recommended live shows.

Special Thanks

I want to give special thanks to several people. Books are not individual projects; they involve many people. They all deserve thanks.

First, I want to thank the publications that published my writings on jazz: TokyoQ, The Japan Times, JJazz.net, the Blue Note magazines, Jazznin, and Jazz Colours.

I want to thank my father, a jazz lover. He played jazz every day at home. Many nights, I asked to leave the door of my bedroom open so I could fall asleep listening to the records he played downstairs.

Thanks to my mom, who pushed me to attend music school when I was three years old and to take piano lessons through high school. She sat through endless concerts, sketching the musicians, helping me to see them better.

Obrigado muito to Marco Mancini, partner in crime, instigator of Jazznin, jazz musician, editor, and all-around jazz fiend. He's someone who can talk about jazz even longer than I can, with or without a drink in hand.

I want to give a big, huge thanks to all the musicians, club owners, wait staff, managers, PR people, CD store clerks, and fans who have helped me understand the vast world of jazz in Japan. Over the years, I have listened to their suggestions and recommendations, and each one has guided me in the right direction.

Special thanks go to my assistant, Kayoko Mohri. She was my student years ago and has been my assistant for years. I can't tell you how helpful she is in both English and Japanese. She runs the calendar on the Jazz in Japan site and can always find any info I need and organize it into comprehensibility. I could never—and I really mean never—have finished this book without her help.

I want to give special thanks to my wife. Although she grew up not hearing jazz, she now asks me to put on Lester Young, Billie Holliday, or that "funky jazz group we heard the other day." I'd love to have back the many evenings I spent in jazz clubs without her, but I feel blessed to have a soulmate who understands me and my musical addictions. Everyone should be so lucky.

ALSO AVAILABLE BY MICHAEL PRONKO

Memoirs on Tokyo Life
    Beauty and Chaos (2014)
    Tokyo's Mystery Deepens (2014)
    Motions and Moments (2015)
    Tokyo Tempos (2024)

The Detective Hiroshi Series
    The Last Train (2017)
    The Moving Blade (2018)
    Tokyo Traffic (2020)
    Tokyo Zangyo (2021)
    Azabu Getaway (2022)
    Shitamachi Scam (2023)

If you enjoyed this book, please consider taking a minute to write a review on your favorite book-related site. Reviews really help indie writers like myself.

And if you're interested in future releases and news and insights from Tokyo, sign up for my newsletter here:

https://www.michaelpronko.com/newsletter/

www.ingramcontent.com/pod-product-compliance
Lightning Source LLC
Chambersburg PA
CBHW030513080526
44586CB00011B/169